MW01092819

The Myth of Apollo and Daphne
from Ovid to Quevedo

The Myth of Apollo and Daphne

from Ovid to Quevedo:

Love, Agon, and the Grotesque

Mary E. Barnard

Duke Monographs in Medieval and Renaissance Studies Number 8

Duke University Press   Durham 1987

© 1987 Duke University Press

All rights reserved

Printed in the United States of America
on acid-free paper ∞

Library of Congress Cataloging-in-Publication Data
Barnard, Mary E., 1944–
The myth of Apollo and Daphne from Ovid to Quevedo.
(Duke monographs in medieval and Renaissance
studies; no. 8)
Bibliography: p.
Includes index.
1. Apollo (Greek deity) in literature. 2. Daphne
(Greek deity) in literature. I. Title. II. Series.
PN57.A49B3   1987   809'.93351   86-29142
ISBN 0-8223-0701-4

For Claudio

Contents

Illustrations

Acknowledgments

I wish to thank Frank Casa, Andrew P. Debicki, Olga Impey, and John Kronik for reading an early version of chapter 4 and for their very helpful comments. I am grateful to James O. Crosby for his judicious reading of the manuscript and for offering valuable changes. I express my thanks to Peter Goldman for skillful editorial suggestions. Finally, I wish to thank Willis Barnstone who read the manuscript carefully and whose many observations have enriched the text.

I am indebted to the American Council of Learned Societies for a research grant that assisted my work. Early versions of chapters 4 and 5 and the appendix appeared in the *Romanic Review* 72 (1981), the *Hispanic Review* 52 (1984), and *Neophilologus* 69 (1985). Permission to reprint this material is gratefully acknowledged.

The Myth of Apollo and Daphne
from Ovid to Quevedo

Introduction

Golden is Apollo's tunic and golden his mantle, his lyre,
his Lyctian bow and his quiver. Golden also his sandals,
for Apollo is rich in gold, rich in possessions, . . . handsome as he is young. . . . No one has his skill. He is the
archer, the minstrel, and he keeps those arts alive. He is
diviner and seer. . . . On his way to Pytho he found an
unearthly beast, a dreadful snake. The god slew him with
a rain of swift arrows, and all sang to Apollo.[1]

So Callimachus exalts Apollo, the brightest god of the
Olympian pantheon. He has beauty, grace, and skill, the gift of
prophecy, and the strength of the unerring marksman. He is the
slayer of Python. But Apollo does not always keep his glorious
bearing, especially as the lover of Daphne. In fact he is a fool,
sometimes grotesque and obscene, and a failure in his erotic
agon. He falls into comic anthropomorphism in Ovid's *Metamorphoses* or becomes the anguished figure burdened with the sor-
rows of the courtly lover in the Renaissance.

Apollo loves Daphne, who is transformed into a laurel to
escape him. This story is itself transformed as it passes from one
version to another, from its popular source in Ovid's *Metamorphoses* to a burlesque treatment in two sonnets by the Spaniard
Francisco de Quevedo. En route the protean figures of the myth
have meant different things to different ages, each age molding
and fashioning the lovers in its own image. In this study, I treat
these transformations from Ovid through the Spanish Golden
Age and place special emphasis on the themes of love, agon,
and the grotesque.

The myth has penetrated virtually every period and most

European cultures, as Yves Giraud documents in his panoramic volume *La Fable de Daphné*.[2] Wolfgang Stechow also gives a broad range vision of the myth in his *Apollo und Daphne*,[3] concentrating largely on its treatments in the arts. My study covers literary manifestations of the tale in Ovid's *Metamorphoses*, medieval commentaries on Ovid, Petrarch's *Canzoniere*, and in two Spanish poets, Garcilaso de la Vega and Francisco de Quevedo. I chose these versions because they offer the most interesting and influential variants in the periods treated.

As the myth of Apollo and Daphne leaves its religious context to enter the world of art and literature, it becomes a field for play, a special vehicle for private aesthetic visions. Ovid's version signals the entrance of the tale into literary history, becoming the principal model for subsequent renditions. To be sure, the term model holds a special meaning for Petrarch, Garcilaso, and Quevedo since, in the Renaissance, imitation of models is an essential principle of creation. Through imitation, the poets typically use this myth to display their classical erudition and rhetorical virtuosity as well as to reveal their aesthetic concerns. Yet to make Apollo and Daphne their own, to make them conform to their own idiom, the poets cannot leave them in their ancient posture. The mythological figures have to acquire a new bearing. They have to be transformed.

Through a kind of artificial mythopoeia, the writers invent new variants for the tale, altering the ancient model, sometimes radically. In Renaissance theories of imitation, this transformative process is compared to bees gathering pollen from flowers and converting it into honey—an image that originates with the ancients and that becomes a commonplace in discussions of imitation.[4] Petrarch, the master imitator of ancient material, warns: "Take care that what you have gathered does not long remain in you in its original state: the bees would have no glory if they did not convert what they found into something different and something better" ("Neve diutius apud te qualia decerpseris maneant, cave: nulla quidem esset apibus gloria, nisi in aliud et in melius inventa converterent," 1.8.23).[5] In the alchemy of imitation, the industriousness of the bees signals the creative energy of the poets, who convert what they inherit from their precursors into elegant variations. In the humanist Renaissance, the poets pay homage to the model even as they transform it. Imitation, therefore, carries with it a double formula: an implicit faith in the original and a freedom to create new poetic visions.

In terms of imitation an exception must be made for Ovid's medieval commentators, since they are not concerned with aesthetic imitation as such. The adaptation and transformation of the ancient model here involve an imposition of meaning in which, through allegory, the mythological figures become symbols and types in the drama of Redemption. Ovid the poet-artificer is for the commentators the poet-sage, the supreme *auctor* who is the unquestionable and authentic source of Christian wisdom.

Douglas Bush has noted that a history of the mythological tradition is largely "an account of the *Metamorphoses* of Ovid,"[6] and he is essentially correct, at least as far as Apollo and Daphne are concerned. The *Metamorphoses* is the main link and model for the numerous versions of the myth. And the themes of *love, agon* (the figurative erotic combat of the enemy lovers), and the *grotesque,* which are featured so prominently in Ovid's version, remain constant, albeit altered and adapted to make them conform to the values of the times. These central themes will constitute the principal lines of inquiry in this study. At this point, however, a preliminary discussion of them is necessary. The myth of Apollo and Daphne will be considered first in the tradition of love and then in the tradition of the grotesque, the agon motif playing a major role in both. It should be noted that in the Middle Ages, agon extends beyond the confines of the erotic and reaches deep into the omnipresent Christian archetypal combat between good and evil.

Originally the Apollo and Daphne myth was an etiological account of the origin of the laurel, one of Apollo's attributes, used in his cult and rituals. Ovid's Apollo and Daphne is the first extant version of the tale that, stripped of its connection with the world of religion, stands as a singular literary achievement. Ovid places the myth in the tradition of Roman erotic elegy, telling an irreverent story of erotic agon: the amorous combat of a god who becomes foolish, as all Ovidian lovers are, and a recalcitrant nymph, who, like all elegiac mistresses, cruelly rejects the impatient wooer. Ovid's treatment is examined in the light of Roman elegy—including the motif of the *exclusus amator*—as well as in his own conception of love in his love poetry, with its treatment of jest and earnest. Ovid's comedy in his amatory poetry is based on a mockery of elegiac conventions: elaborate erotic games seen with the malice of the sophisticated bystander, whether viewed from the double perspective of the

participant-observer of the *Amores* or by the fully detached on-
looker of the *Ars amatoria*. Mythology plays a large role in the
banter, especially as *exempla*. And if the object of the humor in
this erotic poetry is love, and myth is brought in to reinforce the
comedy, in the tale of Apollo and Daphne the converse is true;
the object of the humor is myth, and love conventions are
brought in to frame the comedy. Ovid's parody and farce of the
lover Apollo is linked to a hitherto unrecognized predecessor,
the travesty of the god on the festive, rambunctious Greek comic
stage—in particular the *phlyakes* of Magna Graecia—casting new
light on his comic treatment of the divine lover and touching on
important implications as to his controversial anti-Augustanism.

In medieval Ovidian exegesis, the tale of Apollo and
Daphne is transformed into an allegory of theological and moral
wisdom. At the heart of this exegetical tradition is the conception of Ovid as a sage, a notion based on the *topos* of the poet as
the wise man who hides truth as he spins his poetic fantasy,
which is meaningless only on the surface and to the untrained
eye. This section examines how the commentators' hermeneutics—allegory and typology—convert the clever, bantering Ovid
into a moral philosopher and theologian. In their readings, love
is no longer a tool of play and caricature but an element in the
Christian ethos; it is sensual love *(cupiditas)* and divine love *(Caritas)*, the two poles in the Christian dualism of good and evil,
and they are both represented in the figure of Cupid. Thus the
emphasis shifts from Ovid's erotic agon to a Christian agon, a
psychomachia, where demonic forces of darkness, symbolized by
Python and other monsters, battle the forces of light, symbolized
by Apollo. The opposing roles of the Ovidian Apollo and
Daphne as pursuing lover and fleeing beloved are interpreted in
ingenious ways to correspond to matters of moral and religious
concerns, ranging from man pursuing wisdom (John of Garland)
to Christ pursuing the recalcitrant Synagogue (Pierre Bersuiere).

After the medieval commentators, Petrarch integrates the
tale into the tortured world of love in his *Canzoniere* and revolu-
tionizes the treatment of the myth. Even though he borrows
from the medieval exegetes, Petrarch liberates the mythological
figures from their roles as symbols and types in the Christian
drama of Redemption, placing them once again on the erotic
stage devised earlier by Ovid. Leaving Ovid's irony and play far
behind, however, the grave Petrarch transforms the lovers, endowing them with a courtly bearing; the modest Daphne becomes a *figura* of the elusive, disdainful Laura, and Apollo is a

projection of the Petrarchan poet-lover, a man fated in his idolatrous obsession to the fragile vulnerability of exile from the
woman.

Petrarch elaborates the erotic agon side by side with a
Christian agon, the conflict between the lover's demons of flesh
and poetic glory, on the one hand, and his desire for salvation,
on the other. The figures and events of the tale of Apollo and
Daphne—Cupid, Daphne, the setting, the chase, the laurel—become mirrors reflecting the fragmentation of the poetic self in its
constant wavering between the earthly and the divine, between
bliss and doom. In Petrarch's postlapsarian universe, a Purgato-
rial corner fraught with battles, failure claims a high place: the
failure of courtly love, of the senses in negative ecstasy, of poetic
language, of the will, of achieving a final Christian resolution.
And the Ovidian tale—a story of failure as the god loses his
Daphne to transformation—serves as a tool to reveal the *Canzoniere*'s multiple failures. Petrarch stands as a significant transition
figure between the Middle Ages and the Golden Age, whose
courtly poets, mingling Ovidian and Petrarchan commonplaces,
create their own agonistic stages for the ill-fated lovers.

The myth of Apollo and Daphne is one of the most popular in the mythological tradition in Spain. Along with other tales
of love—Hero and Leander, Pyramus and Thisbe, Venus and
Adonis—the story of the fugitive nymph and the scorned Olympian holds a special fascination for Golden Age poets, especially
for *petrarquistas,* who use the myth as an eloquent statement of
the longing for unattainable love and the suffering of the rejected lover. As with other mythical personages in sixteenth- and
seventeenth-century poetry, Apollo and Daphne are not quite
restored to their ancient form after their Christian eclipse in the
Middle Ages, for Golden Age poets continue the transformative
imitation so masterfully carried out by Petrarch. These poets
adapt Apollo and Daphne to their own idiom, dressing them in
contemporary garb, paralleling, as it were, the practice of many
painters of the age, whose iconography of the gods betrays the
taste of their time: resplendent Venuses in Renaissance finery
and gallant Marses in courtly armor; naked, distorted Mannerist
Daphnes or frightened, dynamic Baroque nymphs. Seventeenth-
century painters treated the gods seriously but often ridiculed
them as in Velázquez's portraits of Mars as an unheroic weakling
and of Bacchus as a drunkard. So too in Golden Age poets, both
serious and comic treatments of Apollo and Daphne abound.

Fully within the courtly tradition, Garcilaso adapts the

mythological figures with all the relish of tears and pain, concentrating on the final stages of the erotic agon, the loss of the woman through transformation. In the manner of Petrarch, Apollo is a mournful lover, clinging to the memory of his loss. Daphne becomes a courtly lady endowed with the exquisite beauty consecrated by tradition. Quevedo, for his part, keeping only one foot on his courtly stage, writes both serious and burlesque versions of the myth. As a grave courtier and Christian poet, Quevedo creates an erotic battle with all the trappings of the cosmological and Neoplatonic values of his day; as a burlesque debaser writing in the antimythological and anti-Petrarchan traditions, he utilizes the myth as a stage for his linguistic extravagances and savage wit.

Love and agon—erotic and Christian battles—mingle in the versions of the tale of Apollo and Daphne with another important but far more complex theme, the grotesque. Daphne's transformation into the laurel, the figure of Apollo as a ravenous dog as he chases his fugitive nymph, and the monsters of the Middle Ages—imposed on the tale by eager moralists—are the three main manifestations of the grotesque. But before outlining the progression this mode assumes in the present study, I need to clarify the term *grotesque*. The grotesque is clearly one of the most elusive of aesthetic categories. The term has its origin in the fantastic decorations found in Roman caves (*grotte,* hence *grottesche*) at the end of the fifteenth century in what had once been the *Domus Aurea,* the Golden House of Nero.[7] These are hybrid fragments in which human, animal, and plant intertwine, creating "monstrous" ornaments that infringe on the laws of nature: a horse with legs of leaves, a man bearing the legs of a crane, and the like. These fantastic, incongruous formations serve as models for the ornamental grotesque of the Renaissance, even though historically the latter is in a very real sense a continuation of the ornamental grotesque of the Middle Ages. Famous among the Renaissance grotesque creations are the paintings of the Papal loggias by Raphael and his school (c. 1515/ 19), the half-human creatures of Luca Signorelli in the cathedral at Orvieto, and those of Agostino Veneziano. The whimsical, fantastic character of the decorative grotesque was welcomed by sixteenth-century artists as the ideal medium to display inventiveness and caprice by creating startling and unexpected forms.[8] But these "dreams of painters," which Giorgio Vasari praises for their novelty and *grazia,*[9] soon incur the criticism of neoclassicists

who, for all their objections, cannot prevent the blossoming of
an immense array of grotesques in both art and literature.

The criticism of Renaissance neoclassicists echoes another
voice from another time, that of the Augustan architect, Vitruvius, a contemporary of Ovid who, in his *De architectura*, condemns the grotesque decorative forms of his times—now causing such a rave in Renaissance Rome—for violating verisimilitude, harmony, and measure. Vitruvius asks in disbelief, "How
can . . . a soft and slender stalk carry a seated figure, and how
can flowers and half-figures rise alternately from roots and
stalks?" (7.5.4.).[10] The monstrous forms that Vitruvius scorns
had, under Alexandrian influence, permeated the architectural
style of his day—friezes and murals boasting of an enormous
outpouring of hybrid forms. And in this propitious climate
Ovid's grotesque of Daphne appears, having been inspired not
only by the Alexandrian taste for hybridization but also by its
treatment of metamorphosis "in progress."

Unlike in Homer, where transformation occurs instanta-
neously, in Ovid and in his predecessors, the Hellenes, "we are
invited to observe the process."[11] In his *Argonautica*, Apollonius
depicts the warrior enemies of Jason emerging from the dragon's
teeth (III.1381–98), the victims of Circe as bizarre assemblages of
man and beast (IV.676–81), and the tears of the Heliades changing into amber as they mourn the death of their brother Phaeton
(IV.603–26). Frescoes at Pompeii and Herculaneum painted in the
Alexandrian manner are telling evidence of this practice.[12] And
so Ovid's hybrid vision of Daphne's transformation into a laurel
is one of the oldest forms of the grotesque. Like its kindred
types, the ornamental "monsters" and Apollonius' incongruous
mixtures, Daphne's transformation defies categorization and def-
inition altogether. Hybrid Daphne is simply a "non-thing" devoid of logical structure and order as we know it, an ambivalent
and anomalous form that has ceased to be human and is not yet
fully laurel. No words adequately describe it; it is as if language
itself were paralyzed.[13] It is what George Santayana calls "the
half-formed, the perplexed, and the suggestively monstrous."[14]

In this paralysis of language and logical structuring,
Daphne's grotesque transformation conforms to Wolfgang Kayser's notion of the grotesque as an intrusion of a strange, incongruous phenomenon into the rational order of nature, the subversion of the familiar world by the uncanny and the absurd,
one of whose manifestations is the juxtaposition of incompatible

elements from different realms of nature.[15] Moreover, Ovid's grotesque Daphne, a moment of human dissolution, also conforms to what Lee Byron Jennings places at the center of a grotesque form. Jennings stresses an element of distortion as the human body undergoes "a change for the worse" in a process of decay or disintegration brought about by an alien force in clear departure from the basic norms of life.[16] Both Kayser and Jennings observe an estrangement from accustomed order, a principle of the alien and chaotic at work. Paradoxically, however, Daphne's grotesque also involves an act of regeneration, an element typical in many grotesques. Daphne's body is destroyed through transformation but in the process it gives birth to another living form, the laurel.[17]

A question that readily comes to mind is this: Can Daphne's transformation in Ovid be considered unnatural, and, thereby, grotesque? We know that underlying Daphne's change—and the theme of transformation in the whole of the *Metamorphoses*—is a cosmology based on the primitive belief that everything in nature is "animated by one and the same life, a portion of which might then migrate from body to body,"[18] an idea that makes tales of etiology such as the laurel's possible. Moreover, is not the notion of a mythological grotesque a contradiction in terms? Mythology has traditionally been regarded as an attempt to elucidate the mysteries and perplexities of human experience; it is an explanation offered by prescientific man for what is unintelligible in life and the cosmos. The grotesque by its very nature, in contrast, must remain on the side of the wondrous and the uncanny; there must be no explanation to shed light on the mystery. As we shall see, the answers to both these questions lie in Ovid's approach to myth, in his urbane toying with once mythical truths. He removes the transformations, including Daphne's, from their religious and metaphysical realms, treats them as poetic fiction, and consequently converts them into an alienated world of uncanny, bizarre forms.

Daphne's grotesque, serious in intent, finds a comic counterpart in the grotesque of the lusty Apollo when Ovid portrays the god as a hunting hound pursuing his fearful, coy beloved pictured as a hare. Whereas Ovid's skeptical urbanity in regard to myth gives rise to the grotesque in the nymph's transformation, his clever handling of the play inherent in the myth itself is the source of the comedy. For Ovid skillfully adds an overlay of parodic exaggeration to the original chase scene of the Greek

Apollo running after the unwilling virgin huntress. (Later in
Ovid's version, Apollo will prove equally foolish when the virgin
escapes the god through transformation into the laurel.) Fancy
and play are intrinsic to the world of myth, as Johan Huizinga
has noted in his *Homo Ludens*.[19] Ovid's predecessors in the tradition of mythical travesties exploit this aspect of the mythical
tales. But play, which once belonged to the sacred sphere, is
now elaborated as irreverent, mocking play, taking place outside
sacred precincts. As noted above, Ovid finds in one of these
predecessors—the *phlyakes* of Magna Graecia, with their outrageous, grotesque figures—antecedents of his foolish Apollo. And
like these festive burlesques, Ovid's comedy of the god signals a
liberation from the sacred. In Ovid's case this liberation represents freedom from the religious and moral strictures of Emperor
Augustus.

The term grotesque crops up here and there in Ovidian
scholarship, especially in L. P. Wilkinson[20] and in Charles Segal's studies.[21] But if the presence of the grotesque in Ovid has
been recognized, it has not been fully clarified. This study offers
an explanation of the nature of the Ovidian grotesque, determin-
ing its role in the framework of erotic agon: how the grotesque
dramatizes the loss of the woman and how it places the lusty
Apollo in comic relief in his descent from divine figure to foolish
lover. Clearly, the kind of grotesque I deal with in this study,
starting with Ovid, is exclusively that of hybridization and at-
tendant notions of distortion, alienation, incongruity, and clashing of incompatibles. My purpose is to demonstrate how the
grotesque functions within the context of ancient, medieval, and
Renaissance aesthetic and intellectual practices.

Each age fashions the grotesque according to its own
norms and values. The Middle Ages combines old and new mo-
tifs and endows the grotesque with distinctive roles. In the commentaries of Ovid's tale of the god and the nymph, the grotesque is used both for purposes of play and as a didactic tool.
Many of the illustrations of Daphne's metamorphosis that accompany the texts exemplify the ludic function, since they are
an extension of the decorative grotesques of antiquity. But more
significantly, as the myth is integrated into the Judeo-Christian
scheme, the grotesque becomes an instrument for teaching moral
truths. Monstrous imagery constitutes the ideal vehicle to make
the distorted world of sin pictorially manifest.

The grotesque makes two brief but significant appearances

in Petrarch's canzone 23 and sestina 30. In the canzone, the poetic persona is transformed into a laurel—an ecstatic moment emblematic of the desired union of the scorned lover with the ineffable Madonna Laura. This grotesque, however, plays a key role in Petrarch's Christian agon between the sacred and the profane. The transformation into the laurel betrays an incongruous assemblage of human and plant akin to hybrids of Petrarch's times, the half-human and half-vegetable forms of the Gothic grotesque. And like many of these grotesques, Petrarch's hybrid has a didactic purpose: to portray the devastating effects of sin. By contrast, the grotesque of the sestina focuses on the erotic agon, the battle between the impassioned lover and the cold woman. The poem depicts Laura as a laurel of diamond branches and gold hair, a grotesque preciosity emblematic of her courtly rigor.

The proliferation of grotesque forms that we find in medieval art continues in the Renaissance, acquiring new impetus from antique models. But if in medieval times grotesque forms are confined mostly to cathedral sculptures and to the marginal drolleries of illuminated manuscripts, in the Renaissance the ornamental grotesque invades many areas. It appears in murals, friezes, and sculptures as well as in tapestries, embroideries, ceramics, furniture, and even in gardens like those at Bomarzo and in palaces like the Fontainebleau Palace in France, with its famous grotesque paintings by Rosso and Primaticcio, and the Escorial in Spain. The grotesque in the visual arts, however, exerts not only a decorative function. It ranges from an ideal technique on the part of the "art-for-art's-sake" *maniera* artists—who, in their efforts to surpass the masters of the previous generation, use the grotesque to display their virtuosity and ingenuity—to a didactic vehicle as in Bosch and Bruegel, where it serves to portray vice and folly. The many functions of the grotesque in art are paralleled by analogous functions in literature, art and literature borrowing freely from each other. Garcilaso and Quevedo deal with two of the most significant literary treatments of the grotesque in the sixteenth and seventeenth centuries: the grotesque as a metaphor for erotic woes and as a tool of the burlesque. Since the grotesque is primarily a pictorial form, its vivid imagery in these poets finds analogues in the visual arts, and where useful I integrate some of these analogues within my discussion. This parallel between the arts is particularly apt for an age in which Horace's *ut pictura poesis* was the object of considerable discussion.

Garcilaso de la Vega, the poet of doleful courtly songs, uses the grotesque in Daphne's transformation, as in Ovid, to dramatize the loss of the woman—here a courtly lady—while the lover Apollo, no longer comic as in Ovid but teary as in Petrarch, looks on. The grotesque fits snugly into the tortured world of the courtly Garcilaso, its distorted, incongruous images reflecting the lack of harmony in a poetic landscape where the lover is forever pained and rejected. I examine Garcilaso's grotesque in the light of *maniera* artists and the emblematic tradition, two prolific sources of grotesque images for the Renaissance.

The book ends with an analysis of the poetics of Francisco de Quevedo, who presents Apollo and Daphne seriously in one poem and wholly irreverently in others. Like Ovid and Garcilaso, he uses the grotesque of Daphne's transformation, with its elements of distortion, to dramatize the loss of the woman, this time as an aspect in a Neoplatonic vision of cosmic convulsion. But Quevedo, poet of a wild imagination, employs a popular fashion of the seventeenth century, namely, the grotesque as a tool of parody. The playful Ovid had already ridiculed Apollo, using ironic barbs and the mock-heroic with touches of farce and the grotesque. Quevedo's comedy goes further. His savage burlesque attacks not only Apollo but Daphne, and, unlike Ovid who uses the grotesque sparingly to taunt his target, Quevedo employs the grotesque as his principal means of derision. Quevedo converts his two mythological figures into cruel, dehumanized caricatures; animalization and puppetry provide the harsh lights of his distorting portrayals, which even descend to the outrageous lows of what Bakhtin has called, in his provocative study of Rabelais, "grotesque realism."[22]

Given the considerable attention paid to the thorny question of the response to the grotesque, I shall devote a few words to it here. The typical response to the grotesque (and *the* response that most modern critics assign to it, taking their lead from John Ruskin's *The Stones of Venice*) is that of ambivalence, a combination of the ludicrous and the disturbing—laughter and something incompatible with it like disgust or horror. But even though this ambivalence is common in grotesque scenes, it is not *always* present. The bizarre of the grotesque does not always elicit fear, horror, or discomfort, nor, conversely, does it always elicit laughter. The manner in which the distortions and deformities of the grotesque are presented will determine our response to them. Many of the frivolous hybrids of the ornamental gro-

tesque of antiquity, the Middle Ages, and the Renaissance do
not provoke an ambiguity of feeling since sinister or discomfort-
ing elements are not present. Horace, in his *Ars poetica,* also
called the *Epistle to the Pisos,* finds this kind of hybridization only
laughable,[23] as does Vasari who calls it "pittura licenziosa e ridi-
cola molto."[24] On the other hand, laughter may be absent from a
grotesque scene. There is no laughter, for instance, in Garcilaso's
version of Daphne's metamorphosis. There are no elements of
mockery or satire in the passage, and the high elegance and
grace, which are part of Garcilaso's serious treatment, blur the
ludicrous aspect of the transformation, preventing laughter from
being evoked. Curiously, Fernando de Herrera, the sixteenth-
century commentator of Garcilaso, regards the latter's transformation of Daphne as merely repugnant.[25] It is evident that each
grotesque scene must be analyzed on its own terms, for each
yields its own unique grotesquerie and generates its own unique
response.[26]

The Myth and Its Background in Ancient Greece

Apollo, the son of Zeus and Leto, is one of the most complex of
the ancient gods. He is a powerful Greek divinity and yet is always unlucky in love. Though his origin remains unknown—an
Aryan origin has tentatively been advanced—he has long been
recognized as the most characteristically Greek of all the gods;
his youthful grace and ideal manly beauty are glorified in both
literature and art. For the Greeks, Apollo is a brilliant figure; he
is the patron god of healing, archery, music, poetry, and, as a
result of a late development in Apolline cult, he is also a solar
deity. The term *Phoebus,* if perhaps not originally meant to denote Apollo's solar character as was once thought, is the epithet
that identifies him as a sun-god. Even though Apollo is associated with primitive forms of worship in his role as a pastoral deity, the god of flocks and herds, he emerges as the champion of
intellectual life, as the philosopher-god who is said to be the real
father of Plato. He is the god of purification and an unerring
prophet, whose oracles, always on the side of high moral and
religious principles, are proclaimed as the supreme authority.
   Apollo's cult was embraced by all Greece, and his most
famous shrines were at Delphi and the rocky island of Delos,
where, as legend has it—the earliest account recorded in the Homeric Hymn to Apollo—the god and his twin sister Artemis
were born.[27] Unlucky as a lover, the objects of Apollo's erotic

fancy are nevertheless numerous. Three of the most famous are Coronis, daughter of Phlegyas and mother of Aesculapius; the somber Cassandra, daughter of Priam of Troy, to whom Apollo gives the gift of divination; and Daphne, the nymph who becomes the laurel tree to escape her eager divine pursuer.

A myth, by its very nature, is fluid. It undergoes constant changes when variants are introduced as the tale migrates from region to region, as it passes in the oral tradition from generation to generation. And the myth of Apollo and Daphne is certainly no exception. As attested in ancient texts, Daphne's original character was quite different than the coy, demure nymph we all know from Ovid's *Metamorphoses*. In this early tradition, she emerges as a rather mysterious figure, endowed with mantic powers. In his *Description of Greece*, Pausanias speaks of her as a mountain nymph, a prophetess interpreter of the oracle of Gaea, the Earth goddess at Delphi (10.5.5).[28] In Diodorus (4.66.5–6) she is the daughter of Teiresias and is identified with the Delphic Sibyl and, in other sources, with Manto (Seeress).[29]

As Daphne enters the erotic world of Apollo, however, she sheds her garb as promantis and becomes the virgin huntress who spurns the god's advances and finally becomes the laurel. This tale surfaces fairly late; the earliest reference to it dates back to the Alexandrian era.[30] The longest account by far of the adventure of Apollo and Daphne is what has come to be known as the Laconian version. Allegedly narrated by Phylarcus and Diodorus of Elaia, it is preserved in varying details in Parthenius, *Erotica Pathemata* 15, Pausanias 8.20.1–4, and Plutarch *Agis* 9. In this account, Daphne is the daughter of Amyclas of Laconia and a follower of Artemis, the chaste goddess of the hunt. Shunning all male companionship, she devotes herself exclusively to the hunt. Leukippos, the son of Oenomaus, king of Pisa, falls in love with the nymph and, in order to be near her, dons a female disguise. Because of his devotion to Daphne and because he surpasses the other virgins in his nobility of birth and hunting skills, Leukippos wins her friendship. The jealous Apollo, however, has Daphne and her companions bathe in the river Ladon. When the virgins strip Leukippos, they discover the deception and kill him. The god pursues Daphne who prays to Zeus for help. The nymph is then transformed into a laurel tree.

In Arcadia, Daphne is the daughter of the river Ladon and of Gaea, the Earth. The Leukippos affair is not mentioned. The legend states simply that when Apollo pursues the nymph, she asks her mother for deliverance. Some sources mention a metamorphosis (cf. Libanius, *Progymnasmata* 13', Teubner VIII, 44); others tell how Gaea, in answer to Daphne's prayer, swallows the nymph and has a laurel tree appear on the spot (cf. Tzetzes, *ad Lycophron Alex.* 6; *Schol. ad Hom. Iliad* I. 14). In the Thessalian version, Daphne is the daughter of the river Peneus and Gaea; this time, the metamorphosis is brought about by her father. After the transformation, Apollo crowns himself with a wreath made of branches from the laurel tree.[31]

Undoubtedly, this myth serves as an etiological account explaining the origin of the laurel, one of Apollo's attributes. Like many of the other Greek deities, Apollo is a god of vegetation, and it is not only the laurel but also the plane tree, the tamarisk, and the apple tree that are sacred to him.[32] But the laurel is by far the most prominent, playing a major role in Apollo's cult, especially at Delphi and Boeotia. Tradition has it, so Pausanias reports, that the most ancient temple of Apollo at Delphi was made of laurel, the branches of which were brought from the Vale of Tempe (10.5.9). In the ritual of divination at Delphi, the Pythoness, the prophetess who gave forth Apollo's oracles, would chew leaves from the laurel to prepare herself for divine inspiration and, in so doing, would also establish communion with the deity. Laurel leaves were also used to adorn the prophetic tripod and the Pythoness herself is said to have worn a laurel crown. At Delphi, the laurel may have been regarded as a prophetic tree, a function fulfilled by the oak at Dodona, for the Homeric Hymn to Apollo refers to the god as speaking "in answer from his laurel tree below the dells of Parnassus" (3.396).[33] One of the god's appellatives, "daphnephoros," was derived from the laurel and related to the ritual of the "Daphnephoria," supposedly a ceremony of purification. And so the laurel, an essential tool in Apollo's religious worship and festivals, was placed in a love story to explain why it was so important to the god: the nymph beloved of the god becomes the tree that forever adorns his locks; the graceful, cherished virgin turns into the graceful, cherished tree. In his *Description of Greece* (10.7.8), Pausanias conceives of the story of Apollo and Daphne as such, and Andrew Lang, the noted mythologist, follows suit. Lang suggests that "people would ask why the deity was associated with the flowers and boughs, and the answer would be readily developed on the familiar lines of nature myth. The laurel is dear to the god because the laurel was once a girl whom he pursued with his love, and who, to escape his embraces, became a tree."[34]

Daphne's different faces in the world of Greek religion—her presence as prophetess, as unwilling beloved, and finally as laurel in numerous rituals (*Daphne* in Greek means laurel)—is not an uncommon occurrence in the realm of myth and cult. For these roles reveal that the nymph, like most mythological personages—an extraordinary example is her own eager lover, Apollo—has proved immensely adaptable to the needs of religious practices. And this adaptability continues as Daphne, along with Apollo, enters the world of literature; both the god and the nymph serve the wishes and whims of writers who, under their own afflatus at times no less magical than that of the ancient holy seers, construct new stages on which the mythical figures play new roles.

1

Ovid's Metamorphoses 1.452–567: Erotic Comedy and Two Grotesques

In his version of the myth of Apollo and Daphne—with its themes of love, agon, and the grotesque—Ovid abandons the mythopoeic role of the story, its function in ritual and cult, and treats it as poetic fiction, answering to the special calling of imaginative play and entertainment.[1] The aesthetic approach to myth that Ovid espouses had already been elaborated in varying degrees in Greek art and letters and by Roman imitators such as Plautus. Stripping myth of its function of interpreting reality and its use in religion, artists and writers use myth as a medium of artistic exploration where freedom of invention rules the day. Ovid's aesthetic approach, however, does not prevent him from using the myth as a disguised political statement against Emperor Augustus. Ovid's comedy of Apollo, the Emperor's favorite deity, betrays his disdain for Augustan religious ideology and moral doctrine.

The myth of Apollo and Daphne, an *aetion* recounting the origin of the sacred laurel so dear to the god, becomes in Ovid's irreverent hands an occasion for his virtuosity as a teller of tales. The Greek etiological legend yields the stuff for a seriocomic story of unrequited love with strong echoes of the trappings of Roman erotic elegy. The key ingredients of the world of elegy are here: love as a madness that overrides reason and common sense, the wanton little Cupid, the rejected suitor, the inaccessible *domina*. And as in his own elegies, Ovid's treatment of the love experience is that of *spoudogeloion* (the mixture of jest and earnest, the mingling of the serious and the frivolous muses), which the ancients bequeath to the Middle Ages and to the Renaissance.[2] The clash between the lusty god and the reluctant virgin is truly an erotic agon, a battle of opposing wills, ending with a frustrated lover and a newly created tree in place of the once "coy mistress."

The grotesque plays a key role in this erotic agon. Transformation is for Daphne a means to escape the world of agon and of men but the grotesque in her change adds drama to the scene as Apollo witnesses what for him is the loss of the woman and of love. Daphne's grotesque is not only a tool of drama, however, but a tool of parody as it sets off the lusty comicity of the deity trapped in Bergsonian rigidity, a foolish lover kissing a bark still throbbing with human life. Apollo is also the victim of a grotesque moment of his own as Ovid pokes fun at the divine lover by dressing him in the guise of a hound as he chases Daphne, who is portrayed as a hare. The comedy of Apollo in this grotesque moment, tinged with both violence and humor, goes beyond the amusing, ironic debasement Ovid contrives for the god before the hound/hare chase. Now animal-like, love assumes new dimensions.

In my analysis I will consider conventions from erotic elegy, epic, the comic tradition of the gods, and the grotesque tradition that inform or serve as background to Ovid's Apollo and Daphne. To examine Ovid's figures in the light of these conventions reveals how uniquely Ovidian they are.

Ovid's comic Apollo belongs to a long tradition of laughter. Comedy among the gods goes back as far as Homer where humor enters the epic genre. Homer treats the ancient gods seriously and, moments later, tells of their scandalous adventures as in the farcical scene in which Hephaestus surprises his wife Aphrodite in the arms of Ares (*Odyssey* VIII). For all his mockery of the gods, however, Homer regards myth and legend as a record of the past. Later the face of myth changes. When the comedy of the gods reaches the theater, it becomes a celebration, a participation in a festive freedom from the sacred, even if this freedom is momentary and in a sense illusory, for it is still tied to the gods and takes place during religious holidays. Striking examples of the travesty of myth on the comic stage are the low burlesque in the Doric farces, comedies of Attica, and the *phlyakes* or mimes of Magna Graecia. Much has been lost of this ancient travesty of myth but the practice was very popular, and it comes to us in all its outrageous humor in pictorial representations, especially on *phlyax* vases with scenes from the stage. If this toying with myth is not the noblest art, it is at least one of the most amusing. And if Homer spared Apollo a comic fall, as we shall see, the burlesque stage did not. Myth becomes progressively detached from notions of history as well as from its

religious base, and in the Hellenistic age its separation is complete, allowing for the gentle humor of Theocritus and the irreverent comedy of Callimachus. Significantly, there is a spirit of
play underlying and tying together the travesties of the gods
that, as Johan Huizinga has shown, is intrinsic to the world of
myth with its wild, unrestrained fantasy.[3]

Ovid's comedy of Apollo is obviously not Homeric—much
has been said about Homer's gods who, unlike Ovid's, keep
their power and grandeur in spite of comic moments—nor does
it share in the crude jolts, obscenities, and buffoonery of the
low, rambunctious Attic comedies and the *phlyakes*. But when
Ovid pokes fun at Apollo, clever mock-heroic touches and subtle
poetic tricks mingle with not so subtle parody and farce, and, as
we shall see, in these latter moments our poet comes close to the
comic theater, with its grotesque elements and its festive humor.
I will also consider Ovid's closest antecedent, Callimachus, with
his mischievous anthropomorphism of the gods. For Hellenistic
Callimachus and for Ovid—in sharp contrast to Virgil who uses
myth for its symbolic value—the mythological tales with their
luxuriantly rich imaginings are a source of literary games; they
are a stage for the poets' wit.

If the comic tradition claims Apollo as one of its own, the
god, along with Daphne, is equally welcome in another well-
known tradition: the grotesque. Their grotesques are but two examples in an enormous outpouring of grotesque imagery that
permeates all stages of antiquity. It was popular in the comic
theater mentioned above, in the ornamental grotesque of friezes
and murals, in terracotas such as those of the Kerch collection,
with its senile pregnant hags, and in the treatment of hybridization, metamorphosis, and "monstrous love" in Hellenistic art
and letters. From the Hellenes Ovid "learns" his grotesque.

Ovid's treatment of Apollo and Daphne is based on the
Thessalian version of the myth: Daphne, daughter of the river
Peneus and of Gaea, the Earth goddess, is pursued by Apollo
and, after asking her father for protection, is transformed into
the laurel. Ovid excludes Gaea from his tale,[4] but introduces a
new character, the notorious Cupid of elegiac renown and his
arrows of opposite effect—one of gold that kindles love and one
of lead that kills all passion. It is fittingly the son of Venus, the
god of love, who sets the stage for this story of frustrated love
by creating the erotic agon, a struggle between two conflicting
and unyielding postures: the rigidity of the modest virgin,

pierced with lead, and the erotic madness of Apollo having been struck by the gold-tipped arrow. The conflict of passion and reluctance is at the heart of Roman love elegy but here it has been exaggerated and intensified, sparking and sustaining the comedy as Apollo attempts to conquer Daphne at all costs.

Brooks Otis has shown how comedy emerges in Ovid's tale through deflation, how the majestic Apollo is converted into a fatuous lover.[5] But Otis does not go far enough in his assessment of Apollo's foolishness. Ovid's comic treatment of this figure rests on a series of psychic transformations. First Ovid strips the Olympian of his divine powers and solemnity and transforms him into a human lover. Foolish in his urgency to capture the elusive Daphne, the deity enters more and more into the realm of comedy. Phoebus appears next in the guise of a predatory hound and lastly as a mechanized figure clutching a tree. Descending, as in a chain of being, the god Apollo becomes human, animal, and machine. Otis is correct in noting that in her recalcitrance Daphne serves as a foil for the comedy (103). But she is much more than that, for to her belongs the transformation, with its grotesque, as well as a secondary theme introduced as Cupid strikes her with his dart—questions of a split identity between her alluring body, which attracts Apollo, and her virgin self. This split is partially mended by the metamorphosis into the laurel.

When Apollo enters the tale, he is a figure of epic stature. Having killed the monstrous Python, the god of the silver bow seems bound for noble deeds, his skill and prowess glowing in majestic battles. But his ambition is thwarted by the god of love. Still exulting over his conquest, Apollo meets Cupid and accuses the little god of stealing his weapon, the bow, made only for the shoulders of the strong and mighty, not for little cupids who deal in insignificant concerns such as love. Apollo is wrong, of course. Defeated by Cupid's arrow, his sole, overriding concern will be love.[6]

This clever detail of the defeat of heroic matters by love is foreshadowed by the poet-lover's own fall at the hands of Cupid in *Amores*, 1.1. As the poet prepares to write an epic in lofty hexameters, the mischievous Cupid steals a foot and converts hexameters into pentameters, the elegiac meter (3–4). Moreover, he wounds the poet with one of his shafts. So love becomes the subject of his verses and, trapped by Cupid, the man must live the uncertain, tormented life of love. Apollo must do likewise.

The once haughty Olympian now suffers the conventional pangs of love: unrequited, he longs, deceived by a misguided hope (496); he burns like wheat in flames (492–95); he cannot cure the wound inflicted by Amor (523–24). In short, the mighty deity has fallen from divinity to become the slave and prisoner of the love god and in a sense of Daphne, the cruel, unreachable mistress. Like the suitor in elegiac love poetry, Apollo is fixed in the rhetorical artifices of the tradition.[7]

In portraying Apollo as both a warrior-god, the killer of Python, and a lover, Ovid draws from two well-known contrasting cónventions, one that regards the god as the patron of epic poetry and the other that makes Apollo the "enemy" of epic, the god of the lyre who cautions Callimachus to "keep the Muse slender" (*Aetia*, 1.1.25) and drives Propertius away from "heroic song" (3.3.13–26). We cannot but think that Ovid is playfully and maliciously "chastising" Apollo for his advice to Callimachus and Propertius against writing epic verses; he deflates the epic Apollo and makes him the protagonist in that "slender" poetry the god himself advocates. In entering the world of love, Apollo is the worse for it. The god is treated in a half-serious, half-mocking vein, reminding us of Ovid's earlier treatment of his elegiac persona, where he mingles elegiac conventions and self-irony.[8] Unlike his predecessors, who take love and the unsatisfied lover seriously, Ovid playfully treats the travails that this wistful creature must endure. Similarly, Ovid endows Apollo with the foibles of the victims of Amor and then subjects him to his typical ridicule. Apollo falls in love at first sight (490)—the elegiac motif of the eyes as vehicles of the experience—and in so doing he is reduced to a comic voyeur (note the sequence of verbs *videt, videt, vidisse, laudat, meliora putat*) as he pleasurably studies his beloved's body:

> videt igne micantes
> sideribus similes oculos, videt oscula, quae non
> est vidisse satis; laudat digitosque manusque
> bracchiaque et nudos media plus parte lacertos;
> siqua latent, meliora putat. (498–502)

> (He gazes at her eyes gleaming like stars, he gazes
> upon her lips, which but to gaze on does not satisfy.
> He marvels at her fingers, hands, and wrists, and her
> arms, bare to the shoulder; and what is hidden he deems
> still lovelier.)[9]

Ovid could have selected any number of enviable charms from the traditional elegiac catalog to exalt this mythological beloved. But in limiting himself to one—the eyes like stars—Ovid shifts our attention from the woman to the lusty lover, the greedy witness. And when Daphne flees Apollo's eyes, the comedy intensifies.

Apollo turns from a passive observer into a threatening, but laughable, pursuer. His subjection to Cupid renders him the helpless victim of *furor*, the erotic madness that afflicts all elegiac lovers, divesting them of self-mastery and reason.[10] We must remember that under the influence of *furor* the lovers of the melancholic Tibullus and the learned Propertius are paralyzed and live in willing servitude and helpless, teary despair. But Apollo—like Ovid's lover in the *Amores*, who can even become a violent rogue (1.7)—springs into action. Moreover, in the figure of the divine Apollo we find the complexity of human love as Ovid sees it, the mingling of pathos and fatuousness, humor and pain, self-pity and pomposity. And this tormented and tormenting feeling is shown in Apollo's speech to Daphne during the chase (504–24), for the god's entreaty is a masterful exposition of the psychology of the lover: his self-pitying submission to his lovesickness (emphasized by the typical *me miserum* of elegiac erotic woes in line 508);[11] his urgency to catch the virgin mingling with his apparent concern for her safety as she runs along rugged paths;[12] his desire to let Daphne know that he is no lowly peasant but a suitor of noble birth and high connections, and only revealing himself as an impotent, impatient fool. Apollo is clearly a failure in "bonas artes," the art of persuasion, which is a mark of successful lovers in ancient literature.[13] (Ovid, the facetious teacher of love, elaborates this notion in his *Ars amatoria* when he instructs the young men of Rome to learn this art in order to seduce their women, 1.459–62). Moreover, as the god chases the poor nymph, the dignified tone of his speech contrasts in incongruous juxtaposition to his wooing-on-the-run, endowing the narrative with mock-heroic touches.

As Apollo's coaxing words fall on deaf virginal ears, the mock-heroic turns into farce and the erotic agon reaches a peak, for now the lusty lover silently but greedily pursues as a fierce, bloodthirsty hound eager to catch its succulent prey. The combination of images of the hunt and sexual aggression, a familiar notion used throughout the *Metamorphoses*,[14] is a means of making fun of Apollo. Divine dignity is totally shattered; lust has further debased Apollo, reducing him from a lover, with very

human passions, to a predatory animal. *Praeda,* as in erotic poetry,[15] has sexual connotations:

> ut canis in vacuo leporem cum Gallicus arvo
> vidit, et hic praedam pedibus petit, ille salutem
> (alter inhaesuro similis iam iamque tenere
> sperat et extento stringit vestigia rostro,
> alter in ambiguo est, an sit conprensus, et ipsis
> morsibus cripitur tangentiaque ora relinquit):
> sic deus et virgo; est hic spe celer, illa timore.
> (533–39)

> (Just as when a Gallic hound has seen a hare in an open
> plain, and seeks his prey on flying feet, but the hare,
> safety; he, just about to fasten on her, now, even now
> thinks he has her, and grazes her very heels with his out-
> stretched muzzle; but she knows not whether she be not
> already caught, and barely escapes from those sharp fangs
> and leaves behind the jaws just closing on her: so ran the
> god and maid, he sped by hope and she by fear.)

In this scene, the grotesque emerges as the human (in his
anthropomorphic form Apollo is for all purposes "human") endowed with animal qualities—resulting in that mingling and
clashing of incompatibles typical of the grotesque. It is true that
Ovid identifies Apollo with a dog and Daphne with a hare by
means of similes and does not actually "transform" them into
these animals. But the way in which Ovid has fashioned his
"cinematic," detailed description of the chase can only make the
reader envision the god and the nymph bearing animal traits,
especially Apollo who, as the target of the comedy, is dressed
with "muzzle," "fangs," and "jaws," clawing at his sexual prey
as he pursues her. Apollo becomes a hybrid in our imagination,
existing in that grotesque interval in which he is neither fully
human nor fully dog but both at the same time. The erotic comedy in this passage, with its grotesque, is no longer the lighthearted banter we had thus far encountered. Animalization has
crept in and changed the tone of the humor. Irony has given
way to cruel caricature.

Apollo's animalization is part of a larger picture in Ovid's
work, the theme of "monstrous" and "forbidden love"—such as
the transformations of lusty gods into animals to seduce their
paramours—which the Hellenistic poets were so fond of and
which Ovid often elaborates to reveal foolish eroticism.[16] The

reason for the treatment of "abnormal" love in the Hellenes has been explained variously as mere sensationalism, morbid delight, or the simple desire to shock. Ovid uses it for his own aesthetic purposes, and one is his clever comedy: for instance, his portrayal of how inordinate lust makes mighty Jove become an irresistibly handsome but silly bull, rollicking on the grass, impatiently awaiting the desired moment to seduce Europa (*Met.* 2.846–75), or his tongue-in-cheek picture of Pasiphaë in love with her bull, wishing she had horns, making dangerous heifer rivals vanish from the herd, and finally "becoming" a cow of maple wood and conceiving the beastly Minotaur (*Ars amatoria* 1.295–326).

When Apollo is placed in the world of "monstrous love," he fares far worse than either Jupiter or Pasiphaë. Ovid's grotesque portrayal of the god goes beyond the playful sketches cited above, for in his lust Apollo becomes, if only figuratively, a ravenous and savage dog. And as he stages his "attack" on his victim, Apollo is not only divested of his majesty but, ironically, of his threatening quality as well (at least for the reader if not for Daphne). The sense of harsh elemental violence conveyed by the hunting hound quickly dissolves into laughter as we picture the god in ridiculous canine costume chasing a rabbit, his obdurate lady love. The grotesque in its distortion—the clash of human and animal, elements that are mutually repellent—reveals the true nature of the lover; Apollo, once the god of light and reason, is now all comic disorder. Taken in by beauty, he becomes mad and foolish. Grotesque dehumanization and animalization for comic purposes will be popular tools of the burlesque in Golden Age Spain, especially in the work of the ingenious Quevedo.

In his use of animal imagery, Ovid uses a subtle play of appearance and reality, a game of "masks," to further poke fun at the lover. At the beginning of his speech to Daphne during the chase, Apollo wants to appear as a "harmless" lover in the eyes of the virgin; he tells her that she is mistakenly fleeing from him as the lamb flees from the wolf, the deer from the lion, and the doves from the eagle (505–6). In the hound/hare scene, however, Ovid mischievously unmasks Apollo by forcing another mask on him, one that distorts and ridicules but also shows the god's true character. By investing Apollo with the rapacity that the god had denied for himself, Ovid not only ridicules the Olympian lover by making him play a ravenous creature hovering over his innocent victim but reveals him for what he is also, a silly liar.

As a background to the chase of Apollo the hound after Daphne the hare, we find the traditional epic chases with their imagery of animal hunt, such as Achilles' pursuit of Hector as a hawk/dove and dog/fawn chase in the *Iliad* (XXII) and Aeneas' pursuit of Turnus as a hound/stag chase in the *Aeneid* (XII). Ovid may have used Virgil as model, for he echoes the *Aeneid's* wind metaphor of the escaping victim. In Virgil, we have Turnus "fugit ocior Euro" (733); in Ovid, Daphne "fugit ocior aura" (502). But the correspondence between the Ovidian hunt scene and the epic chase goes beyond mere parallels. It involves, in effect, a poetic trick. Ovid probably knew that the informed reader would draw parallels between the two and in so doing would see the deity, once "the brightest among the bright Olympians," buried deeper still in the quagmire of an ignoble comedy. Although Apollo is dressed through epic language in the same guise as Aeneas and Achilles, he is worlds apart from these two epic heroes, and the contrast makes him even more laughable; instead of chasing a military foe, our god is shown rabidly pursuing his unwilling lady, who, like an ancient Richardsonian heroine, flees from him to safeguard "her most treasured possession," her virginity. This unfavorable comparison of Apollo the lover with epic figures adds insult to injury since the god, the divine killer of Python and the ideal of nobility and strength, had already lost his epic stature as a result of Cupid's assault and now is explicitly revealed in all his weakness as his lowly erotic dalliance harshly and comically jars with the self-contained, noble world of epic.[17]

It is at this point in the narrative, the farcical scene of a ludicrous Apollo chasing Daphne like a ravenous dog, that Ovid reminds us of a not so distant comic past—the Greek theater, with its grotesque as a tool of parody. Apollo (this time unaccompanied by Daphne) had already been the subject of mockery on the Greek stage. This comedy of the god is, as it were, the other side of the Greek Apolline coin, since Apollo was the deity who represented ideal manly beauty, whether in art or poetry, and stood for order, dignity, and moderation. And, even though there is evidence that the god's cult was not totally lacking in frenzy and in untamed rapture, the predominant qualities of Apolline religion were seriousness and solemnity. But if the Greeks used reason and moderation in their worship of Apollo, they did not spare him their sense of humor and spirit of play, which were abundant. A short digression into the Greek burlesque of myth and Apollo's role in it will show how Ovid's Olympian belongs to a long uninterrupted tradition of laughter, where the gods are mocked and abused.

The roots of the travesty of myth are very old. We find humor and laughter in the folklore of primitive peoples, where serious myths coexist with comic ones, where the deities are at once venerated and ridiculed.[18] This "ritual laughter," which in later times disappears from the sacred sphere, is preserved in agrarian festivals in which obscene raillery is a constant element, as in the Attic spring festival of the Anthesteria—clowns and jesters in wagons hurling insults and abuse against the bystanders. It is also evident in the Roman Saturnalia, in processions of victorious generals where praises mingle with insults, and in funeral processions where a similar mixture is uttered against the deceased.[19] In Greek religion, the spirit of gaiety and play is preserved in the cult of Dionysus, and it is not surprising that the origin of comedy in Attica is connected with the *komos* or revel performed in honor of the god. In these revels (whether the phallic processions of the Rural Dionysia and the festival of the Lenaea, or simply animal masquerades) the *komasts*—cheerful, wild followers of Dionysus—would sing licentious, derisive songs and make fools of the bystanders. It is this coarse, abusive, often obscene, humor that appears upon the comic stage and needles even the Lord of the Festival himself in whose sacred domain it all took place. Comedies became an official part of the cult of Dionysus in the fifth century and were performed in his festivals—as early as 486 B.C. in the elaborate City Dionysia—along with dithyrambs, tragedies, and satyr plays. So we have reverence of the god's deeds and adventures in the tragedies, and mockery and abuse in the comedies, as in Aristophanes' *Frogs* (405).[20] Dionysus is of course not the only one mocked. Exalted heroes of legend such as Herakles and Odysseus, Zeus, the highest god, and even the solemn Apollo are not spared.

Evidence of a comic Apollo comes to us not from Attica but from Magna Graecia, the Greek colonies of southern Italy, on *phlyax* vases. Contemporary with Athenian Middle Comedy, c. 400/330 B.C., these vases depict scenes from the low burlesque called *phlyakes* or mimes.[21] Like their ancestor, the old Doric comedy that had had such a strong influence on Attic comedy itself, these mimes have as one of their main themes the travesty of myth. As these mimes evolved, the myths that were burlesqued were not the mythical tales themselves but the versions in the all too famous tragedies. *The hilarotragodia*—as the parody of tragedy was called—was given literary form by Rhinthon of Syracuse at the end of the fourth century B.C. Only a few fragments of this "cheerful tragedy" survive. However, numerous vase paintings that have come down to us offer a good idea of how these plays were represented on the stage. Even though he was not mocked as often as Herakles and Odysseus, the fact that Apollo was mocked at all in the *phlyakes* gives us an indication that there must have been more burlesques of the god, even in Athens, and that evidence is simply not extant. But what is left is indeed revealing.

A *phlyax* vase now in the Hermitage Museum in Leningrad (fig. 1) depicts a burlesque of Apollo and Herakles as the latter comes to Delphi seeking purification after having killed his tutor, Linos.[22] According to the story, when Apollo refuses to absolve him, Herakles steals the tripod, and Athena and Zeus finally reconcile them. This scene is represented in serious art, as in the pediment of the Siphnian Treasury at Delphi (fig. 2). The vase, on the other hand, presents the encounter as ludicrous slapstick. Herakles stands on the holy tripod onto which he has jumped, holding a club in his right hand; with it, he threatens Apollo. The god appears lowly and ridiculous perched on the roof of his temple where he has fled to keep both the bow and the laurel (the sacred branch of purification) from being snatched away by Herakles. Prissy, effeminate, cowardly, and crowned with his omnipresent laurel garland, Apollo dons the typical grotesque costume of Doric farce and Attic comedy: flesh-colored tights (intended to simulate nudity), the short and thickly padded garment showing bulging paunch and buttocks, a protruding phallus, and a mask with huge eyes, wide nostrils, and gaping mouth. (This exaggerated, distorted costume is the chief means of burlesque degradation not only for Herakles and Apollo but for all the mythological figures who dare appear on the comic stage.) Apollo gazes greedily at the basket of fruit and cake that Herakles temptingly offers. We can guess the rest. Apollo will reach out for the basket, Herakles will strike him with the club, and the god will fall in the basin of holy water beneath him and lose his attributes to Iolaus, who is eagerly waiting to grab them. Apollo and Herakles are predecessors of stock characters of the Roman stage, the greedy blockhead and the clever hunchback who appear later in the *commedia dell'arte*.

Apollo's unsuspected comic bath is a forerunner of Quevedo's burlesque of the god; defeated in his attempt to woo Daphne, this seventeenth-century Apollo will tumble not into a basin of holy water but into a pot of dark, tasty cooking sauce where bay leaves customarily float.

Another *phlyax* vase, found in Apulia and now in the British Museum (fig. 3), shows Apollo, the god of medicine, as a quack doctor upon his arrival at Delphi. On the stage are a bag, a bow, and the god's scythian cap. Apollo is garbed in the costume of comic actors—tights, grotesque mask, and phallus—tending the sickly Cheiron. The centaur is helped onto the stage by a companion; both of them are wearing ugly, comic masks as are the nymphs of Parnassus who watch the scene from above.[23]

Another possible evidence of a comic Apollo is found on a crater—a vessel for mixing wine and water—in Naples (fig. 4). It shows a young man standing next to an old man—both ludicrous in appearance—handing a woman what appears to be a baby in swaddling clothes. One of the explanations given to this scene is that of Apollo giving Ion to the Pythia.[24]

And so in the theater, as in Ovid's *Metamorphoses*, the grotesque is an effective device to comically degrade its sacred subject—the mighty Apollo. The theater effects grotesque deformation through disfiguring bulges and distorted masks, Ovid through animalization. And in both we have not only a disintegration of divine character but also of what Apollo symbolizes in the world of cult and ritual—dignity and solemnity. But is this comedy an imposition from without, something alien to the world it is taunting? The answer is no. For the Greek travesties of Apollo and Ovid's caricature spring from a spirit of play that belongs to the miraculous, fantastic world of myth itself. Johan Huizinga in his *Homo Ludens* defines play as "a free activity standing quite consciously outside 'ordinary' life as being 'not serious,'" a time of mirth and freedom that nevertheless carries its own order.[25] To this time belong "the wild imaginings of mythology" where "a fanciful spirit is playing on the border-line between jest and earnest" (5). And it is the play inherent in the unbridled fantasies of myth that the Greeks captured and elaborated in their burlesques—a practice that the Romans continued, especially in the comedies of Plautus, the Atellan farces, and the mimes, performed in their festivals in honor of the gods, fittingly called *ludi*.[26] And Ovid's comic vision of Apollo in urgent, amorous pursuit places him in the center of this free "magic circle" of play alongside the travesties of the stage.

In the midst of Ovid's humor there is also a touch of what has been called the "festive element" in the comedy of the theater. The laughter in this comic theater is carnival laughter, laughter that mocks and derides, but that is also a triumphant laughter, effecting a secret liberation from restraints, from the awe and respect of the sacred, from social constraints, from law and order.[27] Travesty of the gods on the comic stage provides a moment of release in humor that is ambivalent—mocking and liberating at the same time—and also paradoxical, for it was enjoyed during religious festivals honoring the gods. The fact that the Romans called their religious holidays *ludi* indicates their conscious participation in the spirit of revel, a time where everyday rules do not apply, where there is freedom to share in the celebration. And is not Ovid in his mockery of Apollo participating in a kind of festive freedom of his own? It is well known that the last two centuries of the Republic (230–30 B.C.) witnessed a decline of religion in Rome, and one of Augustus' wishes (one that ultimately failed) was to restore old religious practices such as that of the Palatine Apollo, the object of the Emperor's devotion. Ovid's jeering of the divinity who commanded the most respect from Augustus may well have been not only literary play but a source of liberation for him, the kind of secret liberation found in the theater during festival days. In his comedy of Apollo the sophisticated poet-rebel becomes a celebrant, freeing himself from the rigid bonds of the sacred sanctions of Augustus. Much has been written about Ovid's anti-Augustanism in the *Metamorphoses*, his rejection of Augustus' religious ideology and his antithetical posture to the Emperor's high moral purpose.[28] His comic Apollo is one of the clearest statements of his unorthodoxy. Laughter, as Bergson wisely suggests, is a social gesture and *lascivus* Ovid (as Quintilian called him) gives his answer to moral Augustus subtly wrapped in this universal mode. And so Ovid's levity in regard to myth pits him, like the comic rituals of the stage, against the Augustan ideals of sobriety and austerity, the virtues of *pietas* and *gravitas*.

Ovid's grotesque caricature of the lover Apollo, which ties his comedy to the theater, is not characteristic of Ovid's burlesque of the gods, sophisticated and urbane as it is. Ovid's laughter is on the whole not rollicking, not that "indecorous rumpus"[29] that is an integral part of the comedy of the gods in Aristophanes' theater, in the *phlyakes*, in Plautus, in the Atellan farces. Ovid's humor is closer in spirit to Hellenistic Callimachus who, in the Alexandrian age—the age of enlightenment—treats

Figure 1. *Phlyax* vase in the Hermitage Museum, Leningrad, no. 1660. Herakles threatens Apollo.

Figure 2. Pediment of the Siphnian Treasury at Delphi. Herakles and Apollo contend for the tripod. Photo Alinari/Art Resource, New York.

Figure 3. *Phlyax* vase found in Apulia, now in the British Museum. Apollo and Cheiron. Reproduced by courtesy of the Trustees of the British Museum.

Figure 4. *Phlyax* vase (crater) in Naples. Apollo giving Ion to the Pythia. Reproduced from Margarete Bieber, *The History of the Greek and Roman Theater*. Copyright 1939, 1961 by Princeton University Press.

myth with the skepticism, genial irony, and lighthearted humor of the sophisticated unbeliever.[30] We have but to recall his playfully ironic scene of the child Artemis climbing on the lap of her father, Zeus, and asking him for an endless list of presents (*Hymn to Artemis*, 4ff.) or his humorous portrayal of Erysichthon who, condemned to eternal hunger for cutting down Demeter's sacred grove, eats everything in sight, even the cat (*Hymn to Demeter*, 107ff.). It is true that Ovid's gods are not Callimachean, those divinities of spoiled whims and bourgeois presence. Ovid's gods, as Otis rightly suggests, must be measured by a Virgilian standard, the comedy stemming from the incongruity created by placing "non-heroic behavior" in a "heroic-epic framework," as in Apollo's lofty words while vainly wooing his Daphne on the run.[31] But in Ovid as in Callimachus, myth is the subject matter of poetry that works as artifice; we applaud what consummate stylists can do with humor and a rich, urbane imagination. Like Callimachus, Ovid shows foolishness not in the coarse, slapstick tumbles of the comic stage but by means of tricks and surprising turns of language, fun and ingenuity based on wit and clever imagery. Also like his Greek predecessor, Ovid often plays hide-and-seek with the reader, making him "discover" the comedy. It is perhaps because of this act of discovery that much of Ovid's comedy eluded many of his critics until fairly recently.

If Apollo the foolish lover belongs to a long tradition of laughter, the chaste Daphne is part of an equally rich tradition, that of virginal huntresses pursued by urgent, divine ravishers. Daphne, like Callisto (2.409ff.), Arethusa (5.572ff.), Syrinx (1.689ff.), and other mythical virgins, belongs to the train of Diana, the virgin goddess of the hunt who makes chastity a binding law, enforcing it on her companions with fanatic zeal. Anyone who wavers must contend with the wrath of this cruel, vindictive deity. Callisto, the innocent, unwilling victim of Zeus' seduction, for instance, is cast out in disgrace from the goddess's band (2.464–65). And not even males who violate Diana's sacred grove escape her punishment, which can be ferocious; the hunter Actaeon, after spying the virgin goddess naked in her bath, is transformed by her into a stag and is then devoured by his own dogs (3.180–252). It is in the light of this zealous, forbidding cult of chastity that Daphne's wish for transformation at the end of the chase must be understood. Early in the story, the nymph had asked her father, Peneus, to grant her perpetual virginity— Diana had hers conferred by her father, Zeus—but Daphne's

beauty forbade the fulfillment of her wish (486–89). And so without protection, as it were, she roams the woods hunting wild
beasts, a place where divine and semidivine seducers are constantly on the prowl for young, virginal flesh. When the anxious
Apollo comes into the scene, in an ironic twist the huntress becomes the hunted. Callisto had been tricked by the wiles of
Zeus, who disguises himself as Diana. Daphne, like Arethusa, is
more successful in thwarting her lover; like Arethusa, she flees
in a chase that ends in a saving transformation. Both lose their
forms, which had enticed their unwanted suitors, and they escape forever the world of lusty lovers. We must keep in mind,
however, that Daphne, unlike other virginal huntresses, becomes averse to love only after having been struck by Cupid's
dart. She, like Apollo, comes under the boy's spell. It is obvious
that Ovid's interest is to bring into focus the total power of love
and the comedy that results in the battle between modesty and
lust. But comedy in erotic agon is not all that Cupid brings, for
his dart of lead introduces a secondary theme into the story,
questions of Daphne's identity, a split between her alluring
body, which attracts Apollo, and her virgin self, which she tries
to protect by fleeing. The metamorphosis mends the scission and
enables the nymph to preserve her identity as a virgin by pro-
curing a refuge away from the lover.[32]

Once the narrative turns from the chase to Daphne's transformation, the tone changes from jest to earnest. As the nymph is
about to be caught by Apollo, she prays to her father to change and
destroy her form "by which she pleases so well": " 'fer, pater . . .
opem! si flumina numen habetis, / qua nimium placui, mutando
perde figuram' " (545–47). The transformation is brought about instantly (548–52) by Peneus acting as deus ex machina:

> vix prece finita torpor gravis occupat artus,
> mollia cinguntur tenui praecordia libro,
> in frondem crines, in ramos bracchia crescunt,
> pes modo tam velox pigris radicibus haeret,
> ora cacumen habet: remanet nitor unus in illa.

> (Scarce had she thus prayed when a down-dragging
> numbness seized her limbs, and her soft sides were begirt
> with thin bark. Her hair was changed to leaves, her arms
> to branches. Her feet, but now so swift, grew fast in slug-
> gish roots, and her head was now but a tree's top. Her
> gleaming beauty alone remained.)

Ovid's scene of metamorphosis is a highly visual spectacle of the assimilation of the human form by the emerging laurel. The nymph is caught in midflight and the sense of impending rigidity is imparted by the ominous clause "torpor gravis occupat artus." Next, the verb *cinguntur*, with its passive voice emphasizing the idea of paralysis, gives the beginning of the encroachment by the plant. The transformation appears as a rhythmic flow, carried out with smooth equipoise. In the gradual paralysis of the nymph, only one pairing of maiden and tree conveys contrast—her swiftness *(pes velox)* and the tree's sluggish roots *(pigris radicibus)*. The remaining pairings stress the similarity between her body and the laurel. Daphne's soft flesh *(mollia praecordia)* is begirt with gentle, delicate bark *(tenui libro)*; her hair becomes leaves, her arms branches, and her head the laurel's top. This smooth conversion, along with the uninterrupted rhythm of the change, conveys the sense of a blending of one form into the other rightly suited for the ontological implications of the metamorphosis. For underlying Daphne's change— and the theme of transformation in the whole of the *Metamorphoses*—is a primitive cosmology in which all living things are animated by one life-principle or spirit, which is then capable of migrating from body to body. The transformation enables Daphne to leave a body split by opposing forces of beauty and chastity and to acquire the physical shape that conforms to her conception of herself as a virgin free from sexuality; she is converted into a nonhuman form, into tree life incapable of passion. By escaping into her arboreal citadel, within which she will be secure from overzealous males, Daphne achieves the ultimate withdrawal from a world threatening to her identity.

The laurel, however, not only "protects" the maiden's identity but paradoxically enables her to retain the characteristic physical feature that had at first attracted the god—her fairness, now preserved in a sexually unassailable form. In like manner, the obduracy of the maiden, her trademark as *dura puella*, remains, for even as a tree Daphne shrinks back from Apollo's kisses (556). But this salvation of "a self in crisis" is not a totally satisfactory solution. In a purely mythical world where nubile young women are perceived in slender, gently swaying trees, this transformation would be regarded as perfectly acceptable. But in the poetic world of the skeptical, urbane Ovid, something else is brewing, including dark elements of disorder that subvert Daphne's apparently tidy transformation. And Ovid's skepticism and disorder give rise to the grotesque.

The grotesque effect of the Ovidian treatment of Daphne's transformation has been attributed by L. P. Wilkinson to the "jaded palate of Hellenistic decadence,"[33] a tradition that Ovid followed. But decadent or not, this tradition, with its transformations presented in gradual unfolding, provided Ovid with the ideal models for his own masterful descriptions of metamorphosis. And the result are vivid portrayals of a human being in the process of becoming something that is not human, and this subversion of the human by the uncanny and alien is at the core of the grotesque in Daphne's transformation. Her change reveals a turbulent confusion of the laws of nature. We see a hybrid, incongruous vision of human dissolution and distortion, in violation not only of natural order but of standards of harmony and proportion as well; leaves sprout from her head, arms become branches, and feet grow into roots.

But is Ovid's transformation of Daphne unnatural—and so grotesque? We know that Daphne's change—sustained by a cosmology that makes tales of etiology such as the laurel's possible—constitutes a passage into a vegetative form of life that involves a healing of her split self. It is also an escape; the nymph "casts off" her sexuality to elude her menacing pursuer. This is an explanation that renders the experience comprehensible, offering a measure of harmony and logic. But it is after all only a *literary* explanation, for Ovid, the unbeliever of myths,[34] uses the story of Daphne as a poetic fiction. For the reader of Ovid's times and for the modern reader, "belief" in myth here entails only that suspension of disbelief that the master storyteller creates in his fascinating, compelling collection of stories. The lack of *literal* credibility in the transformations highlights their bizarre and uncanny aspects; it opens the door to the grotesque, to the realm of distorted forms that intrude and subvert our everyday world by their irrational, alien presence. What we have here are two points of view: the "old" primitive belief in transformation and a "new" skeptical view, Ovid's and our own, which can only regard Daphne's transformation as a vision of dehumanization. Transformation becomes for us something other than what it was intended for. The laws, mythical laws as it were, that the transformation once obeyed are no longer valid; so, what was perfectly natural in that world of mythical forms is for us unfamiliar and alien. By wrenching these forms from their religious, metaphysical realm, by denying them their customary mythopoeic function and treating them as poetic fiction, Ovid focuses on their strange, aberrant presence.

And philosophy, the rational leveler, is equally unhelpful in providing a system to explain away Daphne's fantastic transformation. It is no more than wishful thinking to use Pythagoras' speech, as some have done, as a philosophical framework unifying the *Metamorphoses* and thereby offering a coherent meaning to the phenomenon of transformation. Pythagoras' words, often cast in lofty Lucretian style, can no more save the transformations from the grotesque than the primitive cosmology alluded to above. Pythagoras' sermon addresses philosophical concerns, briefly telling us of metempsychosis—an invisible journey of souls after death to new abodes in a cyclical, unending process (15.165–72)—and dwells upon universal change, where nothing lasts under the same appearance. His words echo Lucretius' atomism and his notions about birth and death (252–58). But Ovid is far from this philosophy. His stories of metamorphosis confront us with a multitude of fantastic happenings whose origin lies in a prerational world where, miraculously and in mid-stream, forms become other forms. Pythagoras' notion of flux in Book 15 and the phenomenon of transformation that Ovid offers in the preceding fourteen books evidently belong to different levels of reality. Pythagoras' speech, with its rational, philosophical tidbits (we must remember that it is not a coherently worked out system), surely cannot serve as the explanation for the whole business of fantastic metamorphosis presented by Ovid. As Hermann Fränkel has suggested, the philosophical sermon does by its very nature stop "short of the miracle."[35]

It is significant that if we venture beyond Pythagoras' rational speculations on the nature of things and examine the *quality* of his notion of flux, we end up with what we may call, for lack of a better term, a metaphysics of the absurd. Pythagoras' theater of nature, forever fluid in constant mutability of forms, is nothing but a universe of random and aimlessly changing matter, which souls briefly inhabit in their own aimless wanderings. And here is where the speech connects—if only in a somewhat elusive way—with the preceding stories,[36] whose transformations (at least those concerning humans) emerge as part of an immense impressionistic tableau of sudden, isolated moments. Such moments of transformation are but capricious, senseless happenings where the veil of the uncanny is strikingly real, where the feeling that something is amiss is constantly present.

It is obvious that Ovid is drawn to the grimmer aspects of the Greek mythical stories, and since he treats these tales not only as poetic fiction but as dramatic, human episodes, it would be difficult to dismiss the transformations as pure fantasy, as events occurring in a never-never land. They exist in a world plausible if only in bad dreams, a world where not only the un- natural and startling are everyday occurrences but the loss of the human is as well. What frequently emerges is what Charles Se- gal has called the "chaotic state of the world-order," a nightmar- ish scheme where helpless figures are victims of lustful, arbi- trary, and dimly comprehensible powers.[37] The nightmarish and ominous qualities are essential dimensions of the Ovidian gro- tesque. This is evident, for instance, in the plights of Io the heif- er (1.635–41) and Callisto the bear (2.477–95) who, having re- tained their minds and feelings, are terrified at seeing themselves trapped in animal forms as in cages of frightening, alien flesh.

The nightmarish is especially keen in those cruel transfor- mations where the human form is horribly distorted, such as those of Arachne as she becomes a spider (6.140–45) or Scylla as she is suddenly aware of a circle of monstrous barking dogs about her waist (14.59–67). And although Daphne's change is mild by comparison, it is still threatening to notions of harmony and order. In her urgency to escape, her transformation becomes ambiguous, offering only a half-solution (and even this half-solu- tion is extreme); according to the ruthless formula, her humanity must be destroyed so that her virginity may be preserved. The grotesque extends beyond the actual transformation as the re- jected Apollo eagerly places a hand on the tree, Daphne's newly acquired refuge, and feels the maiden's heart still beating be- neath the bark (554). But paradoxically, as the nymph departs from her human form and descends forever into the world of mindless, unreflecting nature, a new life takes shape—that of the laurel. Daphne's metamorphosis is also a moment of regen- eration and thus participates in that ambivalence typical of gro- tesque forms: the collision of sinister, "demonic" forces with those that are life-giving and creative.[38] This additional ambigui- ty of the transformation between loss and renewal is later high- lighted—not without one of Ovid's characteristically humorous twists—when the river gods meet Peneus and do not know whether to console him for the loss of his daughter or congratu- late him because obviously Daphne has become Apollo's sacred tree (577–78).

There is one more aspect that must be mentioned before

we turn to Apollo's comedy, and this concerns an important quality of Ovid's grotesques—what has been called the "play-urge" in the creation of grotesque forms. The "play-urge," "the desire to invent and experiment for its own sake," is especially strong in the grotesque, "where the breaking down and restructuring of familiar reality plays such a large part."[39] This is particularly true for Ovid, the master storyteller.We cannot ignore the relish with which this most pictorial of poets elaborates masterful descriptions of human deformation and all its grim consequences. I believe that this "play" is behind the paradox that confounds those critics who wonder how a writer as urbane as Ovid could produce such darkly unsettling scenes.

Daphne's grotesque not only adds drama to the loss of the maiden, but its ominous presence, as the human slips away, blends with the foolishness of Apollo to produce a scene that is both disturbing and humorous; as the lover places a hand on the tree and feels the heart palpitating beneath the bark, he embraces the branches as if they were Daphne's arms and kisses the wood (553–56). And so comedy, this time fraught with ambiguity, has entered the narrative once again. Here we have another one of those moments of ambivalence that run as a leitmotif throughout the *Metamorphoses*, this time created as Ovid juxtaposes the serious alongside the play and wit, the pain of transformation seen with his sophisticated, ironic detachment. Sometimes the mixture of the comic with the serious occurs in the experience of the process of transformation itself, creating a response of incompatible feelings found in so many grotesques: disquiet and amusement as when Io, turned into a heifer, wants to talk but can only moo (1.637), or horror and something like a mocking, contemptuous laughter as when Arachne is cruelly transformed into a spider—her hair, nose, and ears fall off, her head and body shrink, and the rest becomes all belly (6.140–44). As Apollo embraces the tree, on the other hand, it is what the god "brings" to the scene of transformation that makes the passage amusing. The humor derives from the kind of automatism that Bergson finds at the root of the comic. The god was obsessed with the idea of catching the desirable, elusive Daphne for so long that once he catches his quarry, now a tree, he stubbornly gives the bark the kisses meant for the girl. This mental obstinacy makes Phoebus comic. His machinelike gesture—giving us a vision of the laurel in the embrace of the persistent and urgent lover—prevents us from empathizing with the god in the

loss of his beloved and detaches us from his plight, creating the
aesthetic distance that is the matrix for laughter.

But even as a laurel, Daphne rejects the god's touch: "refugit tamen oscula lignum" ("even the wood shrank from his
kisses," 556). It is then that Phoebus realizes that Daphne is
gone forever and immediately proceeds to deliver a paean:

> "at, quoniam coniunx mea non potes esse,
> arbor eris certe . . . mea! semper habebunt
> te coma, te citharae, te nostrae, laure, pharetrae;
> tu ducibus Latiis aderis, cum laeta Triumphum
> vox canet et visent longas Capitolia pompas;
> postibus Augustis eadem fidissima custos
> ante fores stabis mediamque tuebere quercum,
> utque meum intonsis caput est iuvenale capillis,
> tu quoque perpetuos semper gere frondis honores!"
> (557–65)

("Since you cannot be my bride, you shall at least be my
tree. My hair, my lyre, my quiver shall always be entwined with you, O laurel. With you shall Roman generals wreathe their heads, when shouts of joy shall acclaim
their triumph, and long processions climb the Capitol.
You at Augustus' portals shall stand a trusty guardian,
and keep watch over the civic crown of oak which hangs
between. And as my head is ever young and my locks
unshorn, so do you keep the beauty of your leaves perpetual.")

The ceremonial solemnity of Apollo's words in this passage can
very well be taken as a fitting pronouncement by a god, whose
characteristics are after all based on this type of seriousness and
nobility. But Apollo's turn from foolish lover to solemn deity is
too abrupt a change—as Daphne/laurel recoils from the god, he
immediately delivers his "If you cannot be my bride, then you
shall be my tree"—and curiously the paean itself appears too
long and solemn. It is evident that Ovid is again up to another
one of his mischievous tricks. Apollo's paean is on the surface a
moment of triumphant self-assertion; he makes the laurel his attribute—the leaves of the bay remaining forever green as they
encircle his youthful, majestic brow—and endows it with a sacred character by proclaiming it an eternal symbol of honor and
victory. One also discerns an apparent touch of tenderness and

some hope of a permanent union with Daphne. But Apollo tries too hard; his hurried, overstated paean, too grandiose, too eloquent a speech—like that of the proverbial lady who protests too much—gives him away. The paean strikes us as a way of achieving a graceful retreat, a means of dignifying his exit from a foolish adventure. But Ovid will not let Apollo off so easily— Daphne escapes Apollo but Apollo cannot escape the clever Ovid. Not only do we see through the pose, but we cannot but chuckle at the duped lover who is forced to accept the laurel wreath in place of his beloved's body. The laurel of victory becomes, paradoxically, a symbol of his amorous defeat. And, since the laurel is Augustus' favorite tree[40] (the emblem of his favorite deity) adorning his palace on the Palatine along with the oak (as Ovid notes in 562–63), the "fall" of the bay from a symbol of triumph to a symbol of defeat may be read as another sign of Ovid's anti-Augustanism, his subtle defiance of the Emperor and his ideology.

The joke is on Apollo doubly, for not only can he not extricate himself from the comic perspective created by Ovid, but the union he seeks with Daphne after the transformation is only a self-deception. Apollo does not confer honor upon the woman and not even upon the *particular* tree she has become, but on the laurel in *general*—the species laurel. Wanting a union with *his* Daphne is but an illusion, another defeat for the boastful god.

After Apollo's paean, Ovid tells how the laurel shakes its top as if in assent to the god's words. This gesture ends the tale with a final comic touch, for now that Daphne is safe behind the walls of her bark, she seems to grant Phoebus her full, if utterly meaningless, consent. Unlike little Cupid who is able to alter lovers, Apollo, as god or man, cannot reach Daphne. He fails. And his failure—unlike that of Orpheus after having lost his Eurydice in Hades—is deprived of pathos or drama. The comic figure alone remains.

In this tale, Ovid characterizes Apollo as a type of *exclusus amator*, the shut-out lover who is denied access to his obdurate lady.[41] Like the traditional excluded lover's *conclamatio*, Phoebus' plea for "admission" meets with failure. And even though the closed door—symbol of both the exclusion of the lover and the mistress's relentless will—is absent, the god finds himself in a very real sense "locked out" the moment Daphne is transformed into the laurel. Phoebus is then forced to sing his song before the bark of a tree that excludes him as completely as the strongest door. But unlike the conventional *exclusus amator*, the rejected Apollo does not sink back into despair and apathetic despondency; the god does not admit his failure in his love affair, and, accordingly, his *paraclausithyron* (the futile plaint of the excluded lover) is not a lament but rather a paean. There is no vigil, no tears, no apparent suffering. And again, unlike the conventional excluded lover, Apollo does not leave the garland "on the threshold," as it were, the symbol of the lover's defeat and sorrow, but instead places it on his head in a stubborn, haughty gesture to regain his badly bruised dignity.

Ovidian scholars speak often of the untragic manner in which Ovid treats many of his tales,[42] offering metamorphosis as an alternative to death or in Daphne's case, we may add, to rape, which to the virgin would be a form of death. Along the same lines, Hermann Fränkel suggests that Ovid's "mild disposition shied from a crushing finale,"[43] and transformation offers a successful compromise. Perhaps it is so for Myrrha who wants to escape both life and death (10.487ff.)—and it is this example that Fränkel cites. But witness Arachne's cruel transformation into a spider, and still more pertinent, Scylla with her waist horribly disfigured by heads of baying dogs. And Daphne encased in her tree, her maidenly zone, as we may call it, for all purposes "dies" to the world of humans. In other words, there is nothing "mild" in Ovid's selection of metamorphosis as a denouement to a given story. Quite the opposite. And if Ovid utilizes the grotesque for comedy, as when he humors Apollo in his sexual rapacity, he also uses it to underline the utter helplessness and, at times, horror in the transformation of figures who have absolutely no choice.

In his Apollo and Daphne, a tale of erotic agon and transformation, Ovid is clearly the skillful creator of both disturbing and comic grotesques, and in his detached urbanity he is also the lighthearted comedian, the poet of *nequitia*. The clever mingling of earnest and jest yields an entertaining story of jilted love in which the beloved—from the beginning in her reluctance through her grotesque transformation to her final leafy bow— serves as a catalyst for the lover's comedy. The divine Apollo, always in the shadow of the nymph's rigid modesty, is forever the fool.

2

The Christianization of the Myth of Apollo and Daphne in Ovid's Medieval Commentators

Ovid's impact on the Middle Ages is enormous. His influence ranges from the Goliards' eulogies of Venus to mythological romances, from Christian adaptations of his tales to secular handlings where the figures of mythology conform to medieval courtly canons. In my analysis of the Christianization of Apollo and Daphne, I will examine that aspect of medieval learning that transforms Ovid the versatile storyteller into Ovid the ethical philosopher and theologian.

In this tradition, the *Metamorphoses* is no longer regarded as a work of literature but rather as poetic history and, above all, as an allegory of theological and moral wisdom. The Bible of the Gentiles—as Ovid's collection of mythological tales was dubbed by the Alfonsine compilers of the *General Estoria*, where Ovid is allegorized at length—was believed to have veiled truth beneath the guise of fable. In this release from the letter of the text, a new kind of imagination is at work—and one very different from Ovid's. Concerned with hermeneutics, it seeks a synthesis of the classical and the Christian and, in its typological readings, a reinterpretation of universal history.

In the Christianization of the tale of Apollo and Daphne, the focus shifts from the seriocomic erotic agon—the love battle between the recalcitrant virgin and her divine suitor—to a *psychomachia*, the battle between the demonic forces of darkness, symbolized by Python and other monsters, and forces of light, symbolized by Apollo. Love discards the purely poetic function it had in Ovid and becomes entwined in the web of ethical and religious meanings imposed on the text. Love appears, above all, as sensual love *(cupiditas)* and as Divine Love *(Caritas)*—both embodied in the figure of Cupid—corresponding to the Christian archetypal dualism of good and evil. The grotesque emerges chiefly in two guises. The first we see in the illustrations of Daphne's metamorphosis, which often accompany the texts—scenes that parallel the playful aspect of Romanesque and Gothic grotesques fittingly called by Bernard of Clairvaux a "ridiculous monstrosity." And the second serves as a didactic tool, appearing in bizarre, fantastic creatures that graphically portray evil.

At the end of the *Metamorphoses*, Ovid tells us his collection of mythological stories are his claim to fame: "Iamque opus exegi, quod nec Iovis ira nec ignis / nec poterit ferrum nec edax abolere vetustas" ("And now my work is done, which neither the wrath of Jove, nor fire, nor sword, nor the gnawing tooth of time shall ever be able to undo," 15.871–72). Curiously, Ovid's fame in the Middle Ages greatly lies in the very "undoing" of Ovid the storyteller by pious good-natured Christians. By denying him the letter—the elegance of style, the clever mischief, the play—medieval commentators help keep alive his name for later use, which if less "edifying" was at least more enjoyable. But before examining the texts of the Ovidian commentators and their treatment of the themes of love, agon, and the grotesque in their readings of Apollo and Daphne, I must say a few words about the presence of Ovid in the Middle Ages and about exegetical allegory, the method used in Ovidian commentaries. These pages will serve a double purpose. First, they will reveal the many faces of Ovid in the Middle Ages—our Ovid allegorized being one of several; second, they will offer a comprehensive picture of the allegorical tradition—one of the most complex and prolific in the intellectual history of antiquity as well as the early and late Middle Ages—and the place of the Ovidian expositors in it. Only in the light of this tradition can we truly explain the commentators' readings of the myth of Apollo and Daphne.

Ovid does not gain wide acceptance in the Middle Ages until the latter part of the eleventh century. The poet's popularity had not diminished with his banishment from Rome by Augustus, and numerous inscriptions of his poems at Pompeii and other cities as well as the use of passages from his poems on the stage attest to this. In the post-Augustan age he is the favorite model of the poets, and his presence in the rhetorical schools of the late Empire is very strong, as the elder Seneca tells us.[1] But as Christianity comes into its own, Ovid's influence declines, even if he is not totally neglected. He is cited by the grammarians, and he is also used, if guardedly, by early Christian writers. Echoes of the *Metamorphoses* are easily discernible in the popular*Mythologiae* of the fifth-century allegorizer Fulgentius and in Prudentius, called "the Christian Ovid" because of Ovidian touches in his antipagan *Contra Symmachum*.[2] But Ovid's circulation is limited and he is eclipsed by other pagan writers, especially Virgil. Rudolph Schevill suggests that the early centuries of the Christian era relegate Ovid to the background because those times are unable to adapt his works to the contemporary systems of philosophy and theology.[3] By Carolingian times, however, it is evident that Ovid's prestige is again on the rise. In a much-quoted ninth-century poem, Theodulph, Bishop of Orléans, notes that even though frivolous things can be found in Ovid, many truths are concealed beneath a false covering, anticipating the moralization of the commentators: "In quorum dictis quamquam sint frivola multa / Plurima sub falso tegmine vera latent."[4] But it is not until the twelfth century that Ovid finally achieves a position of eminence similar to the one held by the sober Virgil in the eighth and ninth centuries.

Ovid becomes many things to many people: courteous lover, preacher, moralist, romancer, philosopher, and even theologian. A secular literature of entertainment hails him as one of its masters. The Goliards and the prolific courtly poets learn much from Ovid, the clever teacher of love, as do others such as the anonymous writer of the influential elegiac comedy the *Pamphilus de amore* and Juan Ruiz, the Arcipreste de Hita, in his *Libro de Buen Amor*. Ovid's influence as *raconteur* extends to the *fabliaux* of the *Gesta Romanorum*, the anonymous *Philomena*, and even to Chaucer and Boccaccio. The moral tradition, on the other hand, makes Ovid part of hagiographic legend and assigns him a prominent place in the *florilegia*, " 'golden treasuries' of ancient *sententiae*."[5] Even the *Ars amatoria* is not exempt from moralization; it becomes an allegory for the edification of nuns. The period from the twelfth to the fifteenth century—the twelfth and the thirteenth are often referred to by Traube's felicitous phrase *aetas Ovidiana*[6]—sees the systematic allegorization of *Ovidius Maior*, that is, the *Metamorphoses*, where the commentators search relentlessly for morality and sacred history. The irreverent Ovid becomes the exalted *Ovidius ethicus-theologus*.

Allegory as a method of exegesis dates back to Homeric apologetics. Plato's well-known attack against Homer and Hesiod in the *Republic* (2.378e) is but an echo of a cluster of angry voices, the loudest undoubtedly being the learned Xenophanes who, more than a century earlier, had ruthlessly spoken against

the impiety and immorality of the two poets. And so Homer's
Greek defenders attempt to justify and correct the god's "scandalous" conduct by reading a hidden meaning into their adventures. Theagenes of Rhegium (fl. c. 525 B.C.), the first known allegorizer of Homer, utilizes physical and moral interpretations to
explain the theomachy; the pagan deities are symbols of natural
forces and moral ideas.[7] Anaxagoras, the cynics Antisthenes and
Diogenes, Metrodorus of Lampsacus and others, continue the allegorical readings of mythical tales. So do the Stoics, especially
Chrysippus, who try to reconcile the myths with their own system in order to give a "philosophic base to their worship of the
gods." The works of these allegorists have since disappeared
and only some of their thoughts are preserved, such as those of
Lucilius Balbus in Cicero's *De natura deorum* and those of Chrysippus in Macrobius' *Saturnalia*. But two works of the first century
A.D., the *Allegoriae Homericae* of the pseudo-Heraclitus and the
Compendium theologiae Graecae by the Stoic writer Cornutus, give
us a good idea of the nature of the allegorists' tireless efforts to
extract truth from the mythical accounts. In the pseudo-Heraclitus—an apology of Homer—Apollo's angry assault against the
defenseless Greeks in the *Iliad* symbolizes a physical catastrophe,
a pestilence brought about by the sun's scalding rays (6.5–6;
14.1–6), and the loves of Zeus and Hera on Mount Ida signify
the union of ether and air, which fertilizes the earth during the
spring (39.1–17). In the moral realm, Athena symbolizes divine
wisdom (28.1), and Aphrodite stands for the folly of love (28.4–
6).[8] At the core of this allegorical tradition, and what ultimately
justifies it, is the notion of the poet as sage, the guardian of philosophy. Unlike the poet-liar whom Plato attacks in the *Republic*,
the irrepressible creator of fictions and false inventions to the
detriment of young minds, the poet of the allegorizers is the
wise man who hides truth in fable. This role of the poet as
"teacher, soothsayer, friend of the gods and friend of men," as
Goethe's Wilhelm Meister calls him in words wrapped in ancient
echoes,[9] is bequeathed to the Ovidian exegetical tradition of the
Middle Ages. The task of the medieval allegorizer is, as it had
been for his ancient counterpart, to lift the poetic veil contrived
by the poet-sage and uncover the wisdom hidden behind it.

Greek rationalism invents another method of interpreting
the gods: euhemerism. This particular hermeneutics exists side
by side with allegory but, unlike allegory, which attempts to find
a "deeper" meaning in myth, it concentrates on a literal inter-

pretation. Stripping the Olympians of their divinity, it creates a spurious history for them; the gods of the Greek pantheon had once been mortals who, through their merits and the worship of their descendants, had been elevated to the level of deities.[10] Both Plutarch in *De Iside et Osiride* and Cicero in *De natura deorum* condemn the impiety of this explanation.[11] But no amount of opposition will kill this creature. The influential pseudo-Heraclitus, for instance, uses it in his *Allegoriae*. Euhemerism, along with allegory, will survive to serve the purposes of other minds and will be used for other reasons.

Allegorized and euhemerized mythology passes into the Middle Ages by several channels. The picture is complex but lines of transmission are readily discernible. Treatises of late antiquity such as Servius' famous commentary on Virgil's *Aeneid*,[12] Fulgentius' *Mythologiarum libri tres*,[13] and Macrobius' *Saturnalia*[14] are treasures of information. *De nuptiis Philologiae et Mercurii* by Martianus Capella,[15] an allegorical secularization of the gods, even though more picturesque is no less influential. After these texts come the encyclopedists such as Isidore of Seville with his erudite *Etymologiae*[16] and Rabanus Maurus with *De universo*,[17] the commentaries on late antique writers such as Remigius of Auxerre's ninth-century commentary on Martianus,[18] and of course the so-called Vatican mythographers.[19] All these works nourish an ever-expanding tradition that, by the time it reaches our commentators, is a well-fed beast. We cannot discount the role of Christian apologetics in this early picture. Its stance toward pagan mythology—at times virulently polemical, at times conciliatory—unwittingly helps keep alive the very "demons" it so harshly attacks. As it turns out, these are illusory demons since, even before the time of Ovid, the pagan deities had become shadows of their former selves, mere metaphors.

The consensus among apologists—Justin, Tatian, Athenagoras, Tertullian—is that the pagan pantheon is either the invention of devils or the euhemerized abode of deified men. Most concede, however—Tertullian is a dissenting voice—that not all of paganism is reprehensible, for in it one finds intimations of Christian wisdom; the heathen poets and sages who lived several hundred years after Moses had read the sacred scriptures and had been instructed by their teachings, even though what they learned was poorly remembered or purposely perverted.[20] Clement of Alexandria goes one step further. In his *Stromata* (VII.2), he contends that the Greeks not only had learned from

Moses and the Prophets but had been inspired in their philosophy by inferior angels.[21] So in the poetry of the ancients, who
were themselves "witnesses" of Christian revelation, many hidden Christian principles can be found and brought forth through
allegorical interpretation. Clement goes so far as to suggest that
in the fabulous tales of their legendary history the ancients "imitated the marvelous deeds which among us and for our salvation
have been accomplished . . . by men of holy life supported by
the power of God."[22] The ancient poet in his mythological accounts is now the guardian of the divine, hiding in his fiction
golden kernels of Christian theology. (Clearly Clement echoes
the ancient allegorizers with their notion of poetry veiling truth,
and if for the ancients the poet was a philosopher in the guise of
a poet, in Clement he is a Christian theologian.) This drawing of
parallels between the Bible and pagan mythology, which was rejected by later Latin theology but cultivated by the medieval
poets, establishes the typological tradition in which the Ovidian
commentators such as the anonymous poet of the *Ovide moralisé*
and Pierre Bersuire will thrive for several decades.

In the myth of Apollo and Daphne, as in the entire world
of ancient myth conveniently "collected" for them by Ovid in his
Metamorphoses, the medieval commentators find a ready-made
shorthand for the exposition of moral and theological thought.
Ovid had removed the myth from its context, emptied it of its
religious baggage, and used it as a field for literary play. In turn,
his "inspired" commentators empty Ovid's demythologized tale
of its poetic value and fill it with the edifying substance of Christian piety. This Christian stage in the development of the myth
of the god and the nymph involves a shift of vision from the literal to the allegorical and representational, from interest in surfaces to a consideration of deeper meaning. And in this allegorical act, the commentators deny the very existence of the Ovidian
characters by denying their poetic literalness as the foolish, jilted
lover and the coy beloved. The Ovidian figures become symbols
of abstract concepts and types in the drama of sin and redemption. In Ovid, myth-turned-play calls attention to itself primarily
as part of an independent, gratuitous act of artistic creation. In
the commentators, the images of myth stand arbitrarily for an
order beyond themselves. They have lost their obvious references and so they exist to represent and signify specific concepts
in a system that determines their meaning and importance. Rosemond Tuve has suggested that the aim of the Christian exegetes

is to render the classics "more meaningful and more contempo-
raneous,"[23] not to bowdlerize them. But in the process of ren-
dering them "more meaningful," the original intent is ignored.
In Ovid we are invited to appreciate craft, in the medieval commentators, to be edified. And the didactic ends of these exegetes
in manipulating the text can nowhere be more clearly seen than
in their treatments of the themes of love, agon, and the grotesque to which I now turn.

Arnulf of Orléans' *Allegoriae super Ovidii Metamorphosin,*[24] a
prose commentary of the second half of the twelfth century (c.
1175), is the first medieval exegesis of Ovid's *Metamorphoses.* In
his treatment of the myth of Apollo and Daphne, Arnulf concentrates on the theme of agon, a physical and a moral agon—the
latter being typically the most important in the medievalized account—where love plays no role. The erotic appears briefly but
is divested of all elements of conflict. The grotesque does not appear; we shall have to wait for the *Ovide moralisé* for our first
glimpse of this mode.

Arnulf introduces his treatise by revealing his method of
interpreting Ovid's stories; he interprets them sometimes in an
allegorical way, sometimes in a moral way, and sometimes in an
historical way, "modo quasdam allegorice, quasdam moraliter
exponamus et quasdam historice." (By allegorical, Arnulf means
physical allegory and, by historical, euhemeristic.) It is evident
that in his exegesis Arnulf purports to give us a key to the un-
derstanding of Ovid; as it turns out, a false key opening up into
a world of Christian visions which, in their capricious usurpation
of Ovid's poetic design, confers upon him a role that the ancients themselves had particularly cherished and the Middle
Ages made its own: the poet as sage, the guardian of truth and
esoteric secrets. In his treatise, Arnulf puts into practice his notion of Ovid the poet as a philosopher, and above all, as a moral
philosopher. This notion is made explicit in Arnulf's "accessus"
preceding his glosses to the *Metamorphoses,* his account of Ovid's
life and works.[25] According to Arnulf, Ovid's purpose in his stories of transformation is moral: "The aim is to speak about
change so that we may think not only about the change which
comes from outside in physical matters, good and evil, but also
about change which comes from within as in the soul, so that it
may lead us back from error to knowledge of the true Creator"
("Intencio est de mutacione dicere, ut non intelligamus de mutacione que fit extrinsecus tantum in rebus corporeis bonis vel

malis sed etiam de mutacione que fit intrinsecus ut in anima, ut reducat nos ab errore ad cognitionem veri creatoris"). And he adds that Ovid's poem leads to the knowledge of divine things through the transformation of corporeal forms ("Vel utilitas est erudicio divinorum habita ex mutacione temporalium"). Clearly, for Arnulf, the allegorical reading of Ovid is an act of discovery rather than what it really is, an arbitrary imposition of meaning. It is not a falsification of Ovid but an affirmation of the true role of the poet and his poetry. The notion of the poet as sage, which has been largely ignored in the studies of Ovid's medieval commentators,[26] is, as it had been for the ancient allegorical tradition, at the center of Arnulf's exegetical allegory and that of those who come after him.

The allegorization of the Python episode in Arnulf is particularly important, for it defines the "medieval" character of Apollo as the killer of dragons and the champion of the forces of light, the key role of the god in the Ovidian exegetical tradition. The combat of Apollo and Python in Greek mythology—the earliest known account found in the Homeric Hymn to Apollo 3.353–74), where the dragon is female—signified in all probability the god's appropriation of the oracle at Delphi from Gaea, the Earth goddess, who is embodied in the vanquished Python.[27] In Ovid the combat serves as a preface to the story of Apollo and Daphne, being at the service of the poet's ingenious storytelling. The triumph over Python arouses Apollo's hubris, the cause of his undoing in his encounter with Cupid who deflates the gloating, majestic Apollo with his golden dart, converting him into a lover and generating the comedy. Arnulf leaves behind both mythopoeic thought and Ovid's play. The dichotomy in the Ovidian text between Apollo the epic hero and Apollo the deflated lover is lost to Arnulf, who sustains the god's epic character even as he confronts his beloved Daphne. Arnulf's Apollo is Homeric, not Ovidian; the emphasis is on Apollo the monster-slayer rather than on his role as lover, a choice well suited to the commentator's moral ends. Moreover, Arnulf's Christian allegory draws upon that glorious, exalted picture of the god that philosophical and religious minds of antiquity had contrived for him, in contrast to the foolish Apollo of the tradition of play and comedy we saw earlier in Ovid.

Drawing from Stoic thought preserved in mythographical texts, Arnulf starts by explaining Apollo and Python as anthropomorphic embodiments of natural forces and their combat as a

cosmic agon. Antipater the Stoic, preserved in Macrobius' *Saturnalia*, had considered the slaying of the serpent by the god as
the salutary effects of the sun's rays on noxious and injurious
vapors generated by heat and moisture (1.17.57). Arnulf, in the
manner of Antipater, interprets the event as the destruction of
pestilent emissions by the sun: "By Python we understand a
noxious moisture of the earth which the sun dries up with arrows, that is, with its rays" ("Per Phitonem noxium terre humo-
rem habemus quem sol sagittis id est radiis suis desiccat,"1.8).
The identification of Apollo with the sun and the sun's rays with
the sun's arrows are commonplaces in Stoic exegesis and are
constant images in medieval physical interpretations.

The cosmic agon becomes a moral agon when Arnulf endows Apollo and Python with meanings from Christian ethics.
Phoebus, divested of his comic garb, is he who is governed by
wisdom *(sapiens)*, and Python signifies deceit *(fallacia)* and false
belief *(falsa credulitas)*. As the sun divides the shadows by means
of light, so does a wise man destroy deceit and false belief by
means of truth and reason. This narrowly fanciful interpretation
is nevertheless deeply rooted in the allegorical tradition. As
Fausto Guisalberti has noted, the explanation of Apollo as truth
and Python as false belief occurs in Fulgentius' *Mythologiarum libri tres* (1.17) and later in the third Vatican mythographer.[28] Apollo as wisdom appears in Fulgentius' allegorization of the fable of
Admetus and Alcestis (1.27), a detail not mentioned by Guisalberti.

The Fulgentian identification of Apollo with wisdom and
truth, however, rings an ancient bell, which makes this interpretation less fanciful than it first appears. In ancient Greece, Apollo was recognized as the "umpire of the intellectual world."[29]
And this role is particularly evident in the legends of the wise
men of Greece as in the tales of the award of the Apolline tripod
to Thales and the palm of wisdom to Socrates; the palm, as is
well known, is one of Apollo's attributes. Maximus Tyrius
"speaks of the philosophic life as that 'which Diogenes chose
freely, the life which Apollo assigned and Zeus commended' "
(Farnell, 242). Empedocles had called Apollo "the divine mental
force of the world," and in Plato's state the chorus of youths
"swear to the truth of their words in the name of the god of
truth, Paian-Apollo (*Laws*, 664 C.)" (243). The identification of
the Pythian Apollo, the oracular deity, with truth and wisdom—
encouraged undoubtedly by the influence of the philosophers—

became a tenet of popular religious thought, along with the idea that "the pursuit of intellectual truth was a divine function and an act of worship" (243). Arnulf does not go this far. It is up to later commentators to assume this task. But by ascribing truth and wisdom to Apollo—his by virtue of ancient worship—Arnulf reendows the god with a dignity and nobility that the playful, irreverent Ovid had denied him. Apollo regains his exalted position—now in the light of Christian morality. In Arnulf, wisdom becomes the Christian intellectual virtue by which man judges all things according to reason. And Apollo's virtue is not only exalted but dramatized as the god—the ideal Christian—is pitted against his old foe, the serpent Python—now the bearer of deceit, the Judeo-Christian motif originating in Genesis 3. The Christianized ancient combat, portraying the triumph of virtue over the powers of darkness, becomes the central motif in the medieval explanation of the myth.

Significantly, the notion of Apollo as the warrior god in a moral combat is not alien to the pagan Apollo. In the epic tradition, Apollo is the mighty god of mighty deeds, the most powerful of the sons of Zeus. In the Homeric Hymn, he is "the wondrous Archer" and "the Lord of valiancy." And even if sometimes he is the terrible god who executes his judgment with terrible fury, as when he sends his arrows of pestilence upon the Achaeans in the *Iliad*, he is most typically the god of law and law-abidingness, whose triumph over Python serves as a symbol of Augustus' victory at Actium—evidence of this found, for instance, on a bowl from Annecy with the inscription "Octauius Caesar Actius," depicting Apollo's victories over Python and the Giants.[30] And this is the Apollo that Arnulf offers us, the god of the mighty bow and the god of righteousness, not the god of the lyre, nor the god who trips and falls in comic, erotic anthropomorphism. Arnulf's Apollo is the god of light, order, and reason. And in his moral exegesis, Arnulf not only denies the poetic reality of the Ovidian Apollo, but in exalting the god Ovid deflates, Augustus' patron deity, he also denies Ovid's act of liberation from the moral and religious principles of the Emperor, embodied in the divine, majestic killer of Python.

Arnulf's moral agon places him in the tradition of the "battle of vices and virtues," one of whose chief exponents is the *Psychomachia* of the early Christian poet Prudentius, who presents personified abstractions in a field of battle.[31] Through this theme of battle, which elaborated Tertullian's famous para-ble on the victory of the virtues over the vices in his *De spectacu-lis XXIX*, the Middle Ages portrays its most profound spiritual conflict—the struggle for man's soul. And this psychologized struggle is but a manifestation of an eternal agon, already discerned by the earliest philosophers and defined by Johan Huizinga in his *Homo Ludens:* "The processes in life and the cosmos are seen as the eternal conflict of opposites which is the root-principle of existence."[32] And this "agonistic structure," the sense of life as the conflict of opposites, is perhaps nowhere more deeply felt than in the Middle Ages, a period that creates an enormous body of literary and iconic imagery to illustrate the contest between good and evil.

Central to the tradition of the "battle of vices and virtues" is the concept of the Christian as warrior, a rubric that defines the Arnulfian Apollo and that, as will be seen later, culminates in the figurative interpretation of the god as a type of the Militant Christ. Life as warfare and the Christian as a soldier who gives battle to the powers of sin is a *topos* that appears in early Christianity. Saint Paul admonishes the faithful as follows: "Put you on the armour of God, that you may be able to stand against the deceits of the devil. For our wrestling is not against flesh and blood; but against principalities, and powers, against the rulers of the world of darkness, against the spirits of wickedness in the high places. . . . Stand therefore, having your loins girt about with truth, and having on the breastplate of justice" (Eph. 6.11–12, 14). And this is what Arnulf captures so well in his moral agon between the divine Apollo and the serpent Python.

The serpent/dragon Python as a symbol of deceit and false belief belongs to an old tradition that conceives of the monstrous as the embodiment of evil, and of course the serpent of Genesis is readily recognizable lurking behind the image. Python—not itself grotesque, for it belongs to the tidy category of dragons—serves nevertheless as a prefiguration of grotesque monsters, demonic "non-things," which we will encounter later in Pierre Bersuire and Christine de Pisan. In their structural confusion, these monsters are immensely suitable for the representation of evil, which for the Christian Middle Ages is spiritual confusion and chaos. The fantastic nature of mythology becomes an ideal ground for the distorted, bizarre images of the grotesque.

By making the figures of Apollo and Python perform an allegorical function in a Christian setting, Arnulf carries Ovid

into the very heart of medieval Christian thought and practice—
vice and virtue clothed in tangible shapes, engaged in perpetual
battle. Only that Arnulf has found his tangible shapes in an already created scheme; he labels them, imposing an arbitrary
meaning drawn from an old chest of allegorized mythology, reminding us of the ancient and medieval illustrations of mythological figures with names tagged on to them in order to reveal
their "true" nature.

Clearly, in Arnulf's treatise, moral agon takes precedence
over Ovid's erotic agon. And even though the theme of love is
not absent, it is subordinated to Arnulf's Christian design (I.9).
Cupid retains his ancient garb as the god of love. But when the
little god strikes Apollo with his dart, Arnulf tells us that Apollo
loves no one but the chaste Daphne. The passage seems to im-
ply that even if the wise man should fall in love, he will not fall
prey to erotic frenzy and moral havoc, for he is controlled by
reason—all that we could expect from a glorious monster-slayer.

And if Arnulf keeps Cupid's ancient presence, he nevertheless Christianizes the pagan Daphne. The nymph is the symbol of virginity—an interpretation that Servius had already made
in his commentary on Virgil (III.91)—and the laurel wreath is the
reward that virgins obtain in heaven for their exemplary life on
earth. Arnulf offers a rationalizing (and charming) touch when
he explains Daphne's modesty as a result of being the daughter
of a river; Peneus' cold waters make this notion fitting since
modesty is the daughter of coldness just as lewdness is of heat.

Two short steps intervene between Arnulf and *Ovide moralisé*, the best known and most popular of Ovid's commentaries.
These are John of Garland and Giovanni del Virgilio, who continue the moral and physical allegory of Arnulf but not without
introducing variations of their own. In John of Garland's *Integumenta super Ovidium Metamorphoseos* (c. 1234), a verse commentary written in 260 distichs,[33] the moral agon between the medievalized Apollo and Python is explained as a battle between two
enemies, the wise man overcoming the wicked and the deceitful
(I.91–92). The laurel wreath represents wisdom, that after which
man's eager spirit strives:

> Mentibus hec arbor sapientum virgo virescit
>   Que quamvis fugiat victa labore viret.
> Est virgo Phebi sapientia facta corona
>   Laurus, quam cupida mente requirit homo. (I.93–96)

(In the minds of wise men this virgin tree grows green. In spite of its flight and overcome with hardship, it continues to flourish. Phoebus's virgin became the laurel garland [the mark of] wisdom, which man seeks with an eager mind.)

In Giovanni del Virgilio's *Allegorie librorum Ovidii Metamorphoseos* (1322–23), a commentary of short prose explanations that are then converted into poetry,[34] Python is the already familiar symbol of deceit and the wickedness of the world and Apollo is the wise man who destroys it (I.8). If the learned John explains the laurel as wisdom, an intellectual virtue, Giovanni makes it a symbol of chastity, a virtue residing in the heart rather than the mind (I.9).

As medieval Ovidian exegesis evolves, it becomes more elaborate and complex. One such work is the anonymous *Ovide moralisé*, probably written by a Minorite in the early fourteenth century.[35] The poem is a rendition of the *Metamorphoses* into French verse with an allegorization at the end of each tale. The Minorite does not restrict himself solely to the Ovidian stories, however, for he introduces fragments from, among others, Chrétien de Troyes, Hyginus, Statius' *Thebaid*, and even Ovid's *Heroides*.[36]

Even though our chief concern is the allegorical commentary of the tale of Apollo and Daphne, a brief look at the Minorite's French rendition of the Ovidian story—an adaptation rather than an actual translation—will give us a glimpse of the medieval exegete in his role as poet and his particular treatment of the themes of love, agon, and grotesque—all three endowed with moral significance. Even though he lacks the poetic energy, the verve and wit of the playful Ovid, the Minorite manages to create some felicitous verses. These moments are, however, few and far between. Moreover, not only do the octosyllabic couplets replacing Ovid's elegant hexameters seem to trivialize the classical account, but the heavily moralized interpolations convert Ovid's cleverly amusing work into a ponderous and at times awkward poem. Our Minorite emerges as an obviously earnest but naive poet-allegorizer.

In the Minorite's poetic rendition of the story, Python, Cupid, Apollo, and Daphne are medievalized versions of their former classical selves. The serpent Python cannot escape being placed on the wrong side of the moral scale. Emerging fierce and proud from the deluge, it immediately calls forth echoes from Genesis; its role is typically to persecute mankind (2647–54). By the same token, the playful sexual appetite that the ancient Cupid represents in Ovid becomes *fole amours,* the sin of *cupiditas.* This is the "mythographical Cupid" that Erwin Panofsky addresses in much detail in his *Studies in Iconology;*[37] nakedness and blindness as signs of moral turpitude are key elements in the rendition of this new, debased little god. In mythography, the *Ovide moralisé* finds the allegorical meaning of its Cupid, describing him (along with his brother Jest) early in the legend of Saturn and his three sons:

> Jocus et Cupido sont point
> Au pointures nu, sans veüe,
> Quar fole amours et jex desnue
> Les musars de robe et d'avoir,
> D'entendement et de savoir,
> D'onnor et de bones vertus:
> Pour ce sont il paint desvestus,
> Et pour ce sont il paint avugle
> Qu'amours et jex mains folz avugle. (672–80)

> (Jest and Cupid are painted
> naked and blind, because foolish love
> and jest strip the wanton of
> clothing and possessions,
> of understanding and of knowledge,
> of honor and virtues:
> That's why they are painted naked,
> and why they are painted blind
> because love and jest blind many fools).

As in Ovid, Cupid's arrows create an erotic agon between the lusty god and the modest virgin, but here the erotic battle assumes a decidedly moral twist. The gold arrow strips Apollo of moral and intellectual virtues, for as the Minorite notes in one of his many moral interjections, love not only ravishes "grant sens" and "bone mours" ("good sense" and "good conduct") but "amours fet les plus sages pestre" ("love turns the wisest into fools," 2964). And the Daphne that confronts this lowly Apollo is not the coy and demure Ovidian huntress but a self-righteous Christian who cries out to her father in moral outrage: " 'Je n'ai cure de mariage, / Ains vuel garder mon pucelage: /

Vierge sui et vierge serai' " (" 'I care not for marriage, / and I
want to keep my maidenhood: / I am a virgin and a virgin will
remain,' " 2857–59).

Daphne is as beautiful as she is chaste. The charms of the
nymph, so briefly alluded to in the *Metamorphoses*, are depicted
in a long and detailed exposition. The Minorite draws from a
canon of beauty that originates with the ancients and is reworked by the medieval love tradition to exalt and glorify the
courtly *midons*.[38] To the stellar conceit of the Ovidian text ("sid-
eribus similes oculos" which is rendered as "iex rians / Que sont
estoiles flamboians" ("smiling eyes / that are bright stars"), the
Minorite adds traits that are frequently elaborated in medieval
and later in Renaissance amatory poetry (2880–900): "crins
blons" ("blond hair"), "bouche petitete" ("small mouth"), "la
face blanche et rosine, / Qui samble rose et flour d'espine"
("white and rose-colored cheeks, / that seem like blossom and
flower of the rosebush"), "lons dois et les blanches mains"
("long fingers and white hands"), "la char qu'ele a blanche et
deugie" ("white and delicate skin"), and, as if not to leave anything within reason behind, a reference to her breasts, "les ma-
meles qu'ele a duretes / Et roondes comme pometes" ("her
breasts are firm / and round like small apples," 2901–2). This catalog of the maiden's charms is not meant as a glorification of the
woman as in the courtly poets, however, but rather as a portrayal of the sensual allurement that can drive a man to perdition.
And so in this erotic exposition, the emphasis is on the moral
debasement of the god, who is, like the Ovidian Apollo, witness
to the nymph's beauty. But if in Ovid the god appears as a foolish voyeur admiring his beloved's charms, here he is carried to a
moral rather than a comic downfall: "[Apollo] voit la potrine et
voit le col, / Qui sont fet pour amuser fol" ("[Apollo] sees her
breasts and sees her neck, / which are made to beguile the wanton," 2891–92).

The transformation, with its grotesque, emerges as the
means to destroy Daphne's beauty, which the nymph regards as
the possible cause of her own damnation ("Me met d'estre a corruption," "leads me to corruption," 3023). This metamorphosis,
with its emphasis on the destruction of beauty, serves in a curious way as an antecedent to the courtly Garcilaso who, as we
shall see later on in this study, uses the disfiguring metamorphosis—and images similar to the Minorite's—for his own poetic
purposes, this time to portray the painful loss of the woman.
The Minorite retains Ovid's images of the nymph's flesh encir-

cled with thin bark and her feet arrested by the laurel's roots. But here beauty succumbs as blond hair becomes green leaves and arms turn into long branches:

> Ses ventres, qui pas n'iere ençains,
> Fu tous de tenvre escorce çains;
> Ses crins dorez et flamboians
> Devindrent fueilles verdoians;
> Ses bras sont en lons rains muez:
> Touz ses cors li est tresmuez:
> Li piez isneaus de la meschine
> Fu tenus a ferme racine. (3027–34)

> (Her sides, which will never swell with child,
> were encircled with tender bark;
> Her gold and flaming hair
> Became green leaves;
> Her arms were changed into long branches:
> Her whole body was transformed:
> The swift feet of the maiden
> were held fast in firm roots.)

As in Ovid, when Apollo embraces the tree, the grotesque persists in the scene as the god feels Daphne's breast trembling beneath the tender bark. The Minorite, in one of those rare instances when his poetry loses its stiffness, skillfully renders this Ovidian moment, now devoid of comic elements: "Il sent le pis chaut et mouvant, / Qui sous l'escorce tenvre tramble" ("He feels her warm and trembling breast, / moving under the delicate bark," 3038–39).

The Minorite's use of the grotesque as the destruction of something morally harmful is not discernible in the many illustrations of this scene that accompany the text. In two of these miniatures, one in a manuscript in the Bibliothèque de l'Arsenal in Paris (fig. 5) and the other in a manuscript at the Kongelige Bibliothek in Copenhagen (fig. 6), Daphne's head is perched on top of the laurel's trunk, itself surrounded by leaves which Apollo, garbed in medieval dress, tenderly touches. These two grotesques, like so many classical grotesque ornaments showing human heads sustained by pilasters or columns, are characterized by a playful, fanciful touch that is so common in the ancient grotesques and in which medieval artists seem to revel. Clearly, this spirit of play is omnipresent in medieval grotesque art: in

the tiny monsters of the anonymous craftsmen of the miseri-
cords, in the enigmatic gargoyles, and, above all, in the marginal
drolleries of myriad manuscripts. These gay decorations display
a refreshing freedom from ecclesiastical constraints, from the rigid tyranny of representation and symbolic signification.[39] Similarly, the Daphnes of our illuminators are ornaments that have "re-
belled" against their "text"; indifferent to its message, these
images seek their meaning in their own bizarre designs, delight-
ing in their own strangeness and frivolity. The gaiety and play
in the pictorial Daphnes are particularly striking in those of the
illustrations of L'Epître d'Othéa by Christine de Pisan: a human
torso with branches from which Apollo gathers leaves (fig. 7); a
skirted laurel the sight of which seems to surprise the divine
lover, whose hair stands on end as a fiery halo—perhaps a clever attempt to simulate the rays of the solar deity as he stands before the tree in anthropomorphic form (fig. 8); a naked Daphne,
a hand demurely covering her genitals, carrying a laurel tree on
her shoulders in place of her head (fig. 9).

The playful ornamental grotesque of the Middle Ages did
not remain free of criticism from its detractors. Every period in
the history of the grotesque gives rise to angry voices that, for
one reason or another, speak against its bizarre, strange presence. Bernard of Clairvaux, in a much-quoted statement filled
with moral indignation, condemns its frivolous presence in the
cloisters of Cluny, an attack that reminds us of that of the architect Vitruvius, who, for essentially artistic reasons, decried these
distorted forms in the Augustan period. Bernard's condemnation
seems to be directed more at the pointlessness of the grotesques,
however—at their meaningless strangeness intruding in a sacred
precinct—rather than at their actual distortions:

> "But in the cloister, in the sight of the reading monks,
> what is the point of such ridiculous monstrosity, the
> strange kind of shapeless shapeliness, of shapely shape-
> lessness? . . . You can see many bodies under one head,
> and then again one body with many heads, here you see
> a quadruped with a serpent's tail, here a fish with the
> head of a quadruped. Here is a beast which is a horse in
> front but drags half a goat behind, here a horned animal
> has the hindquarters of a horse. In short there is such a
> variety and such a diversity of strange shapes everywhere
> that we may prefer to read the marbles rather than the
> books."[40]

We can only guess what Bernard might have thought of the playful Daphnes gracing the pages of commentaries meant for moral and religious edification. But if he had regarded them as unfavorably as the hybrids of Cluny, he may have found some consolation in the thought that grotesque forms were also used as a didactic tool in Ovidian exegetical texts—a popular function of the grotesque in the Middle Ages—in order to depict evil conquered by the forces of righteousness. These forms will be studied later when I consider Bersuire and Christine de Pisan.

The commentary on the tale of Apollo and Daphne in the *Ovide moralisé* reads like that of a pious and ingenious biblical exegete. This should come as no surprise, however, for biblical exegesis with its allegorical interpretations provides the Ovidian commentators, especially our Minorite, with a handy model for their methods in interpreting Ovid's tales. Philo of Alexandria had used the allegory of Homeric apologetics and of the Stoics to interpret the Old Testament,[41] and the Church Fathers, having Philo as their enlightened predecessor, applied it to all Scripture. But the Fathers found another method of interpreting the Bible that also proved appealing to Ovidian commentators: the typological method that Saint Paul had adapted from the midrashic exegesis of Palestinian Judaism.[42] In Paul's typology, characters and events in the Old Testament are prefigurations of characters and events in the New Testament and its history of Redemption. So Adam becomes a type of Christ, the "figure of him who was to come" (Rom. 5:14), and the union of Adam and Eve typifies the bond between Christ and the Church.[43] Typology applied to the *Metamorphoses* is the *Ovide moralisé*'s main contribution to Ovidian exegesis. Drawing heavily on previous commentators, the Minorite also offers physical and moral explanations, including a euhemeristic touch of his own. Here only the typological will be analyzed in detail, since it is wholly new and adds another dimension to our portrait of the medievalized Ovidian characters.[44]

Even though the allegorical method we have studied thus far and typology are commonly placed under the generic term *allegory*, a distinction must be made between the two. A typological interpretation—allegorical in the widest sense since one thing stands for and signifies the other—differs from the allegorical in one important respect. As Erich Auerbach has noted, in allegory "at least one of the two elements combined is a pure sign, but in a figural [typological] relation both the signifying and the signified facts are real and concrete historical

Figure 5. Miniature, *Ovide moralisé*, Apollo and Daphne, Ms. 5069 fol. 4r, Bibliothèque de l'Arsenal, Paris, fourteenth century. Photo Bibl. Nat., Paris.

Figure 6. Miniature, *Ovide moralisé*, Apollo and Daphne, Ms. Thott 399 fol. 45r, Kongelige Bibliothek, Copenhagen, c. 1480.

Figure 7. Miniature, Christine de Pisan, *L'Epître d'Othéa,* Apollo and Daphne, Ms. Harley 4431 fol. 134v, British Library, c. 1405/10. By permission of the British Library.

Figure 8. Miniature, Christine de Pisan, *L'Epître d'Othéa,* Apollo and Daphne, Ms. Bodley 421 fol. 60r, Bodleian Library, Oxford, c. 1460.

Figure 9. Miniature, Christine de Pisan, *L'Epître d'Othéa,* Apollo and Daphne, Ms. 74 G 27 fol. 83r, Koninklijke Bibliotheek, The Hague, c. 1450/60.

events. . . . It is essential . . . that neither the prefiguring nor
the prefigured event lose their literal and historical reality by
their figurative meaning and interrelation."[45] Typology is essentially an interpretation of universal history in which every historical event has its place "on the plane of providential design
by which the event is revealed as a prefiguration or a fulfillment
or perhaps as an imitation of other events."[46] When the Ovidian characters take their cozy places in this providential design
as types in the drama of Redemption in the *Ovide moralisé*, they
are more than fabulous creations in a tale not to be believed;
they become in a sense historical presences. And if we find
this typology unconvincing, it is nonetheless unmistakably
sanctioned by patristic voices from a learned past—Clement of
Alexandria's, in particular. With his notion of ancient mythology
as "legendary history," containing imitations of deeds from the
history of Redemption, Clement finds a devoted follower in the
Minorite. Ovid the philosopher has turned into Ovid the theologian.

In his typological interpretations of the tale of Apollo and
Daphne and what we have regarded as its preface, the Python
episode, the Minorite concentrates on the themes of agon and
love. His typology clearly excludes the grotesque.

Apollo as a *figura* of Christ and Python as a *figura* of the
Devil immediately alert us to their combat as a Christological
agon, the victorious battle of the Savior of mankind over Satan,
the champion of the forces of evil. The identification of Apollo
with Christ is ingenious but it contains no surprises. It is based
chiefly on Apollo's ancient roles as sun-god, the god of healing,
and the philosopher-god, whose identifying trait is wisdom. All
three roles bear easily identifiable parallels with Christ in his
Messianic mission. Since a figural relation is established by similarity, Apollo, his glorious mythical presence already known and
exalted in the medieval expositors' moral allegory, is eminently
suitable for the role. The pagan sun-god becomes "Solaus et lu-
miere du monde" ("Sun and light of the world," 2673, 3222),
and "Solauz qui tout home enlumine" ("The sun that illumines
all men," 3223). The Minorite borrows his imagery from Scripture to describe his Apollo-Christus. In the Biblical text Christ is
depicted as the "Sun of justice" (Malachias 4:2), "the true light,
which enlighteneth every man" (John 1:9), and the "light of the
world" (John 8:12). His coming is described as the rising of the
sun, "the Orient from on high hath visited us; To enlighten

them that sit in darkness" (Luke 1:78–79), and his Transfigura-
tion is all glory and radiance, "his face did shine as the sun: and
his garments became white as snow" (Matt. 17:2). This solar imagery had been appropriated by the early Christians from Hellenistic star cults in order to give visual expression to the "mystery, revealed and fulfilled . . . the Logos made Flesh."[47]

The identification of Apollo and Christ continues by association. Both in ancient and medieval times, Apollo is regarded
as the god of medicine; in the physical allegory of the Stoics,
Apollo is often called the god of healing because of the salutary
effect of the sun's rays (cf. Macrobius, *Saturnalia*, I.17.14 and the
third Vatican mythographer, 8.15), and in the euhemeristic treatment of the gods in Isidore of Seville, Apollo appears as the dis-
coverer of medicine (IV.III.1–2). In the *Ovide moralisé* the ancient
healer becomes the Healer of mankind:[48] "Mires qui set toutes
les cures / Et d'erbes toutes les natures, / Qui puet tout malade
et tout mort / Saner et resourdre de mort" ("Healer who knows
all the cures / and the nature of all herbs, / Who can heal the
sick / and resurrect the dead," 3227–30). In similar fashion,
Apollo, the now familiar god of wisdom, becomes the instrument of Creation (3281–82) and Wisdom Incarnate: "[Dieus] fist
sa sapience descendre / En terre et char humaine prendre, / Si
fist sa char a mort livrer, / Pour nous garir et delivrer / De mort
et de l'infernal cage" ("[God] made his Wisdom descend / To
earth and take on human flesh, / He made His flesh a prey of
death / To save and deliver us / From death and the infernal
cage," 3313–17). As in the previous cases, the Minorite draws
upon Orthodox Christian thought for these two concepts. The
Fathers of the Church, harmonizing Saint Paul's notions of the
preexistent Christ ("the power of God and the wisdom of God,"
I Cor. 1:24) and the Johannine doctrine of the Logos, identify
Wisdom with the Word. So that which is predicated on the Logos in John (Creation and Incarnation) is also attributed to Wisdom.[49]

Python, the monstrous reptile, is a *figura* of the Devil. Just
as Satan—who appears in Genesis in the guise of a tempting,
malevolent serpent—reveals himself openly in the New Testament (Matt. 4.3–11; Rev. 20.2), so does the monstrous creature
of the Ovidian text unveil his true nature in the *Ovide moralisé*.
Python brings damnation and slavery to mankind (2666–68). The
slaying of Python by Apollo, which typifies the victorious agon

of the Militant Christ over the Devil and the liberation of the human race from the yoke of sin (2675–78), reveals the Minorite as
a truly ingenious exegete with an inordinate desire to cover all
possible grounds. In the combat there is typology on three levels. Christological figurism, the defeat of Satan through the Messiah's Passion, is followed by a mystical typology; the Pythian
games established in memory of Apollo's victory typify the
struggle of each Christian, as part of the Mystical Body of Christ,
against the powers of Temptation. This leads to an eschatological
interpretation,[50] for the laurel wreath awarded in the Pythia is
the type of the award achieved by the blessed in Heaven: "Il
aquerra par sa victoire / Coronne en pardurable gloire"
("Through his victory he will win / The crown of eternal glory,"
2735–36).[51]

 The identification of mythological figures with Christ—
Apollo being one of several—belongs to an old tradition that
must be dealt with lest we think that our Minorite's typology is
more original than it really is. This tradition goes back at least as
far as early Christian artists who, lacking an artistic tradition to
fall back on, borrow details from ancient art with which to portray the Messiah, his life and ministry. Ancient iconography of
pagan characters—Herakles, Hermes, Orpheus, Apollo—whose
attributes and exploits parallel those of Christ, served as appropriate models for the many representations in mosaics, sarcoph-
agus carvings, and the many frescoes of the catacombs. Orpheus, the tamer of animals, proves a popular figure to
represent Christ the Good Shepherd.[52] The borrowing from pagan imagery is also popular with the writers of hymns, for
whom the adventures and travails of the figures of myth provided the ideal imagery for Christ's redemptive acts, especially his
battle against the forces of evil. The Easter hymn, "Morte Christi
Celebrata," relying on the memory of the faithful to recall the
Orpheus who went down to Hades in his unsuccessful search
for Eurydice, calls Christ "Noster Orpheus," a successful Orpheus who saves the church from the underworld.[53] A similar
parallel, this time between Christ and Apollo the ancient monster-slayer, prompts the author of another Easter hymn—believed to be Paulinus of Nola (c. 354/431)—to hail Christ as the
true Apollo, the slayer of Satan. This is one of the earliest attempts to describe the Christological agon by using Apollo's
combat with Python:

Salve, O Apollo vere, Paean inclyte,
Pulsor draconis inferi!
In triumpho nobilis!
Salve beata saeculi victoria,
Parens beati temporis![54]

(Hail, O true Apollo, famous Paean,
Killer of the infernal dragon!
Noble in triumph!
Hail the blessed victory of the age,
Begetter of blessed time!)

The combination of pagan and Christian imagery in early Christian art and hymnology is, however, simply a question of aesthetic opportunism. Drawing from a rich arsenal of ancient images, these early artists fulfill their expected tasks of bringing to the faithful vivid, convincing portrayals of Christ the divine redeemer in human form. There was no attempt to find a Christian message in the pagan figures themselves. This task was being fulfilled in other quarters, especially by the Fathers. We saw how Clement endows the ancient poet with the authority of a theologian in whose verses there are prefigurations of the story of salvation. And this habit of thought was to persist and culminate with such ingenious commentators as our Minorite.

The *Ovide moralisé*'s typological interpretation of Daphne leaves behind the theme of love along with the role of the nymph as obdurate beloved, and concentrates solely on her role as virgin. The maiden is a type of the Virgin Mary, the epitome of virginal beauty and perfection (3241–42, 3244). At this point in the commentary the Minorite adds the kind of clever but excessive and naive detail that often plagues Ovidian commentaries; Apollo's gesture of crowning himself with the laurel typifies the act by which God takes on human form in Mary's womb. Just as Apollo is enveloped by the wreath, so is Christ enfolded by the Virgin's body (3246–49).

The full burden of the erotic and its typological meaning is placed on the shoulders of little Cupid. In his typology, the Minorite invests Cupid with an awesome role: *cupiditas*, erotic love (*fole amour*), the force that strikes the flesh and causes perdition, becomes *Caritas*, Divine Love (*bone amour*), that which affects the soul and leads to salvation.[55] (The Minorite is careful to point out the extraordinary notion that Cupid is actually God, by which he means the Holy Spirit, the Third Person of the Trini-

ty.) The sublimation of the erotic in the figure of the pagan god
of love is extremely successful in the Middle Ages, a cliché that
will survive well into the Renaissance to the delight of emblem
writers in whose riddles Cupid/*Caritas* luxuriates with his halo of
rays, often teaching a personified human soul the mysteries of
Divine Love. If Cupid stands for *Caritas,* it follows logically that
his golden dart should symbolize the fiery flame of *Caritas:* "l'en-
brasant flame / Dont Dieus en s'amour nous enflame" ("The all-
embracing flame / With which God in his love inflames us,"
3385–86). The language of profane love is again sublimated. The
pagan imagery of the flames of erotic passion, an obligatory element in the elegiac and courtly descriptions of the lover, is
Christianized and transformed into the fires of Divine Love by
which God inflames the heart of the faithful. The idea of the
fiery arrow of *Caritas* is another image with a lasting currency.
We have but to recall the well-known *Ecstasy of Saint Theresa* by
Bernini where the Saint swoons back in mystical rapture as a
smiling angel—his right hand delicately holding the arrow of Divine Love with which he has just pierced Theresa—looks on.

As has become abundantly clear, the medieval commentators I have examined deny both the reality of the Ovidian figures
and thus the reality of the poet himself. The Ovidian text does
not function on the literal level; its words do not bear their expected referents but are signs of encoded moral and theological
messages which the commentators decode in the manner of
scriptural exegesis. And this particularly holds true for the Minorite. In his study of Callimachus, Bruno Snell notes that "the
cultured man, the scholar, delights in his sensation of standing
above the world, without being committed to it."[56] Despite the
anti-Augustan touches in his treatment of Apollo, Ovid emerges
as an embodiment of this ideal; his urbanity, his sophisticated
detachment from his material, his playful comedy places him
above society, religion, and even the emperor himself. The Minorite's Christian hermeneutics, endowing the pagan figures
with a typological meaning, places Ovid in the currents of sacred
history. The commentator has been inspired by the kind of te-
leology that Meyer Schapiro explains in his study of the Joseph
scenes on the Maximianus throne in Ravenna, a Christian work
from late antiquity: "The universe—nature and history—is satu-
rated with Christian finality, everything points beyond itself to a
formal system evident in the analogical structure of things, due
to a divine intention working itself out in time."[57] Ovid's charac-

ters are brought into this tidy Christian universe and made to
partake of sacred time. The poet, in turn, has been transformed
into the "soothsayer," the proto-Christian who holds the magic
wand of Divine Truth.

Whereas the *Ovide moralisé* concentrates on the themes of
love and agon in its commentary, Pierre Bersuire offers an interesting variation by bringing the distorted forms of the grotesque
into the theme of agon.

The Benedictine Pierre Bersuire was born in the thirteenth
century and died in 1362. Having joined the Franciscan Order in
his youth, Bersuire, like Rabelais—a monk so very differently
cast—later left the Franciscans to join the Benedictines. At the
papal court in Avignon and later in Paris, Bersuire made influential friends including both Philippe de Vitry, who gave him a
copy of the *Ovide moralisé*, which undoubtedly influenced his al-
legorizations of myth, and Petrarch, who was not only to offer a
lasting friendship but would also influence his work. Bersuire
was charged with heresy in 1350 or 1351, possibly for being sus-
pected of "dabbling in magic of some sort,"[58] and he was re-
leased in 1355. A prolific writer, he composed the *Reductorium
morale*, a moralized encyclopedia, the *Repertorium morale*, a moralized dictionary, and a translation of the Roman historian, Livy.

Bersuire devotes the fifteenth book of the *Reductorium morale* to his exegesis of Ovid's *Metamorphoses*. This Ovid moralized, appropriately called *Ovidius moralizatus*, was detached from
the *Reductorium* at an early date and circulated independently. It
contains two sections. The first part, *De formis figurisque deorum*,
presents iconographical descriptions of pagan deities and their
attributes, starting with the planetary gods arranged in the order
of their spheres, Apollo as the sun-god typically occupying the
fourth sphere. Then Bersuire endows these images with his allegorical and typological interpretations. The second part is divided into fifteen books, corresponding to those in the *Metamorphoses*, in which Bersuire explains Ovid's tales, borrowing heavily
from previous commentators.[59]

In the prologue to *De formis figurisque deorum*, Bersuire justifies his allegorical readings of pagan material by alluding to a
familiar image: the poet as sage. The poet in his fables, like Sacred Scripture in its parables, seeks to demonstrate truth in cryptic form. And so Bersuire's purpose is to search in poetry for
moral principles and the mysteries of the faith. In his reading of
the pagan past, Bersuire is the only one of the Ovidian exegetes

to allude to the famous simile of the *spoliatio Aegyptiorum*, a *topos* originating in Exodus 12:35 and used by early Christians to justify their borrowings from the Graeco-Roman heritage. Just as the Hebrews despoiled their enemies of jewels and gold in their flight from Egypt, so should the Christians steal from the pagans in order to enrich their own tradition. Bersuire presents a variation on the image: "[quod] que de thesauris Egipciorum tabernaculum federis edificet & componat" ("[one] would build the tabernacle of the covenant from the treasures of the Egyptians," p. 2. 8–9). This is a possible allusion to the Scriptural reference concerning Moses and his learning in the wisdom of the Egyptians. But the message is clear: it is not only licit but highly desirable to take from one's foes what is useful. It is evident, however, that a topic that was used with great religious zeal by the early Christians has degenerated into a convention. Bersuire repeats the "enemy's" own words to reinforce this borrowing: "fas est ab hoste doceri" ("it is proper to learn from an enemy," *Met.* 4.428).

Agon and the grotesque are the key elements in Bersuire's iconography of Apollo and its allegorical interpretation. The iconography is based on Petrarch's *Africa* (III.157–73), with its detailed description of Apollo's attributes and of Python and the grotesque three-headed monster borrowed from Macrobius' *Saturnalia*. I will deal only with the latter two here. The humanist Petrarch offers a dramatically poetic description of the three-headed monster:

> At iuxta monstrum ignotum immensumque trifauci
> Assidet ore sibi placidum blandumque tuenti.
> Dextra canem, sed leva lupum fert atra rapacem,
> Parte leo media est, simul hec serpente reflexo
> Iunguntur capita et fugientia tempora signant. (160–64)[60]

> Beside him sits a monstrous beast, three-mawed;
> mark how he fawns, placated when the god
> rewards him. Triple heads he has; the right
> a dog's, the dusky left a raging wolf's,
> and in the midst a lion's. These are joined
> by twining snakes that show the shrinking skull. (193–98)

Bersuire wastes no time in poetic niceties. In dry prose, he writes:

> sub pedibus eius erat pictum quoddam monstrum terrificum cuius sc. corpus erat serpentinum triaque habebat

capita, caninum s., lupinum & leoninum que, quamvis in-
ter se essent diversa, in corpus unum tamen coherebant &
unam solam caudam serpentinam habebant. (p. 17, 33–38)

(Beneath his feet was portrayed a frightening monster
whose serpentlike body had three heads—a dog's, a
wolf's, and a lion's—which although separate from one
another were united to one body and had a single serpentine tail.)

Unlike Petrarch who delights in the imagistic and pictorial elements of Apollo's iconography,[61] Bersuire does not forget for a
moment that his *Ovidius moralizatus* is a manual for preachers
and that his main concern is to instruct. For his didactic message, with its victorious moral agon, he uses two important ingredients, the grotesquery of the three-headed monster and the
clever touch of placing Apollo on top of the creature.

Following the iconography of Apollo is the allegorization,
a veritable "mirror for prelates," in which the moral agon is explained in detail. The grotesque three-headed monster incarnates
evil. It is a symbol of malicious and wicked sinners who are
dogs in their flattery, lions in their ravaging, and wolves in their
flight. Even though these sinners may be hostile among themselves, they are united in one serpentine tail, that is, confederat-
ed in evil against others. Bersuire relies on contemporary Christian thought for his representation of sinful man. In his
Consolation of Philosophy, Boethius explains what is behind this
general picture of moral and spiritual degradation:

To give oneself to evil . . . is to lose one's human nature.
Just as virtue can raise a person above human nature, so
vice lowers those whom it has seduced from the condition
of men beneath human nature. For this reason, anyone
whom you find transformed by vice cannot be counted a
man.
      You will say that the man who is driven by avarice
to seize what belongs to others is like a wolf; the restless,
angry man who spends his life in quarrels you will com-
pare to a dog. The treacherous conspirator who steals by
fraud may be likened to a fox; the man who is ruled by
intemperate anger is thought to have the soul of a
lion. . . . In this way, anyone who abandons virtue ceases
to be a man, since he cannot share in the divine nature,
and instead becomes a beast.[62]

Boethius' notion of evil is adapted and expanded in the Middle Ages. But in medieval texts the representation of man surrendering himself to sin, to his inner bestial nature, is not limited to mere animalization as in Boethius; it also involves the use of the monstrous and the grotesque. In Odo of Cluny, the *chimaera* symbolizes libido, and in the third Vatican mythographer carnal love is a grotesque composite monster, born from sick men's dreams—words that echo Horace's well-known characterization of the genesis of hybrid forms in his *Epistle to the Pisos*—bearing "the head of a lion, the belly of a goat, and the tail of a serpent."[63] The violation and corruption of nature in these grotesque creatures, composed of "dismembered" animal parts assembled in chaotic fashion, mirror spiritual and moral corruption. Such disorder is, for the Christian Middle Ages, the inevitable wages of sin, which in itself signifies the absence of order and reason. This notion culminates in the portrayal of the demonic as in the comic devils of the mystery plays, who often bear animal snouts, horns, and scaly or hairy bodies,[64] or in the exquisitely perverse little monsters that torture Saint Anthony in Martin Schöngauer's *The Temptation of Saint Anthony*, which clearly belongs to this tradition (fig. 10).[65] Bersuire's grotesque monster is right at home among these wild, fallen creatures. And if Bernard of Clairvaux's "What is the point?", his angry question about the playful and meaningless hybrids of Cluny, were now directed to these creatures and Bersuire's hybrid, we would have an answer. Here the grotesque has a clear meaning. For these fallen grotesques, sin is their stamp and their message. Being free from structural constraints, distorted, as if the very nature of their moral transgressions gave them the liberty to be so, they are powerful vessels for the communication of the immensity of sin, an idea ever present in the mind of the medieval Christian.

By placing his grotesque evil creature beneath Apollo's feet, Bersuire completes his own message: the graphic portrayal of the victorious moral agon, the triumph of virtue over vice. For, while the monster stands for sinful man, Apollo is the good judge or prelate who must always tread upon this frightful creature, heeding the exhortation of Psalm 90:13: "Super aspidem & basilicum ambulavi & conculcavi leonem & drachonem" ("I walked upon the asp and the basilisk and trampled under foot the lion and the dragon," p. 18, 38–39).[66] In depicting Apollo/the good prelate standing in triumph on the three-headed creature representing sin, Bersuire imitates the standard manner in which Christian iconography illustrates "the victory of Christianity over

all its adversaries,"[67] counting with an endless number of pictorial analogues. From an early date Christian art had visually translated Psalm 90:13—Bersuire's mention of the psalm shows his
acquaintance with this tradition—in order to illustrate the ultimate triumph of virtue over evil. Thus holy figures stand upon
devils and dragons, and Christ is depicted standing upon conquered animals (fig. 11) or treading on the deadly sins. Bersuire
himself does not neglect this most powerful image of the Messiah's redemptive function. He adds a Christological interpretation of Apollo and the monster in which Apollo is the Sun of
Justice rising above "those with three heads—that is, the proud
and shameless princes of the world" (p. 20, 52–53).

Bersuire's moral agon also embraces Python. In the *Africa,*
Petrarch merely mentions that the serpent lies on its back (168),
but Bersuire makes a point of telling us that Apollo slew Python
with one of his arrows (p. 17, 44–45), emphasizing once again
the conquering role of Apollo, who as the good prelate must be
prepared to attack, punish, and correct Python, who in turn represents serpentine sinners. In the Christological agon, Python
plays once again his old role as the Devil (Bersuire designates
him as Lucifer), defeated by the arrow of the cross (p. 20, 51–
52).

Bersuire's interpretation of Apollo *in bono,* as a good judge
or prelate, is accompanied by a contrasting interpretation of him
in malo where he is called *exterminans* ("exterminating")—a term
used in medieval mythography to denote the destructive powers
of Phoebus-Apollo, the sun.[68] Bersuire also declares Apollo an
idol through whom the Devil gave oracles at Delphi. He signifies
the evil prince or prelate exterminating the poor and innocent
subjects, and he is, moreover, the image of the Devil because of
his sins. In this scheme of conquering evil powers, Python
stands for the needy *(pauperes)* who are wounded by arrows of
cruelty and malice; the three-headed creature, keeping its sinful
nature, signifies in turn the ruler's impious officials who are
steeped in false flattery, treachery, and ravage (p. 19, 2–30).

In dressing Apollo as a judge, prelate, and prince, Bersuire parallels the pictorial representations of the gods found in
medieval astrological manuscripts.[69] In these illuminated texts
the classical divinities are conceived as figures of contemporary
society, a practice derived from Arabic writers and illustrators
who depict the planetary deities in nonclassical costumes and
who assign them new attributes. Thus in a Christian astrological

manual of the middle of the fourteenth century, Jupiter is portrayed as a gentleman carrying gloves and Mercury as a bishop
holding a crosier and a book. This tradition is also followed by
the illustrators of mythographical treatises. In an illustrated manuscript of the *Fulgentius metaforalis* by John Ridevall (Cod. Palat.
1066, Bl. 218v), Apollo is portrayed as a medieval prince in full
armor, bearing a crown, brandishing a bow and arrow, and
holding a crow on his lap.[70] Similarly, as we shall see later in an
illustrated manuscript of Christine de Pisan's *L'Epître d'Othéa*,
Apollo is equally at ease in knightly costume. These different visions of Apollo demonstrate how far his "medievalization" had
reached in the fourteenth century; prince or knight, Christ or Satan, wise judge or evil prelate, and totally un-Ovidian, his many
faces in the Middle Ages attest to the transformative power of
the figure, though his transformations during this period often
border on the naive and even on the ridiculous.

Bersuire is the only medieval commentator to present conflicting interpretations of Apollo, making him play the leading
role in the moral agon both in the world of light and in the
world of darkness. It is true that Bersuire's work is a manual for
preachers and as such he must show both sides of the moral
coin, as it were. But I believe that his dualistic vision of Apollo is
prompted by the crisis of faith of the fourteenth century, a convulsive moment whose imprint appears in many forms and guises.[71] For Bersuire, living in the midst of this crisis, the combat
between good and evil becomes more real and immediate than
for his fellow commentators. It is clear that the forces of darkness can invade the world of light and hold their own as the crisis itself reveals. And so by giving evil equal footing with virtue,
Bersuire wants to focus on the threat evil poses. Pursuing the
tension in the clash between good and evil, Bersuire extends the
dualistic play of contradictory forces to his interpretation of the
myth of Apollo and Daphne.[72]

Bersuire's retelling concentrates on the chase and typically
transforms Ovid's erotic agon into a theological and a moral
agon: Apollo is both the Devil and a type of Christ; Daphne
stands for the Christian soul, on the one hand, and sinful humanity and the synagogue, on the other. In his demonic role,
Apollo pursues the nymph just as Satan persecutes the human
soul through temptation. Yet as the god of wisdom and a type
of Christ, Apollo tries to establish a union with sinful humanity
who flees, vilifying his love. Daphne, as the symbol of the un-

Figure 10. Martin Schöngauer, *The Temptation of St. Anthony*, Musées de la Ville de Strasbourg, c. 1470.

Figure 11. Mosaic, Il Redentore, Palazzo Arcivescovile, Ravenna, early sixth century. Photo Alinari/Art Resource, New York.

yielding synagogue, is pursued by Apollo-Christus in His efforts to convert her to Christianity. "Dana synagoga" is transformed into a laurel from which the wood of the cross is fashioned, an obvious reference to the crucifixion of the Messiah by the Jews. Christ bestows upon the cross all manner of privileges and benefits. While previous commentators resolve tension into affirmation and glorify the power of virtue, Bersuire places emphasis on the tension itself as he portrays evil conquering in the same fashion as virtue and just as often.

From the fourteenth century on, Bersuire's *Ovidius moralizatus* is perhaps the most important source of mythographical information about "medievalized" classical divinities. After Bersuire the image of a conquering Apollo standing on the grotesque three-headed monster is a primary mode of representing the god. The image appears in the anonymous *Libellus de imaginibus deorum* (c. 1400),[73] where the emphasis lies on the purely iconographical, as Jean Seznec has pointed out.[74] This mythographical handbook of the images of the gods focuses, as does Petrarch's *Africa*, on the scene's pictorial qualities—finely captured in the delicate pen drawing in Cod. Reginensis 1290 reproduced in Seznec (177, fig. 68)—and leaves behind the allegorical trappings of Bersuire.[75]

By contrast, in a miniature appearing in a manuscript of Christine de Pisan's *L'Epître d'Othéa* (fig. 12),[76] a moral agon is easily discernible. Christine's work, written at the end of the fourteenth century, is not a commentary on Ovid's *Metamorphoses* as such but a collection of one hundred "Textes" in octosyllables—"story moments," as Rosemond Tuve calls them,[77] as well as descriptions of pagan gods and ancient dicta—based primarily on classical legend and myth. Each "Texte" is followed by a prose gloss and a prose discussion, the latter called "Allegorie." Both serve as a chivalric code, a true "mirror for knights." Christine's allegorical method follows the tradition of Ovidian exegesis and many of her interpretations of the pagan gods are gathered from the commentators. In the "Allegorie" to Texte 9, Apollo the sun, by which all truth is revealed, offers a virtuous example to emulate: "that man scholde haue in his mouthe the trouthe of the verray knyghte Ihesu Crist and flee all falsnes."[78] Christine ends with a quotation from the Bible: "Super omnia vincit veritas." The sober Christine does not mention the three-headed monster, keeping clear of all fantastic allusions. But her illustrator, obviously wanting to portray not simply a virtuous

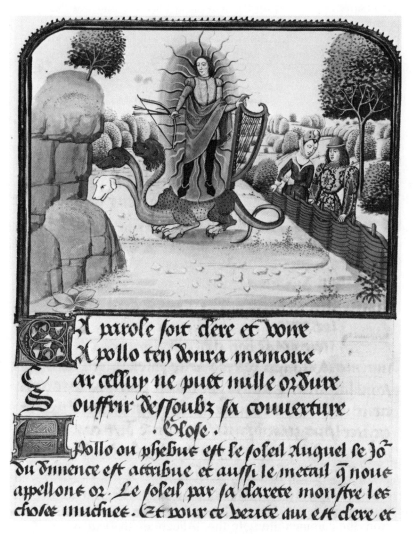

A parole soit clere et voire
Apollo ten donra memoire
ar cellup ne puet nulle ordure
ouffrir dessoubz sa couuerture
· Glose ·

pollo ou phebus est le soleil Auquel le Jo͞
du dimence est attribue et aussi le metail q̃ noue
appellont or. Le soleil par sa clarete monstre les
choses muchiees. Et pour ce beute qui est clere et

Figure 12. Miniature, Christine de Pisan, *L'Epître d'Othéa*, Ms. 9392 fol. 12v, Bibliothèque royale Albert Ier, Brussels, c. 1455/61. Copyright Bibliothèque royale Albert Ier, Brussels.

knight's victory over falsehood but a glorious victory, borrows the grotesque creature from the iconographical tradition of Bersuire and the *Libellus,* and contrives what for him clearly defines the triumph. He paints Apollo dressed as a knight, enveloped in a halo, with rays shooting forth from his body. The god is suspended over the creature, and two witnesses in medieval garb look on, evidently serving as spectators of such a praiseworthy, valiant figure.

It is no accident that the pictorial images of myth become popular in the Middle Ages and express the edifying messages of Christian piety, especially in the fourteenth century when Ovidian exegesis reaches its peak. These classical images, captured in iconographic stillness in Bersuire and in the many miniatures illustrating manuscripts such as Christine de Pisan's *Epître,* ideally qualify for what Johan Huizinga has identified as one of the factors that dominate late medieval religious life:

> The spirit of the Middle Ages, still plastic and naive, longs to give concrete shape to every conception. Every thought seeks expression in an image, but in this image it solidifies and becomes rigid. By this tendency to embodiment in visible forms all holy concepts are constantly exposed to the danger of hardening into mere externalism. For in assuming a definite figurative shape thought loses its ethereal and vague qualities, and pious feeling is apt to resolve itself in the image.[79]

Medieval commentators discover Christian meanings supposedly latent in ancient images. Through allegorical interpretations they impose rigid concepts on these images, making fixed abstract ideas equivalent to figures in order to satisfy theological and moral ends. Love, agon, and the grotesque are accordingly resolved and codified in fixed images: divine and corrupt love, *Caritas* and *cupiditas,* are embodied in Cupid; the moral agon of wisdom against deceit and the Christological struggle of Christ and the Devil are seen through the figure of Apollo battling Python; and the grotesque is conveyed in human and bestial distortions—at times merely playful, at times flashing evil or its correction—in chapbook and church. The ancient figures have obviously lost their Ovidian presence and, fossilized in Christian postures, have become mere signs and figures, receptacles for an alien thought.

The Christianization of myth continues into the Renaissance, thriving along with secular visions of the gods, and we will encounter it again in our analysis of Quevedo. But before entering the Golden Age we must turn to Petrarch, who is the first to reclaim Apollo and Daphne from the medieval commentators, and who will serve as a model for Garcilaso and Quevedo.

3

Agon, Ecstasy, and Failure in Petrarch's Canzoniere

Petrarch, the dreamer and visionary, integrates Ovid's tale of Apollo and Daphne in his *Canzoniere*—that blissful and tortured song of the self in love—rescuing it from the Christian allegorizers. He utilizes its pictorial images, with their splendidly evocative powers, in his lyrical reflections on earthly and spiritual concerns. The themes of love and agon, and instances of the grotesque, take center stage in a complex web of conceits and emblematic images, highlighted by moments of ecstasy in which the lover unites with the object of his brooding eros, the ineffable Laura.

Petrarch largely divests the Ovidian tale and its figures of the ethical and theological trappings of medieval exegesis. And even though a few remnants remain—as when Laura, in her Messianic role, carries a laurel branch, a symbol of chastity and victory over the flesh—he brings back once again the theme of erotic agon so prominently featured in Ovid. But Petrarch leaves behind Ovid's careless exuberance, his ironic distancing, his play, and endows the tale with the earnest vulnerability of the grave, sentimental courtly lover. In the *Metamorphoses,* the erotic agon between the lover and the beloved is couched in the commonplaces of elegiac love and is colored by Ovid's typical half-serious, half-comic stance. Steeped in the courtly tradition of his day, much of it inherited from the ancients, Petrarch sidesteps Ovidian jest and concentrates on complaints and lamentations, exaltation of beauty, and the pain of female rejection. In his creative imitation of the ancient tale, the virgin Daphne is a *figura* of the chaste Laura. Apollo, keeper of the sacred bay and frustrated lover, is no longer the Ovidian fool or the medieval divine monster-slayer, but a projection of the courtly Petrarchan lover.

The erotic agon is accompanied by a moral agon: the con-

flict between the sacred and the profane, the antithesis that had
been abolished by the *dolce stil nuovo* and Dante but, in Petrarch,
reappears in all its tension and complexity.[1] In a sense, this
dualism of the profane and the sacred places Petrarch in the tradition of the "battle of vices and virtues," so dear to moralists of
the Middle Ages. Petrarch's *psychomachia* is defined in his *Secretum*. The Augustine of the *Secretum* tells the erring lover Francesco that the latter's two great concerns ("speciosissimas curas"),
love of woman and love of literary fame ("amor" and "gloria"),
are the secular snares that will lead to his damnation.[2] In the
Canzoniere, the conflict between the earthly and the divine and
the persona's constant wavering between them, contribute to the
vision of the poetic self as an elusive and fragmented presence, a
self as "scattered" as the lyric "fragments" *(rime sparse)* that it in-
habits.[3] The figures and events in the tale of Apollo and
Daphne—Daphne, the laurel, Cupid, the setting, the chase—
serve as mirrors of Petrarch's Christian battle of the flesh and
spirit and share in the fragmentation.

   Daphne, in both her virginity and her role as elegiac beloved, becomes an ideal *figura* of Laura. Laura is a courtly lady
typically chaste and sensual. But if her perfect chastity is at
times envisioned as a way to heaven, her sensuality is both
blissful and dooming. She offers earthly delight and, in her role
as Medusa, perdition. The laurel is a symbol of both earthly
cares (woman, glory, poetry) and moral virtue (especially chastity). Cupid is seen as the bearer of carnal delight and spiritual
death. The setting, a rural landscape as in Ovid, is an earthly
paradise and a Dantean dark and thorny wood. In the chase motif, the lover seeks the woman, but the "contrite" Christian
withdraws and searches for peace away from her. Apollo, the
ancient lover, does not take part in the Christian conflict of flesh
and spirit. His lofty presence as god of poetry and solar deity
lends a certain nobility to the work, and as a lover he becomes a
rival to Petrarch's lyric persona.

   The fragmentation of the Ovidian figures and events reveals that the *Canzoniere* is above all the narrative of a self in crisis. And failure is the stamp that marks the revelation. For Petrarch's story is also a story of failure: failure of the erotic quest,
failure of language as the poet tries in vain to give concrete
expression to his vision of an earthly, yet divine and evanescent
woman, failure of the will that holds the lover bound to his
earthly cares, failure of the senses as he is caught in ecstatic rap-

ture (often an anguished, negative ecstasy), and at the very end, failure to achieve a Christian resolution to the conflict between the sacred and the profane. As we shall see, Petrarch also uses the figures and events of the tale of Apollo and Daphne, itself governed by the failure of the god to reach the nymph, to reveal these multiple failures.[4]

In Petrarch's elaboration of the Ovidian story, the grotesque, previously undetected, makes two brief but significant appearances: the first in canzone 23, the second in sestina 30. In the canzone, the lover is transformed into the laurel. This transformation is emblematic of the union of the lover with Laura—a moment of intimate union in ecstasy—and of the rupture and fragmentation brought about by sin. In the sestina, the grotesque is a graphic portrayal of the woman's courtly insensitivity. It is a harsh laurel of diamond branches and golden locks, a monstrous preciosity.

Robert Durling writes of the centrality of Ovidian metamorphoses in the *Canzoniere*,[5] and Daphne's transformation is the most significant. It is a means of depicting the elusiveness of Laura. Moreover, this moment in which Daphne's fragile form is violated helps define the complex psychology of love. The ontological instability and uncertainty of transformation are ideal for an erotic scheme where the desire for earthly things is, according to the Augustinian formula, a disorienting, scattering experience. In typical medieval fashion, transformation is also a means of graphically portraying the lover's fall into the chaotic world of sin. Paradoxically, there are moments when worldly desire brings peace and integration (for instance, in moments of ecstasy, as in canzone 126), but these moments are few, and the overall tenor of the piece is one of constant flux and fragmentation.

If the images of myth are a vehicle to convey meaning, they also contain a substratum that can never be fully explored or fully explained: shards of a shadowy archaeological past haunt Petrarch's poetic passages, adding an aura of mystery. Petrarch's poetics feeds on mystery, on veils that hide meaning and allow for a hermetic poetry whose intricate puzzles, when deciphered, give the reader aesthetic pleasure. In his Coronation Oration, Petrarch makes this evident by drawing distinctions between history and poetry, lauding poetry for not revealing things outright as history does: "Poetry . . . is all the sweeter since a truth that must be sought out with some care gives all the more delight when it is discovered."[6]

Some of the veils are provided by Petrarch's emblematic
images, and his use of the Ovidian tale of Apollo and Daphne is
consistent with this practice. The images function as emblems
proper in that they are visual allegorical designs, symbolic vehicles for the illustration of ideas. Petrarch's symbolic bent readily
ties him to Ovidian medieval exegesis. Mario Praz writes that
Petrarch's use of emblems "must be considered in the light of
the medieval theory which saw in the fables of the poets fore-
shadowings of scientific and philosophic mysteries, regarding
them . . . from a point of view akin to that from which hiero-
glyphics were afterwards to be interpreted," that is, as a "purely
ideographical form of writing."[7] For both the Ovidian exegete
and the emblematist Petrarch, poetry is writing wrapped in allegorical veils that must be pierced to reach meaning; it is writing
that must be painstakingly decoded. But there are significant differences between the Ovidian exegete and Petrarch. For the exegete, the code exists in an inexhaustible trove of Christian morality and theology, which he gathers and imposes on the poetic
text. Petrarch's code is buried in the text itself. His poetry is self-
referential, and so his code exists in a complex web of symbols
and conceits adapted in original ways from pagan, biblical, patristic, and medieval sources.

Cupid—Petrarch calls him Amor, as did his predecessors
the Roman elegists—is the first of the Ovidian characters to appear in the *Canzoniere*. Sonnet 2 tells of Cupid's unexpected assault, and from here on he is omnipresent, the number of references to him ranking second only to those concerning Laura.
Petrarch's Amor bears all the traits of the classical Cupid. As if
rescuing the god from one of the many medieval texts where he
traditionally appears blind—a sign of his moral turpitude—Petrarch restores his vision and brings him new life:

> Cieco non già, ma faretrato il veggo,
> nudo se non quanto vergogna il vela,
> garzon con ali, non pinto ma vivo. (sonnet 151)

> (Not at all blind I see him, but bearing
> a quiver, naked except where shame veils
> him; a boy with wings, not depicted but
> alive.)[8]

This newly reborn Amor is the skillful artificer of the man's eros.
With traditional bow, arrows, chains, and even a fashionable

knightly armor, he turns the lover's life into one of eternal war, the *topos* that Ovid puts into vogue in *Amores* 1.9. As in Ovid's *Metamorphoses*, Amor's assault on the lover is a chastisement. The Ovidian Apollo berates Cupid for usurping his mighty bow and then is punished for his thoughtless words. Similarly, the undoing of Petrarch's lover results from his scorn of Amor, in his case living in careless freedom, disdainful of the erotic yoke (canzone 23.6). Both lovers provoke Amor's wrath and are then trapped in his power.

Petrarch wishes to capture the power of erotic love when he resurrects elegiac Amor. The kind of love that Cupid brings to the Petrarchan lover is in part that of *furor*, love as an incurable illness that overrides reason and deprives the victim of will and sanity. This concept goes back to Roman elegy. The playful Ovid makes fun of it in his own poetry, and utilizes it in the *Metamorphoses* to mock Apollo. But in the *Canzoniere* this malady does not bring rage and comedy, as in Ovid, but tears, as in Propertius and Tibullus. And the failure of the will this love creates is charged with Christian significance. In the *Secretum*, Saint Augustine links Petrarch's love to the ancients' by calling it *aegritudo* and *insania*, and blames it for Petrarch's moral conflict.[9] Lack of will had turned the Ovidian Apollo into a fool, but in Petrarch it has serious consequences, for it keeps the lover from taking a nobler course, from meditating on his mortality and accepting the dictates of the divine. Cupid emerges as the creator of both the erotic agon and the moral agon.

Cupid is not only the elegiac Cupid of the ancients, however, but a courtly Cupid, for the love he inflicts upon the lover in the *Canzoniere* is love that combines erotic desire with a devotion to a higher object.[10] Petrarch's love emerges both as an erotic idolatry and a spiritual quest, the latter typically a means of ennobling the lover. Catullus had called his Delia *divina puella*, and Propertius had placed his Cynthia among the goddesses. But these attempts at divinization are but exaltations of the beauty of the elegiac mistress. Petrarch's Laura is the object of similar praise and more, for she is deemed divine not only because she is beautiful but also because she is virtuous.

Amor, the creator of the lover, is also the molder of the poet's style. But if Amor dictates the rhymes and inspires the weary poet, at the end the latter must recognize the insufficiency of poetic language to capture the evanescent, divine Laura. Thus Amor's inspiration carries with it a touch of failure. The god, who first "set free" the poet's tongue, provides wit, time, pen, paper, ink (sonnet 309), but all in vain. The poet finally asks wearily: "Come poss'io, se non m'insegni, Amore, / con parole mortali aguagliar l'opre / divine" ("How can I, if you do not teach me, Love, / with mortal words equal divine works," canzone 325.5–7). Amor and the poet fail, and the failure of poetic language parallels the failure of the erotic quest. The divine Laura who eludes the mortal word is as elusive in her earthly guise, the cruel beloved who stays forever distant in her obligatory courtly rigor. And just as the ancient Cupid serves Petrarch to bring into focus the failure of poetry to capture its true object, as we will see, so the ancient Daphne highlights the failure of the erotic quest.

Amor also takes the guise of an artist and a poet of sorts as he sculpts the lover's weeping and writes Laura's name with a diamond in his heart (sonnet 155); he is also the gardener who opens the poet's left side and plants the bay in the middle of his heart (sonnet 228)—Laura, the desire for poetic glory, and Petrarch's very poetry are born with this gesture. The classical Amor performs the miracle and the self-absorbed lover and poet suffers and delights, bound in his earthly shackles. But Amor's gesture carries with it a touch of doom. The left side, where the heart is traditionally located, is also the side of desire and irrationality, and in the *Canzoniere*'s spiritual tension between the sacred and the profane this fact is not innocent. It has important implications. Amor's horticultural magic is a threat to the Christian lover, and this threat is made clear in other poems when the poet reveals the dark side of the little god. Sonnet 290 brings us a blind Amor, what Erwin Panofsky calls a mythographical Cupid, whose blindness "puts him . . . on the wrong side of the moral world."[11] This fallen Amor, seen earlier in the discussion of the *Ovide moralisé*, is the force that carries the harried lover to spiritual death, to possible damnation:

> Ma 'l cieco Amor et la mia sorda mente
> mi traviavan sì ch'andar per viva
> forza mi convenia dove Morte era.

> (But blind Love and my deaf mind
> led me so astray that by their lively
> force I had to go where Death was.)

Protean Amor, the creator of the poet and the lover, also

fashions the woman, the adversary in the erotic agon. The craftsman of verses becomes the craftsman of Laura's beauty that enchants and traps the poet. Amor "spins and weaves" the gold to fashion Laura's blond hair (sonnet 198); in astonished wonder the poet asks where Amor has gathered the gold for the blond tresses, the rose, the fresh and tender frost, the pearls, the celestial singing that make up Laura's radiant loveliness (sonnet 220).

And it is the presence of this enchanting woman, forever visible to the mind's eye of the lover, that Petrarch attempts to recreate in his verses, to fix in a timeless present. Miraculously, imagination enables the poet to "sculpt" the woman's beautiful face in a place (canzone 50.65–67), where it cannot be moved by force or art, and then constantly contrives "poetic" images to recapture it. Memory, in turn, feeds the imagination; images cast in the magic language of the *dolce stil nuovo,* where the woman becomes the divine *donna angelicata,* transfigure Laura, however imperfect the act, "within a magic timelessness."[12] Petrarch wishes to evoke this sense of timelessness when he selects the modest Daphne, the mythical beloved, to recreate the disdainful Laura. Daphne, the recalcitrant virgin forever eluding the lover, is the ideal vehicle, not simply because she belongs to a mythical universe of timeless images but because Petrarch makes her a *figura,* a prefiguration of Laura. Laura's life as a courtly *midons* becomes a fulfillment of the life of Daphne as a *dura puella.* Present and past become one, and time is thereby abolished.

Daphne comes into Petrarch's historical present to stand for Laura and *be* Laura, and as many times as Petrarch can bring forth the mythical beloved, eternally unchanging in figurative recall, as many times can the nymph successfully fulfill her task as the "impersonator" of the woman. As in biblical typology where "at any time, at any place, Adam falls, Christ sacrifices himself, and humanity, the bride of the Song of Songs, faithful, hopeful, and loving, searches for Him,"[13] so does Daphne appear at any time, at any place, beautiful and elusive, to perform her "act." But just as she appears in an instant out of her ancient "sleep," she must disappear as quickly. For if the poet can bring Daphne into the present—transcending time and fixing her in an eternal now—the ancient beloved, by her very nature, must frustrate the poet's attempt to keep her there, constantly recreating Laura. For Daphne, eternally unchanging in figurative recall means also eternally unchanging in her escape from the lover. If she can be

brought into the present as often as the poet desires, he will be
forced to lose her just as many times. Hopeful, knowing full
well that his words are no more than wishful thinking, the lover
muses:

> et non se transformasse in verde selva
> per uscirmi di braccia, come il giorno
> ch'Apollo la seguia qua giù per terra! (sestina 22.34–36)

> (and let her not be transformed into a green wood
> to escape from my arms, as the day
> when Apollo pursued her down here on earth!)

Moreover, Petrarch must also deal with the inevitable elusiveness of the medium he has chosen to reconstruct Laura's image,
for words are as elusive as the woman. And of course the poem
itself must always end.

If Cupid provides the poet with the inspiration and the
noble style to recreate the woman but falls short in providing
him with the words to match the divine side of Laura, Daphne
is, by the same token, only partially successful in fulfilling Petrarch's expectations. Daphne provides him, for an instant, with
the woman suspended in time. But like Cupid, she fails. In her
case she fails to give the poet the woman in an eternal now.

To the presence of the ancient beloved corresponds the
presence of the ancient laurel, converted, like Daphne, into a
tool to recreate Laura. The laurel is paradoxically both emblematic and self-referential. John Freccero has denied the laurel all referential value:

> [F]or the laurel to be truly unique, it cannot *mean* any-
> thing: its referentiality must be neutralized if it is to re-
> main the property of its creator. Petrarch makes of it the
> emblem of the mirror relationship *Laura-Lauro,* which is to
> say the poetic lady created by the poet, who in turn cre-
> ates him as poet laureate. This circularity forecloses all ref-
> erentiality. . . .[14]

Freccero is correct in pointing out that this "mirror relationship"
does exist in and for itself. But the notion of self-referentiality
must be qualified. Inasmuch as the laurel is an emblem, it is referential, a sign pointing beyond itself to signify something other
than itself, something other than merely a tree. And the emblematic relations Petrarch creates are made possible and ren-

dered convincing because they initially rely on a set of meanings that have been established prior to the writing of the *Canzoniere*. The laurel can be a successful emblem of the woman because in the ancient past it is the tree into which Daphne, a *typos* of Laura, is changed. In the ancient cosmology of migrating forms, the bay is "Daphne transformed." In other words, the laurel tree has gathered unto itself the necessary connections to serve as a successful sign for Laura, the antitype of Daphne. Similarly, the laurel is a symbol of poetic glory for the ancients as well as for Petrarch. But if the meanings that the laurel yields in its emblematic and figurative referentiality are initially sought in the ancient past, once they reach the Petrarchan poetic cosmos they become the poet's own, establishing relations in and for themselves. Ultimately, the laurel emblems do become self-referential. And this can nowhere be better seen than in sestina 30, "Giovene donna sotto un verde lauro." This sestina also illustrates Petrarch's skillful imitation of the Ovidian material, focusing on the woman's transformation into the laurel.

"Giovene donna" depicts the idolatrous dimension of Petrarch's love for Laura,[15] rendered chiefly through images of the woman and the laurel. The sestina also makes evident the complex mechanism that, through memory and the imagination, generates poetic images for Petrarch. Here, as in much of the *Canzoniere*, Laura's reality is tenuous. The woman recreated in the lover's imagination first appears in dim outlines, later is fused with the laurel, and at the end she appears only as the laurel, her sign.

The poem opens with a vision of Laura as the poet first sees her, under the laurel tree:

> Giovene donna sotto un verde lauro
> vidi più bianca et più fredda che neve
> non percossa dal sol molti et molt'anni;
> e 'l suo parlare e 'l bel viso et le chiome
> mi piacquen sì ch'i' l'ò dinanzi agli occhi
> ed avrò sempre ov'io sia in poggio o 'n riva. (1–6)

> (A youthful lady under a green laurel
> I saw, whiter and colder than snow
> not touched by the sun many and many years,
> and her speech and her lovely face and her locks
> pleased me so that I have her before my eyes
> and shall always have wherever I am, on slope or shore.)

The word *vidi* ("I saw") in the second line not only makes memory a silent conspirator in bringing the woman into the present
but is the mechanism that makes possible the kind of poem Petrarch wants to write. The sestina is fanciful, visionary, and full
of startling turns, instability, and ambiguity. Memory by its very
nature deforms, blurs, and transforms. It thus allows for a fragmented and disintegrating reality, a reality constantly being
transformed into yet a new reality capable of further fragmentation and transformation.

In this first stanza, the woman and the laurel are separate
entities; she is young and so is the laurel in its youthful green-
ness. She is also beautiful, with a lovely face and hair, and cold-
er than snow, the latter a reference to Laura's cruelty in her disdainful courtly stance. Here Petrarch establishes the key notion
that governs the poem, the woman's rigor.

In the second and third stanzas, two laurel images tell of
the unattainability of the woman. An *impossibilia* dramatizes the
lover's inability to reach shore, an ambiguous emblematic image
possibly referring to the lover's inability to reach the distant
woman: "Allor saranno i miei pensieri a riva / che foglia verde
non si trovi in lauro" ("Then my thoughts will have come to
shore / when green leaves are not to be found on a laurel," 7–8).
Since the laurel tree is an evergreen, it is evident that the lover
will never reach his goal. In the third stanza, the faithful lover
pledges his loyalty to Laura by vowing to always follow the
shadow of the laurel: "seguirò l'ombra di quel dolce lauro / per
lo più ardente sole et per la neve, / fin che l'ultimo dì chiuda
quest'occhi" ("I shall follow the shadow of that sweet laurel / in
the most ardent sun or through the snow, / until the last day
closes these eyes," 16–18). The lover does not say that he will
follow Laura herself but the shadow cast by the laurel, the magic
space under the tree where the woman was first seen. In these
two stanzas the woman and the laurel are still separate.

Then something happens that distorts the imagery and
threatens the very identity of the lover. Laura's eyes appear,
those eyes that throughout the *Canzoniere* enrapture and dazzle
the man. The eyes melt him as the sun does the snow (21) and
the lover becomes a river of tears that is led by Love "to the foot
of the harsh laurel / that has branches of diamond and golden
locks" ("a pie' del duro lauro / ch'à i rami di diamante et d'or le
chiome," 23–24). Rapture so enthralls the lover that it paralyzes
the logical ordering of thought. His imagination, free from the

shackles of reason, distorts reality and makes him not only envision himself in watery transformation, but makes him conceive the woman in a grotesque image. It is a grotesque preciosity in which the cold and lovely woman of the first stanza now merges with the laurel, which is not green as in the beginning nor sweet as in the third stanza, but harsh, corresponding to the hard, "cold" stone *(diamante)* that defines the unmoving Laura.[16] Even if we are to understand that emblematically the laurel is Laura and the branches are her arms, the initial picture on our first reading is of a laurel with actual locks on white diamond branches. The grotesque vision is not only precious but monstrous as human, diamond, and laurel mingle and clash. It is as if the woman, cruel and distant, had become a kind of insensitive monster. The notion of the unattainability of Laura, referred to in the second and third stanzas, here reaches its peak.

In this grotesque image, Petrarch is working with an Ovidian reminiscence, the transformation of Daphne into the laurel, a fact that Robert Durling points out in his study of this sestina (11). But it is not only to the Ovidian images of Daphne's arms and hair transformed into leaves and branches *(Met.* 1.549) that the reader must refer to here, but also to the last line of the metamorphosis, "her gleaming beauty alone remained" ("remanet nitor unus in illa," 552), and to the line that depicts Daphne/laurel shrinking away from Apollo's kisses, "refugit tamen oscula lignum" (556). In these two lines Daphne's beauty is preserved in the laurel, and her recalcitrance is reflected in her rejection of Apollo's touch. And it is both recalcitrance and beauty that Petrarch echoes in his grotesque Laura. Daphne transformed into the unfeeling plant is Laura transformed into the harsh laurel— both escaping the "embraces" of the lovers. But in the sestina it is no longer the Ovidian Daphne and no longer the Ovidian laurel, for in making the ancient images self-referentially his own, it is now Petrarch's Laura and Petrarch's laurel.

From the grotesque vision, partly woman, partly laurel, Petrarch proceeds to two laurel images that center on Laura's characteristic rigor and the love-religion of the poet. In the fifth stanza, Laura becomes "my idol carved in living laurel" ("l'idolo mio scolpito in vivo lauro," 27). The woman's body, hardened into laurel, is an idolatrous construct, totemic, harsh in its pitiless stillness. Then after having shed all human traits, including her outline imposed on the tree, the woman becomes fully laurel, remote in time and presence:

sempre piangendo andrò per ogni riva,
per far forse pietà venir ne gli occhi
di tal che nascerà dopo mill'anni,
se tanto viver po ben colto lauro. (33–36)

(always weeping I shall go along every shore,
to make pity perhaps come into the eyes
of someone who will be born a thousand years from
now—
if a well-tended laurel can live so long.)

The "well-tended laurel," undoubtedly that green laurel planted
by Cupid in the heart of the poet and nourished by suppliant
tears in sonnet 228, is now but the sign of Laura reincarnated,
who will be born in a thousand years and who will perhaps
choose to give her pity to the poet.

The progression in the Ovidian transformation of Daphne
from human to hybrid to laurel is followed in Petrarch's extended visionary "transformation" of Laura from youthful lady, then
to hybrid form, and finally to laurel. But if in Ovid the bay becomes an object of reverence for Apollo, here it elicits more than
reverence; it is an object of worship and adoration. This worship
is, however, self-defeating and hopeless, for it is bestowed on an
evanescent figure who forever eludes the lover. The gradual disappearance of the Petrarchan woman parallels Daphne's step-by-
step transformation into the laurel. In Petrarch, Laura becomes
more and more remote as she too turns into a tree. The vague
picture of Laura in the first stanza gives way at the end to an
even vaguer vision of the woman. *Someone (tal)* is the word that
marks her presence now projected into a distant future, along
with only her sign, the omnipresent laurel.

The recreation of the woman imagistically by means of
laurel images is accompanied by constant linguistic recreation,
games of paronomasia with the woman's name to capture her in
a web of sound patterns.[17] Paronomasia functions phonetically
the way emblems function imagistically in that both hide and reveal meaning at the same time. It is a device that creates linguistic veils, allowing for that hermeticism and difficulty that in Petrarch's poetics gives pleasure to the reader deciphering the text.
Laura's name echoes in the familiar words "l'aurora," "l'aura,"
"l'ora," "l'oro," "l'aureo" and, of course, "lauro." One of the
most noted of these wordplays describes the breeze gently swaying the laurel and the woman's golden hair: "L'aura che 'l verde

lauro et l'aureo crine / soavemente sospirando move" (sonnet
246). Laura's presence is called forth emblematically (the breeze
and the laurel are signs of the woman), but the paronomastic
construct lends the verse its strength in its incantatory litany-like
cadence. It is as if language itself had taken a magic life of its
own, awakened by the overriding need to render and sustain
the woman's presence, if only through the constant repetition of
sounds. In these numerous games of paronomasia, each word
emerges in effect as a kind of hybrid as if Petrarch were phonetically recreating the woman's transformation into the laurel. Each
word evokes both the woman and the laurel, and the tangle of
sounds parallels the many images of metamorphosis where the
woman and the bay are fused and confused. In the *Canzoniere*,
paronomasia recreates Laura in sound in the same way that she
is recreated in images. Laura's presence is fragmented, as her
eyes, hair, face, arms, hands appear in effect as if scattered on
the landscape and are then assembled by the reader in order to
reconstruct a unified image.[18] Similarly, the echoing sounds scattered on the page are gathered to fashion Laura's name.

The recreation of the woman by means of paronomasia
carries with it, as everything in Petrarch's poetry, an element of
defeat. Laura is captured and fixed in sound as words appear
again and again, drifting and echoing across the page, but the
words are soon gone. Given the elusive nature of language, the
poet possesses the woman as long as the echoes last; when the
poem is done, the process must start anew. Laura's presence in
sound is ephemeral, merely suggested, evoked in the fleeting instant of an echo.

Laurel images, often accompanied by transformation as in
sestina 30, are the most common vehicles to circumscribe and
define the woman, however imperfectly. But they also define the
man. In canzone 23, for instance, a key laurel image "belongs"
to the lover; he is transformed into the bay, and this typically
ambiguous emblem reveals the profound impact his earthly
chains, Laura and poetic glory, have on him. Throughout the
Canzoniere, Laura is continually transformed in the poet's imagination and, caught in the magic spell of the dazzling woman,
he, in turn, is transformed into her mirror images—a laurel, a
swan, a rock, a fountain, a voice, a stag. Canzone 23 conveniently gathers these transformations, and Ovid's mythological figures are here easily recognized—Daphne, Cygnus, Battus, By-
blis, Echo, and Actaeon.[19] Ovid's world of flux, of mutability of

forms, provides the poet with ideal images to tell his story, capturing the instability of erotic desire and moral disorder, accompanied by touches of uneasy stability. The man's transformation into the laurel (41–49) is a significant moment in the complex narrative of the self in love, an ecstatic self as it confronts the woman.

Early in the canzone (15–20), Petrarch explains the psychological state of the lover trapped by "fierce desire" *(fera voglia)* and by recollections of the first time he saw Laura, here referred to as "one thought" *(un penser)*. This one thought brings about a paralysis of reason, surrender of the will, loss of self, and oblivion. These conditions constitute the rites of passage for the lover's entrance into the ecstatic, mysterious world of mythical transformations:

> E se qui la memoria non m'aita
> come suol fare, iscusilla i martiri
> et un penser che solo angoscia dàlle,
> tal ch'ad ogni altro fa voltar le spalle
> e mi face obliar me stesso a forza,
> ch'e' ten di me quel d'entro, et io la scorza. (15–20)

> (And if here my memory does not aid me as it is
> wont to do, let my torments excuse it and one
> thought which alone gives it such anguish that
> it makes me turn my back on every other and makes
> me forget myself beyond resistance, for it holds
> what is within me, and I only the shell.)

What Petrarch describes here is the dark night of aridity before the lover's ecstatic union with the woman. The transformation into the laurel is the emblem of this union. But before we examine this transformation, it would be instructive to look at other ecstatic moments that appear in the *Canzoniere,* for they shed light on what happens to the lover as he becomes the bay.

Ecstatic moments in Petrarch are couched in the language of Christian mysticism: a closing of the mind to external phenomena and suppression of the senses and reason, a loss of self, of identity, as the mind falls into a state of oblivion, uniting with the ineffable.[20] The self is in effect "standing elsewhere," transported from its immediate surroundings. For Christian mystics, the ineffable is God; for Petrarch it is the divine, evanescent, beautiful Laura from whom emanates that "ineffable sweetness"

(*ineffabile dolcezza*) that dazzles and paralyzes the lover. Laura
takes him into ecstasy, and canzone 126 captures this moment:

> Così carco d'oblio
> il divin portamento
> e 'l volto e le parole e 'l dolce riso
>   m'aveano, et sì diviso
> da l'imagine vera,
> ch'i' dicea sospirando:
> "Qui come venn'io o quando?"
> credendo esser in ciel, non là dov'era. (56–63)

> (Her divine bearing and her face and her words and
> her sweet smile had so laden me with forgetfulness
>   and so divided me from the true image, that I was
> sighing: "How did I come here and when?" thinking I
> was in Heaven, not there where I was.)

The exterior world is blissfully transfigured by the divine yet
sensual woman (even the reality of the true Laura—"l'imagine
vera"—fades), and the lover is transported in raptured forgetful-
ness to a heavenly abode of total peace and rest. He experiences
in effect a beatific vision, Laura having usurped God's role. He-
retical in its implication, this passage is the clearest example of
the lover's idolatry of the woman, the man having been totally
absorbed by her "holy" presence.

Moments of ecstasy—in effect flashes of ecstasy, for the
experience comes briefly rather than in extended visions—can be
easily multiplied. In sonnet 167 Laura is an enchantress, a heavenly siren whose song binds the lover's senses with sweetness;
in canzone 73 the lover, his reason dead, surrenders his will to
the woman and, dazzled by her eyes, lives in joy (22–39). In the
conventional terminology of ecstasy, when the mind becomes
enraptured, the body, detached from the mind, often takes on
new traits. In sonnet 175, the lover's first encounter with Laura
is described as "the time and the place where I lost myself" ("il
tempo e 'l loco / ov'i' perdei me stesso"), and the man, his identity gone, becomes something other than himself:

> solfo et esca son tutto, e 'l cor un foco
> da quei soavi spirti i quai sempre odo
> acceso dentro sì ch'ardendo godo.

> (I am all sulphur and tinder, and my heart is
> a fire lit by those gentle words which I

> always hear, so aflame within that I joy
> in my flames.)

The changes in the lover's body initiate him into the cult of the
mysterious woman. He enters her realm, loses himself, and is
readily transformed, reaching a momentary union with her presence. Her words kindle a fire in which he, transformed into tin-
der and sulphur, burns joyfully. The lover's metamorphosis is
the physical analogue of a spiritual component, ecstatic feeling
and union exemplified through a transformation. The lover's
transformation into the laurel is, as will be seen shortly, equally
a moment of ecstasy.

    While the lover finds peace, joy, and exultation in these
ecstatic moments, at other times he finds anguish and pain in
what one might call negative ecstasy. In these dark moments,
Laura has the petrifying, baneful power of the Medusa. Unlike
Dante, who is able to cover his eyes and save himself from the
sight of the Medusa outside the gates of Dis in Canto IX of the
Inferno, the lover of the *Canzoniere* can neither resist nor avoid
Laura's eyes. So Laura/Medusa turns his terrified heart into marble (sonnet 197). She is fearsome, plundering the lover's heart
and turning him into stone (canzone 23.72–80). Laura's power is
total and magical. She not only transforms the lover, but her
eyes are his norm (canzone 73.56). He even takes on her changing appearance: "my breast which takes its form from your varied aspects" ("il petto / che forma tien dal variato aspetto," canzone 72.59–60).

    The man's transformation into the laurel, one of Laura's
"varied aspects," presents ecstasy both as a celebration and as a
hopeless moment of anguish. The change is brought about by
Cupid and by the woman herself:

> ei duo mi trasformaro in quel ch'i' sono,
> facendomi d'uom vivo un lauro verde
> che per fredda stagion foglia non perde.
>   Qual mi fec'io quando primier m'accorsi
> de la trasfigurata mia persona,
> e i capei vidi far di quella fronde
> di che sperato avea già lor corona,
> e i piedi in ch'io mi stetti et mossi et corsi,
> com'ogni membro a l'anima risponde,
>   diventar due radici sovra l'onde
> non di Peneo ma d'un più altero fiume,
> e 'n duo rami mutarsi ambe le braccia! (38–49)

(those two transformed me into what I am,
making me of a living man a green laurel that
loses no leaf for all the cold season.
   What I became, when I first grew aware of
my person being transformed and saw my hairs
turning into those leaves which I had formerly
hoped would be my crown, and my feet, on which
I stood and moved and ran, as every member answers
to the soul,
   becoming two roots beside the waves not of Peneus
but of a prouder river, and my arms changing into
two branches!)

This transformation is prefaced by lines 15–20 quoted above,
which tell of the lover's first encounter with Laura, a thought
that holds everything within him, making him forget himself
"beyond resistance." He remains "only the shell." The man has
surrendered his self and his will to the woman, and now his
"shell" is molded and transformed by her and Cupid into the
green laurel, her sign. Lover and beloved are one. This is clearly
a moment of rapture. As in sonnet 175 mentioned above, the
transformation is the physical analogue of ecstatic trance; the
body changes and is absorbed in union with the woman. The
transformation is the peak of an ecstatic experience that has its
origin at the moment of meeting Laura. Now the lover is "elsewhere," in the universe of his enchantress. This is an example of
negative ecstasy, for the lover is terrified by Laura, the bearer of
pain, who governs the passage.
   Union through transformation is a familiar notion in the
vocabulary of mysticism. Saint John of the Cross, the Spanish
mystic, employing erotic imagery to convey mystical rapture,
writes in his *Noche oscura* of "amada en el amado transformada"
("beloved in the lover transformed"). In his commentary to the
poem, the mystical union is explained as the "union of the soul
with God which is consummated in the soul's transformation in
God—a union which can come about only when the soul attains
to a likeness with God by virtue of love."[21] Love transports and
transfigures; it is the force and the impulse behind the union
both for Petrarch's lover and for Saint John—erotic in the former
and divine in the latter. The secular lover, like John the mystic,
mingles with and is absorbed by the object of his love. It is a
moment of affirmation, yet anguished and fearful, as he rises to

union with the cherished woman and, by extension, with the laurel of poetic glory, a poetic salvation for the lover as he becomes the poet laureate.

This moment of celebration, however, carries an element of defeat for both the courtly lover and the Christian. First, the lover reaps only an illusory union with the woman for it is, after all, a sublimated bond with her symbol. The courtly lover's union with Laura, like Apollo's union with Daphne in Ovid's *Metamorphoses,* is merely a form of self-deception, since the sensual woman is left behind. The surrogate union becomes a phantasm and an ultimate failure. As in Ovid, the laurel—the symbol of honor and glory—becomes paradoxically a symbol of the lover's defeat in the erotic agon. To the Christian it is still a more profound defeat, as the man yields to his dreams of poetic glory and to the earthly Laura, both of which tangle the lover in their erotic snare, leading him astray, away from God and along the road to perdition. The transformation into the laurel is in effect a rich emblem of the lover as sinner.

The Augustinian notion of love for earthly things *(cupiditas)* as the cause of mutability, instability, and disorder is captured in this moment of transformation, when the lover is not only fragmented and divided from his former self but hurled down to the subhuman world of plants. And as the grotesque is unveiled, the sinner emerges. The lover unites with the laurel in hybrid clash: hair turns into leaves, feet into roots, and arms into branches. Echoes of medieval Christian notions of sin come to mind: man corrupted by vice abandons his reason, becoming, in the process, less than a man. This metaphysical notion springs from the belief that the rational soul gives the body its form—its structure and order. The corruption of man by evil is equivalent to his losing his soul, his form, and a physical metamorphosis is a way of graphically portraying this loss. D. W. Robertson writes of the medieval idea that "a man corrupted in some way by . . . sensuality might exhibit animal characteristics, or even plantlike features."[22] When Petrarch's lover surrenders to the sensual Laura, he also surrenders what is "within" him (20)—that is, his soul—becoming mere matter ("la scorza," "the shell") to be shaped according to the whims of Laura/Medusa. Like Odo of Cluny's *chimaera* and the many composite monsters of the Middle Ages, which, in their wild, chaotic violation of structural order represent spiritual degradation, the idolatrous lover's grotesque union with the laurel—a symbol of his vices,

woman and poetic glory—mirrors his moral transgression. Moreover, the incongruous union of human and laurel, suggesting a
conflict between the two, represents the lover's struggle with
what he regards in moments of contrition as his baser self.

Petrarch's grotesque is typically paradoxical and ambivalent, like most grotesques. It belongs to an alienated world of
distorted forms that speak of dark, threatening forces, and yet it
also brings forth regeneration and life. To the Christian Petrarch,
the dark side of the grotesque represents a loss of humanity,
emblematic of contamination with sin; its regenerative aspect—
marked by the laurel's evergreen freshness (40)—is celebratory, a
positive, even though anguished, occasion of the birth of the
lover and the poet laureate.

The transformation into the laurel is a moment of illumi-
nation and recognition—the revelation of the man as lover, poet,
and sinner, captured in one cryptic image. Petrarch the visionary
has availed himself of Daphne's metamorphosis as a model for
the lover's metamorphosis, making it speak in clear, though hidden, tones of the mysteries of love and poetry. Even though Petrarch keeps close to the Ovidian model in his imitation, including its key note of paralysis, he clearly invests it with new
meaning. Daphne's rigidity—her limbs overcome by heavy torpor and her swift feet arrested in sluggish roots—mirrors her
virginal modesty. The transformation leaves her unawakened,
changed into a tree incapable of feeling. The paralysis of Petrarch's lover, on the other hand, as his feet become two roots,
is emblematic of spiritual paralysis. The man is caught in the
petrifying power of the Medusa, who carries death in her eyes.
The man enters this fantastic realm through memory marked by
the word *vidi*, which reveals the lover as a witness and narrator
of his own metamorphosis. As noted earlier in the analysis of
sestina 30, memory by its very nature blurs and distorts. And
here memory merges the lover and the laurel in unnatural, grotesque union just as in the sestina it had merged the woman and
the laurel.

Petrarch uses Daphne's metamorphosis to give expression
to what lies behind the lover's "silence." As in traditional ecstatic moments where there is a loss of speech in the presence of
the transcendent, the poet's voice fails as he confronts the ineffable Laura. Paralysis of language is a common complaint in the
Canzoniere, where words constantly miss the mark. Excessive
pleasure is an "obstacle to my tongue" ("s'atraversa / a la mia

lingua"), the poet writes in sonnet 143; his wit becomes frozen
and his voice remains trapped in his breast in the presence of
Laura's beauty (sonnet 20). Even though Petrarch's display of el-
oquence makes his assertions suspect, the reader realizes that
the poet is deeply conscious of the fact that words alone are in-
adequate. They are powerless to evoke glorious visions of the
woman or the rapt moment of meeting.

And so he uses the language of myth to offer, pictorially
at least, an intuition of what for him represents the ultimate in-
communicable experience; to fall in love with a profoundly sensual yet celestial creature. Through this use of the ancient images, Petrarch shares with his religious contemporaries the habit
of giving concrete form to abstract notions. Johan Huizinga has
suggested that this habit "was an irresistible tendency to reduce
the infinite to the finite, to disintegrate all mystery."[23] For pious
Christians the need to give concrete form to religious thought is
born from their desire to understand and render the divine in
simple terms. For Petrarch the use of concrete, pictorial images
is similarly a means, however imperfect, of grasping the un-
graspable. Whereas for the everyday Christian this act of concret-
izing the ineffable is ultimately an act of genuine, if naive, piety,
for Petrarch it represents an act of heresy and a perversion. Endowing Laura with the epithets commonly reserved for God—
divine and ineffable—Petrarch contrives images to portray the
lover's union with her. Saint Augustine writes of God: "He
alone is ineffable, Who spoke and all things were made. He
spoke and we were made; but we are unable to speak of Him."[24]
In the *Canzoniere,* Laura usurps God's role. Petrarch is unable to
"speak" of the woman, and she, the ineffable magician, "creates" the lover and the poet laureate in silence, not speech, in
what is for the man a second birth. Idolatry is Petrarch's constant curse and blessing.

If the transformation into the laurel dramatizes the lover's
moral agon—the conflict with his earthly chains—in terms of a
hybrid clash, the landscape dramatizes it in a dialectic portraying
his wavering between the profane and the sacred. The setting
emerges both as a haven of peace, repose, and beauty and as a
threatening Dantean wood.

The former is a sylvan landscape, a setting also utilized
with insistent frequency by Ovid in his *Metamorphoses*—an idyllic
rustic setting of dense forests, lush grass, shade, flowers, water,
and gentle breezes. Petrarch creates scenery that, like Ovid's, is

"vague, exotic, and suggestive,"[25] constructed chiefly from the conventional elements of pastoral. The suggestiveness and vagueness not only make possible the atmosphere of mystery and mythical fantasy that permeates both works but also contribute to the successful use of landscape as a symbolic frame for the action.[26]

Ovid places Daphne in secluded woods that are a place of refuge for the nymph, a symbol of her innocence and purity. Like the transparent pool of Narcissus or Diana's sacred grove, Daphne's woods are the sheltered realm of a virginal way of life. Petrarch also places Laura, the antitype of Daphne, in a sheltered wood. The woods of the chaste Laura are not only secluded, however, but they exhibit the characteristics of a typical *locus amoenus* with its luxuriant physical delights. Virginity and sensuality are the woman's basic traits, and nature participates in their revelation and celebration. Laura's presence is scattered everywhere throughout the landscape. Her feet and eyes move through "the shady cloister" of the lovely hills (sonnet 192). She is the gentle breeze that awakens the flowers in the "shady wood" (sonnet 194). At times it seems as if Petrarch's woods are endowed with numen, the presiding spirit being of course the woman, as in sonnet 176:

> Parmi d'udirla, udendo i rami et l'ore
> e le frondi, et gli augei lagnarsi, et l'acque
> mormorando fuggir per l'erba verde.
>
> (I seem to hear her, when I hear the branches and
> the breeze and the leaves, and birds lamenting, and
> the waters fleeing with a murmur across the green
> grass.)

Everything is alive with Laura's presence. These woods are her world, her private, almost sacred domain, a frame for her ideal beauty as in the epiphanic canzone 126 where the lover, as he searches for Laura, introspects and calls forth her image. She is of the woods and, like Daphne, who is transformed into the laurel and literally becomes part of the landscape, Laura is one with nature. The woman is the laurel, the breeze, the dawn.

When guilt enters the lover's conscience, however, the inner vision changes and his darker, remorseful side is projected upon the landscape. These lovely, friendly woods—a veritable earthly paradise—are transformed into an evil and dangerous forest filled with thorns. According to Virgil in *Aeneid* 6, those who die for love become, in the underworld, wanderers in a dark wood.[27] Petrarch endows the Virgilian image with moral significance; the lover becomes not only a wanderer but a captive, the unwilling "dweller in the shady wood," where he humbly and urgently prays to God for deliverance (sestina 214.28–30). In these ominous woods, the once sweet Laura is now the harsh beast *(aspra fera)*, an image that defines her courtly cruelty but also her deadly sensuality (sestina 22). Like the woods, the pleasance is transformed. It becomes a paradise before the Fall, where serpents lurk amidst the flowers and the grass, and if the eyes are enchanted by its splendor, it is only to ensnare the unsuspecting soul (sonnet 99). This polarity in the landscape had already been anticipated in Ovid's *Metamorphoses*, with its ambiguous landscapes, where a sheltered, inviting place of refuge calls forth its opposite. As Charles Segal writes:

> The landscape symbolical of virginity may thus suddenly become the landscape of lustful sensuality; images of sanctity may become images of desire. The shaded pool of Diana may symbolize virginity in the stories of Callisto and Actaeon; but such a pool may entice to sexual surrender, not restraint, in tales like those of Narcissus, Salmacis, Arethusa.[28]

The change in the landscape is often effected by figures who threaten and entice, the darker powers that so often govern the action of the *Metamorphoses*, such as Jupiter in the story of Callisto (2.409ff.), Salmacis in her seduction of Hermaphroditus (4.306ff.), and Alpheus in his lusty chase after Arethusa (5.572ff.).

Apollo has a similar role in the Daphne episode. Because of him, the nymph's solitary, virginal woods, a place of happy freedom from love, become a place of entrapment, the lonely witness of her possible undoing. Moreover, lust visibly transforms the landscape; suddenly it becomes rugged and thick with brambles as Apollo chases Daphne (510). In Petrarch, the sensual Laura becomes the threatening figure who destroys the peace of the landscape. The lover, like Daphne, must traverse a rugged path "full of snares and thorns" (sestina 214.25). But in the *Canzoniere's* Christian framework, this road is most surely the road to perdition.

The motif of the road is closely linked to the image of the chase, an Ovidian theme well-suited for the poet's moral agon. The chase, like the setting, clearly portrays the lover's vacillation between salvation and perdition. In his guise as pilgrim and wanderer, the lover constantly pursues Laura, later to withdraw in fear and guilt. In an image reminiscent of Apollo's chase after Daphne, who escapes like the wind, Petrarch's lover hopelessly runs after the woman who, free of the "snares of Love," flies before his slow pursuit (sonnet 6).

When guilt and shame oppress the lover, the sensual Laura is envisioned as the bearer of evil. In sonnet 209 the lover is a fleeing, wounded deer, an image taken from Virgil's picture of Dido in the *Aeneid* (4.69–73). The lover attempts to escape the woman, and by extension his irrational desire, signaled by the arrow embedded in his left side:

> Et qual cervo ferito di saetta
> col ferro avelenato dentr'al fianco
> fugge et più duolsi quanto più s'affretta,
>
> tal io, con quello stral dal lato manco
> che mi consuma et parte mi diletta,
> di duol mi struggo et di fuggir mi stanco.
>
> (As a hart struck by an arrow, with the poisoned
> steel within its side, flees and feels more pain
> the faster it runs,
>
> so I, with that arrow in my left side which destroys
> me and at the same time delights me, am tormented
> by sorrow and weary myself with fleeing.)

The Actaeon episode in canzone 23, the lover transformed into a stag by Laura in the guise of Diana and pursued by his hounds (147–60), presents a similar picture—the flight of the Christian from the erotic enterprise and its spiritual death.

Apollo, Daphne's lover and pursuer, does not figure in the Christian agon. He does, nevertheless, play a key role in the *Canzoniere*. His very presence confers an exalted nobility on Laura; the woman is the antitype of Daphne, and the fact that she is Apollo's beloved gives her a glorious dignity. In order to make Apollo fit for this task, Petrarch must transform the god. He rescues Apollo from the medieval exegetes and divests him of his Christian roles as a symbol of wisdom and a type of

Christ. He also rescues him from Ovid by eliminating his role as a foolish lover. Apollo appears as the lofty god of poetry, and at one moment Petrarch asks him to exercise his power by defending the "honored and holy [laurel] leaves / where you first and then I were limed" ("difendi or l'onorata et sacra fronde / ove tu prima et poi fu' invescato io," sonnet 34).

These verses establish the link of the lyric persona with Apollo, for both are lovers and poets. And here the lovers are doubly caught since the leaves stand for both poetry and Laura, and the saving of the leaves will signify the preservation of both the woman and poetic glory:

> sì vedrem poi per meraviglia inseme
> seder la donna nostra sopra l'erba
> et far de la sue braccia a se stessa ombra.

> (Thus we shall then together see a marvel—our lady sitting on the grass and with her arms making a shade for herself.)

The "marvel" (*meraviglia*) referred to in these lines not only points to the startling vision of arms that are like branches making shade, but also to the fact that miraculously both Apollo and Petrarch's lover will be able to contemplate the woman in peaceful repose rather than in flight. Laura remains typically elusive, however, for the woman who will be preserved if the laurel is saved is a Daphne/Laura who belongs to the imagination, in that interval of uneasy fusion of tree and woman, when the mythical and the unreal prevail.

The ambiguity of this last image of Laura also reveals the ambiguity of the figure of Apollo himself. Divine and lofty, the god is nonetheless a defeated lover, who never reaches the woman. Defeat in love is Apollo's trademark, whether in Ovid or Petrarch. But if Ovid employs Apollo's defeat to create his comedy, revealing the foolish god who must accept the glorious laurel as a substitute for the woman, Petrarch uses defeat to define his courtly Apollo. Courtly lovers are, by their very nature, defeated lovers.

Apollo is not a fool in the *Canzoniere,* and unlike the Ovidian Apollo who tries to regain his lost majesty through his paean to Daphne, Petrarch's Apollo never quite loses his majesty, even when he sheds tears. The god seems to accept his defeat in the *Canzoniere,* or at least he does not hide it. In sonnet

43, he anguishes over the loss of the woman: "mostrossi a noi qual uom per doglia insano / che molto amata cosa non ritrove" ("he showed himself to us like one mad with grief / at not finding some much-loved thing"). As we shall see, this agonistic Apollo will be Petrarch's legacy to the Spaniards Garcilaso and Quevedo.

We have seen an ambiguity in Apollo as both the divine protector of the laurel and as the defeated lover. There is another ambiguity in the fact that for all the nobility that Petrarch confers upon Apollo, the god awakens jealousy in the lover. Apollo becomes his rival and as such is not allowed to appear more than a few times in the *Canzoniere*, and when he does he is either distant, looming high in the sky as the Sun, or he is the object of a brief address or a brief description. It would appear that by trying to ban the god's presence, Petrarch could also ban the threat of the divine lover. But Petrarch knows that the god's glorious image is vital to his verses and that he cannot be banished altogether. Thus occasionally Apollo makes his presence felt. The rivalry, however, is very real and the poet sets up isolated scenes of love victories and defeats for the lover and for Apollo. In sonnet 115, the lover achieves a small victory over the god, who appears in the guise of Sol, when Laura turns away from Sol to give her attention to the lover. In sonnet 188, Sol pays back in-kind when he ignores the lover's anxious pleas and disappears. The ensuing darkness makes the cherished place where Laura was born (and where the lover's heart dwells with the woman) vanish from sight.

Petrarch's defeated lover emerges, like Apollo before him in the *Metamorphoses*, as an *exclusus amator*, the excluded lover who is barred from his lady's presence. But there are differences between these two jilted lovers. The Ovidian Apollo had transformed his *paraclausithyron* (the lament of the excluded lover) into a paean to regain his dignity after his foolish wooing of the woman. Petrarch's song—the entire *Canzoniere* is in fact his song—is both a paean of praise to the woman, and, as the traditional *paraclausythiron*, a song of sorrow. This sorrow is caused by Laura's recalcitrance when she is alive and by the lover's loss of the woman and final exclusion after her death. Whereas in the *Metamorphoses* the loss of Daphne yields the laurel, in the *Canzoniere* Laura's death implies a double loss; not only does the lover lose the woman but the laurel of poetry as well. While the arrogant Ovidian deity dons the garland triumphantly, the defeated Petrarchan lover must relinquish the coveted leaf.

The loss of the laurel and the end of the *Canzoniere* occur as the poet realizes that his earthly Laura is gone forever. Laura herself reveals this to the lover. In canzone 359, "Quando il soave mio fido conforto," Laura, having cast off her role as the cruel courtly enemy and become *salvatrice,* appears to him in a vision and tells him that her blond hair and her beautiful eyes have been earth for many years (60–61). A virtual Beatrice, she points the way to heaven by admonishing him to liberate himself from his mortal cares and turn to God. Laura bears two small branches, one of laurel and one of palm, both symbols of victory and a tribute to her moral virtue:

> "Palma è vittoria, et io giovene ancora
> vinsi il mondo et me stessa; il lauro segna
> triunfo, ond'io son degna
> mercé di quel Signor che mi die' forza." (49–52)

> ("the palm is victory, and I when still young
> conquered the world and myself; the laurel
> means triumph, of which I am worthy, thanks
> to that Lord who gave me strength.")

The laurel has changed hands and roles. It is no longer the poet's: the symbol of poetry and the sensual woman. The laurel now belongs to a Christian Laura and it stands for the triumph of the spirit over the flesh. As in Ovidian exegeses of the Middle Ages, especially Arnulf of Orléans' commentary and the *Ovide moralisé,* the bay is the heavenly reward for an exemplary life on earth. Laura has become one of the blessed and her chastity has merited the victorious garland. The fact that the palm accompanies the bay is particularly significant. In Old Testament typology, the palm stands for both victory over death and sacrifice, an apposite symbol for Laura's messianic role.

Petrarch had already used the laurel to praise Laura's chastity as in canzone 29, in sonnet 295 (along with the palm), and in sonnet 313. But in these three poems, the lover is riding the full tide of his passion for Laura. In canzone 359, on the other hand, the man's love is informed by the recognition that the woman's body has turned to dust and that she is but naked spirit ("spirito ignudo")—words that ring with undisputed finality. And this recognition renders the woman's chastity useless to the poet. In other words, Laura's chastity without her sensual allure is no fitting matter for Petrarch's courtly poetry. The destruction of Laura's body is also the destruction of poetry and of poetic fame, and thus, as sonnet 363 reports, the glorious laurel gives way to the lowly elm and oak:

> Morte à spento quel sol ch'abagliar suolmi,
> e 'n tenebre son li occhi interi et saldi;
> terra è quella ond'io ebbi et freddi et caldi,
> spenti son i miei lauri, or querce et olmi.

> (Death has extinguished the sun that used to dazzle me, and my eyes though whole and sound are in darkness; she is dust from whom I took chills and heat; my laurels are faded, are oaks and elms.)

The transformation of the lover's laurels into elms and oaks carries echoes of mythical beginnings. Before the laurel came into being, as Ovid tells us at the end of the Python episode (so as to inform the reader of the etiological value of the tale of Daphne), the oak was awarded to the Pythian victors and Apollo himself would bear a garland from any tree (448–51). Petrarch has returned to the times before the laurel when the oak and other trees fulfilled the bay's roles. These times bore witness to the exploits of the epic Apollo, the killer of Python, not to the adventures of the lover. The woman had yet to appear. Thus the period before the laurel was a period when love was silent. Silence will soon be our poet's lot.

      The woman and the laurel gone, the lover turns to God "stanco di viver, non che sazio" ("weary of life, not merely satiated," sonnet 363). Like the Ovidian Apollo who tries to turn his defeat into a triumph after his hopes of obtaining Daphne have vanished, the lover seeks his own victory in Christian salvation when he sees that after his loss he is left with no other recourse. And so his contrition is suspect. Moreover, the loss of the sensual Laura is an attempt to bring about a Christian resolution to the *Canzoniere*. But the turn is too abrupt and is thus unconvincing. Not surprisingly, the last two sonnets and the final *Vergine bella* are prayers for salvation rather than statements of conversion. We must bear in mind that Petrarch's very first poem was a palinode, a confession of his error and his repentance. This poem and the last establish a circularity that negates the poet's very claim to conversion. As Giuseppe Mazzotta notes: "The implied link between beginning and end gives the poetic sequence a circular structure which challenges the possibility of renewal and leads the reader to suspect that the moral claim is the ambiguous expedient by which the poet attempts to constitute his own self as an 'authority.' "[29] The erotic agon has disappeared at the end of the *Canzoniere* but, always ambiguous, the moral agon remains unresolved.

4

The Grotesque and the Courtly
in Garcilaso's Apollo and Daphne

To speak of the grotesque in connection with Garcilaso de la Vega may be startling, for such a mode seems an unlikely intrusion into the world of this luminous poet, whose scenes of idealized beauty and nature represent the epitome of Renaissance classicism in Spain. But in Garcilaso there are also tortured landscapes and violent passages that serve as correlatives for the pain and desperation of the courtly lover caught in the drama of unrequited love and of the lady's death. This is the Garcilaso who turns to the grotesque to illustrate the ultimate moment of loss, the loss of the woman. His mythological sonnet of Apollo and Daphne, with its disfiguring metamorphosis, portrays the grotesque destruction of the lady and the grief that this destruction spawns. The disharmony that abounds in Garcilaso's courtly world is often reflected in images contrary to nature. And the grotesque, characterized by a violation of nature and the established order, cannot but serve as a perfect device to mirror this disharmony.

As a backdrop to Garcilaso's grotesque stand the numerous physical grotesques of the period, incongruous inventions startling in their departure from the verisimilitude and ideal forms of Renaissance classicism. Among these we find the whimsical fancies of monsters and hybrids of the ornamental grotesque, the "dreams of painters" that permeate the plateresque art of Spain; emblems filled with bizarre images including mythological scenes of metamorphosis; and numerous compositions of *maniera* artists. These latter artists' disregard of classical norms, especially in their deliberate distortion of harmonious proportions, leads to grotesque deformations, an aesthetic practice culminating in Arcimboldo's composite monsters and Cambiaso's "cubic men." It is to the *maniera* style that we owe the distorted Daphnes that are, as will be seen, Garcilaso's pictorial analogues.

This period's fondness for the marvelous and the fantastic nurtures a rich mythological tradition with images of the grotesque, and Ovid's *Metamorphoses*—a world of fanciful creatures and strange transformations where the human and nonhuman merge—is its main source. Garcilaso stands at the beginning of the mythological tradition in Golden Age poetry, and his grotesque is the point of departure for a series of mythological grotesques, the best known of which is Góngora's Cyclops in the *Polifemo*.

For his treatment of Apollo and Daphne—the first reworking of this myth in the Golden Age[1]—Garcilaso uses Ovid's version as a model for the transformation and Petrarch for his portrayal of the divine lover. Garcilaso's tale of the god and the recalcitrant nymph illustrates the final stages of the erotic agon, the lover's loss of the woman through transformation. Yet, while his imitation recaptures the essence of the Ovidian story, Garcilaso subverts and distorts the myth by placing it in his highly artificial, dolorous world of courtly love.[2] In his retelling, Apollo is not a comic, self-deluding deity in newly consecrated laurel leaves, but a disconsolate, courtly mourner; and Daphne is not a modest virgin who suffers a mild transformation while gaining the protective citadel of the bay, but a courtly lady harshly destroyed by the bay, which remains as a sign, a gravestone of her death. The grotesque contained in Garcilaso's sonnet is all the more surprising for being encased in the mellifluous lines of elegant, measured Renaissance speech:

> A Daphne ya los braços le crecían
> y en luengos ramos bueltos se mostravan;
> en verdes hojas vi que se tornavan
> los cabellos quel oro escurecían;
>   de áspera corteza se cubrían
> los tiernos miembros que aun bullendo 'stavan;
> los blancos pies en tierra se hincavan
> y en torcidas raýzes se bolvían.
>   Aquel que fue la causa de tal daño,
> a fuerça de llorar, crecer hazía
> este árbol, que con lágrimas regava.
>   ¡O miserable 'stado, o mal tamaño,
> que con llorarla crezca cada día
> la causa y la razón por que llorava![3]

> (Now Daphne's arms began to grow and turn
> into long branches;
> I saw her hair, which had made gold a blur
> of darkness, becoming green leaves;
>   her tender limbs, which still were trembling,
> were being covered by coarse bark;
> her white feet were piercing the earth
> and turning into twisted roots.
>   And he who was the cause of such damage,
> by dint of weeping made this tree grow
> from tears with which he watered it.
>   O miserable state, o huge calamity,
> that from his weeping each day should grow
> the cause and reason of his weeping!)

I will examine the innovations wrought by Garcilaso on the Ovidian myth, including the role of the grotesque in his vision of Daphne's transformation; the relation of his distorted design to artistic notions of his age, in particular to the aesthetic of the *maniera* and to emblem literature; the function of the grotesque in his courtly poetics; and the role of the courtly Apollo.

In his rendition, Garcilaso strips the transformation of the elements of paralysis of the Ovidian model and, endowing the nymph with the traditional beauty traits of the courtly lady, focuses on her deformation and destruction. To stress the laurel's baneful nature, he converts Ovid's "gentle" bay into a menacing and even "ugly" plant. These changes bring about an intensification of the grotesque. The similarity between the maiden and the tree, which Ovid stresses to show the harmony in Daphne's ontological quest, gives way to a dramatic contrast between the soft, exquisite woman and the rough, twisted tree. A world of ideal beauty is destroyed by the coarse and involuted. The grotesque in Garcilaso is used for its visual impact: to dramatize both the loss of the lady and the pain of the lover who witnesses that loss.

From the very beginning of the sonnet, the intensification of the grotesque elements is evident. Ovid's terse "in ramos bracchia crescunt" becomes a description of how Daphne is stretched apart as her arms elongate into branches:

> A Daphne ya los braços le crecían
> y en luengos ramos bueltos se mostravan.

Next, the tree covers Daphne from head to foot in a downward movement of loss. In three stages the emerging laurel destroys

an element of beauty in Daphne's body: her golden hair, her soft
flesh, and her white feet.

Ovid's "in frondem crines . . . crescunt" becomes

> en verdes hojas vi que se tornavan
> los cabellos quel oro escurecían.

> (I saw her hair, which had made gold a blur
> of darkness, becoming green leaves.)

Ovid's verse, devoid of modifiers, merely tells of the transformation; Garcilaso's antithesis, with its chromatic elements of change
from gold to green, conveys not only the destruction of beauty
but of ideal beauty, for the hyperbolic description of Daphne's
golden hair belongs to the conventional catalog of charms consecrated by tradition. By investing Daphne with the traditional
golden hair of amatory poetry, Garcilaso places her alongside the
exalted elegiac *domina* of the ancients, the troubadour lady, and
the Petrarchan beloved.[4]

But it is in the second quatrain that the grotesque emerges
in all its force, for the plant brutally destroys Daphne's body.
Ovid's depiction of how the nymph's soft sides are encircled
with delicate bark, stressing the similarity of the girl's body to
the texture of the laurel, gives way to a violent image in the new
scheme:

> de áspera corteza se cubrían
> los tiernos miembros que aun bullendo 'stavan.

> (her tender limbs, which still were trembling,
> were being covered by coarse bark).

By substituting *áspera* for *tenui*, Garcilaso sets forth a dramatic
contrast between the softness of the maiden and the coarse texture of the tree. Moreover, the addition of "que aun bullendo
'stavan," with the participle *bullendo* conveying the feeling of
palpitating flesh and the adverb *aun* reinforcing the presence of
human life in the nymph, creates a juxtaposition where the
throbbingly beautiful is smothered by the clutching rough bark.

The last conversion continues the deformation of pulling
and stretching seen in the first two lines of the sonnet. The Ovidian *pes velox* becomes *blancos pies,* and *pigris radicibus* gives way to
torcidas raýzes. The antithesis of the Latin verse, which shows the
ceasing of the swift flight of the virgin, in Garcilaso becomes a
horrible image. The maiden's white feet are thrust into the
ground and twisted into roots:

los blancos pies en tierra se hincavan
y en torcidas raýzes se bolvían

The reference to white feet, like the golden hair motif, is a figure consecrated by tradition corresponding to the Petrarchan *candido piede*. Thus the metamorphosis preserves the notion of the destruction of ideal beauty.

Clearly, in Garcilaso's grotesque there is a greater degree of distortion than in the Ovidian model, and thus the scene is filled with more incongruous tension and disquiet. In Ovid, the presence of a cosmology that explains Daphne's transformation as a "transmigration" from human to laurel adds a measure of harmony and weakens the impact of the grotesque: Daphne escapes Apollo and finds a suitable—if not totally satisfactory— abode for her virginity. And of course, at the end of the transformation, Ovid tells how Daphne's fairness, her "gleaming," remains: "remanet nitor unus in illa." Although the *unus* subtly records that the rest of Daphne is gone, the reader is also aware that the beautiful maiden has become a beautiful tree.

In Garcilaso, the absence of the ancient notion adds to the abnormality of the grotesque scene. Moreover, Garcilaso ends Daphne's conversion with the most violent image of the deformation sequence, as if to emphasize the fact that the "ugly" tree is completing its destructive mission. In line nine, he sums up Daphne's metamorphosis as a *daño*, a blight caused by Apollo. In Ovid, when at the end of the tale Daphne/laurel shakes her top as in assent to Apollo's solemn paean, her gesture not only provides a final comic touch to Ovid's lighthearted story—for now that Daphne is safe behind the walls of her bark, she seems to grant Phoebus her full, if meaningless, consent—but it also seems to affirm, however tenuously, her salutary arboreal state. In Garcilaso, on the other hand, Daphne's body, covered and disfigured by a shroud of tree life, disappears, and along with it all traces of the human Daphne. The loss is complete. In her place stands an inanimate, unfeeling plant upon which the impotent lover can do nothing but shed his tears.

Garcilaso's quatrains rest on a symmetrical structure, for the antitheses that convey the change (*braços-luengos ramos; verdes hojas-cabello [de] oro; áspera corteza-tiernos miembros; blancos pies-torcidas raýzes*) give perfect balance and equilibrium to the composition.[5] This poised symmetry, however, is not accompanied by the expected repose but by restless vitality. Like Ovid, Garcilaso conveys the movement of the transformation by the alternate motion of the antitheses. But Garcilaso intensifies the illusion of dynamic unfolding by using the imperfect tense, by placing the verbs at the end of each line—creating a rhythmic, musical *íanaban* rhyme—and by introducing enjambments, the type that Dámaso Alonso characterizes as *encabalgamiento suave,* in order to stress the uninterrupted progress of change. The increased dynamism also increases the grotesque effect, for it makes the process of disintegration more vivid.

In his commentary on the sonnet, Fernando de Herrera noted that the verb *vi* in line three was used by Garcilaso to comply with the exigencies of the meter.[6] But the verb is essential in the scene and has several functions. The lyric speaker gives concreteness and credence to the event by becoming a participant in a mythological past that was revealed to him. The *vi* also works as an imperative, a call urging the reader himself to see, to open his visual imagination to the scene of transformation. But paradoxically the verb functions as a distancing device in the scene; while the reader is urged to see, he must do so through an intermediary. Since the spectacle of transformation is conveyed through the medium of the lyric speaker as reporter, the violent disfiguration of the nymph comes to the reader indirectly, as something spoken of. This human intermediary spares the reader a direct confrontation with the deformation; his intervention, through the *vi,* subtly serves to veil the scene's brutality.[7]

Since Garcilaso fashions the scene of metamorphosis as a recollected revelation—"I saw," not "I see"—the poem takes on a kind of visionary quality. The lyric speaker was a witness and participant in a fantastic scene, and the visionary quality of his recollection renders the experience convincing, a condition that the present ("I see") would not have allowed. For while the present suggests historical truth, the past frees the witness to invent a "memory" of things, to present his vision in his own time and place. The dimension of memory, by its very nature, allows for a distorted and exaggerated vision, a deformed world of the imagination where it is licit for women to be converted into trees and grow, fed by their lovers' tears.

There is a curious ambiguity in the use of the first person *vi,* for it not only indicates the participation of the lyric speaker in the scene but also suggests the presence of Apollo, who is, like the poetic *persona,* a witness to the gradual disappearance of the lady. This intimate connection between Apollo and the lyric voice of the conventional Renaissance love-poet is not fortuitous, for Apollo as the spurned lover is an ideal figure for Garcilaso's world of unrewarded love.

Garcilaso contrives a new ending for the Ovidian legend by endowing the Olympian with pain and tears—a wholly un-Ovidian touch—and makes him a projection of the agonistic persona of his courtly poems: the lover who experiences the loss or death of the beloved. In this sense Apollo is the poet's alter ego and the myth becomes in part a tableau to portray with dramatic immediacy the pain of thwarted love. This enables the poet to express his own love-suffering, yet to observe that suffering as a spectator. By distancing himself from his pain, the poet provides a stage for his *dolorido sentir*, embodied in the "actor" Apollo. When he depicts Apollo's grievous state in the plaintive "¡O miserable 'stado, o mal tamaño" of line twelve, he is not only expressing commiseration for the god, but it is as if he were lending Apollo a voice, *his* voice, to give utterance to unmitigated grief. The doleful exclamation, suggesting both Apollo and the lyric speaker, contains an ambiguity similar to the one elicited by the verb *vi*.

The emphasis on visualization conveyed by the *vi* underscores the pictorialism of the scene of transformation. Garcilaso was undoubtedly aware of the graphic qualities of the design, for, in his Third Eclogue, Daphne's metamorphosis is embroidered by a naiad on one of four tapestries depicting thwarted love affairs (three mythological fables—Orpheus and Eurydice, Apollo and Daphne, Venus and Adonis—and a story from the poet's pastoral world, the adventure of Elissa and the shepherd Nemoroso). Here I will glance briefly at the eclogue, since in it Garcilaso offers a second version both of Daphne's grotesque change and the link between the lyric speaker and Apollo.

Garcilaso's iconic imagery places him in that "venerable convention" of literary pictorialism, whose motto, the Horatian "ut pictura poesis," inspires so much Renaissance poetry, and which counts Homer's description of Achilles' shield as its archetype in poetry.[8] Garcilaso has as one of his literary antecedents Ovid's account of the tapestries of Pallas and Arachne (*Met.* 6.53–69) and, from more recent vintage, the Eurydice tapestry in Sannazaro's *Arcadia* (Prose 12). It must not be forgotten, however, that classical fables were a favorite subject for decoration in the sixteenth century, especially in Italy, and during his extensive stay there Garcilaso could not have avoided seeing the mythological frescoes, paintings, and tapestries that graced the palaces and homes of the nobility. It is therefore no accident that a tapestry tells the tale of Daphne in the Third Eclogue. Garcila-

so is following not only a literary tradition but an artistic one as
well.[9] (Garcilaso's link to the visual arts will be treated later.)

In the tapestry of Apollo and Daphne, the naiad presents
the story in three stages: Cupid's vengeance, the chase, and
Daphne's metamorphosis. The last, our only concern here, differs from the sonnet's rendition. The eclogue states:

> Mas a la fin los braços le crecían
> y en sendos ramos bueltos se mostravan;
> y los cabellos, que vencer solían
> al oro fino, en hojas se tornavan;
> en torcidas raýzes s'estendían
> los blancos pies y en tierra se hincavan;
> llora el amante y busca el ser primero,
> besando y abraçando aquel madero. (161–68)

> (But finally her arms began to grow
> and turn into leafy branches;
> and her hair, which was brighter than
> fine gold, was turning into leaves;
> her white feet were stretching into twisted
> roots and piercing the earth;
> the lover weeps and searches for her former self,
> kissing and embracing the wood.)

Since it is the river nymph who is recording the event, Garcilaso
excludes the role of the lyric speaker as witness and omits the *vi*
of the third line of the sonnet. To comply with the numerical exigencies of the stanza, he also excludes lines 5–6, the smothering
of Daphne's vibrating body by rough bark.[10] Although this omis-
sion attenuates the grotesque element, enough distortion is left
in the ecphrasis to make the transformation jar in the idyllic
world of the eclogue, whose stylized splendor Garcilaso depicts
at length (57–88). It is evident, however, that by juxtaposing the
destruction of the nymph with the beauty and serenity of the
pastoral setting, the eclogue goes further than the sonnet in
stressing the unnaturalness of the beloved's death and thereby
the dramatic impact of the loss. Note that this scene is second in
the tapestry sequence, which presents a crescendo of violent destruction of the loved one, culminating in the vision of the decapitated Elissa, the beloved of Nemoroso, one of Garcilaso's
pastoral masks. As is to be expected, and to underline the horror
at the lady's death, in this last tapestry the contrast of beauty

and brutal death reaches a peak as the mutilated body of the
fair, delicate nymph lies on the verdant, luxuriant pleasance
(225–32).[11]

    The use of the tapestry to depict Daphne's transformation
serves as a distancing device, a role fulfilled by the *vi* in the sonnet. Here in the eclogue the reader is twice removed from the
scene, for it is the naiad's vision, which is then embroidered on
the tapestry, that reaches us. The disfiguration of the beloved
was perhaps too crude to present directly. A sign of Garcilaso's
Renaissance sensibility is revealed in his effort to contrive ways
to mitigate its impact: an artistic construct in the eclogue and, in
the sonnet, a reporter who lends us his eyes to view the
nymph's deformation.

    If in the sonnet the *vi* suggests a mingling of presences in
which Apollo and the poetic *persona* are subtly confused, in the
eclogue they are linked in other equally complex and subtle
ways. The lyric self appears in two guises: as the speaker-narrator who introduces the mythical world of the nymphs and describes their embroidered stories, and as Nemoroso, the poet's
pastoral mask, whose plaint for the dead Elissa we first heard in
the First Eclogue and who now reveals himself in the fourth tapestry as a grieving, disembodied voice in the nymph's epitaph.
Thus unlike the sonnet where only Apollo becomes an "actor,"
here the god and the lyric self—in the veiled presence of a pastoral disguise—appear "on stage," characters in unhappy tales
of love, linked in their self-torment and memories of death.
Apollo's suffering serves as a prefiguration of Nemoroso's, and
both are observed by the speaker-narrator with impassioned ob-
jectivity. The play of perspectives in the eclogue—the secondary
pictorial plane of tapestries and the splitting of the lyric self—enables the speaker to remain fully detached from his love-suffering, a task only half-achieved in the sonnet.

    Garcilaso's contorted design of Daphne's transformation
belongs to what I will call the "Mannerist phase" in the iconography of the Daphne theme. A relation between the arts is particularly appropriate for an age in which the conception of the
Sister Arts, with its notion of the poet as pictorial imagist, was
an integral part of aesthetic canons. I have dispensed with a discussion of a zeitgeist possibly reflected in the sonnet, an elusive
quest at best, or questions of a literary Mannerist style. At present, literary Mannerism is caught in a tangle of definitions, none
of which, in my estimation, offers a satisfactory solution. Its

study has been frequently reduced to the impressionistic analo-
gies between art and literature popularized by Wylie Sypher and
Roy Daniells, or the unconvincing "Angst-mannerism" of a Hauser so obviously influenced by modern preoccupations with tension and anxiety.[12] Until a more workable approach is found, its
usefulness as a critical tool must be questioned. My aim is to
make some suggestive relations between the sonnet and a visual
tradition accessible to Garcilaso.

There is a close affinity between Garcilaso's Daphne and
the representations of the nymph by practitioners of *maniera*.
The world of *maniera* is one of artifice and invention; the figure
is treated like an ornament fashioned in distorted elaborations,
revealing the strains to which the classical idiom of the High
Renaissance—with its reliance on reason, harmony, and perfect
proportions—has been subjected.[13] The Mannerist figural treatment leaves its imprint on the iconography of Daphne's metamorphosis. And such representations, notably the Farnesina
fresco attributed by some to Peruzzi and by others to Giulio Romano, 1510–12 (fig. 13),[14] and a copper engraving by Agostino
Veneziano, c. 1515/18 (fig. 14), in which the degeneration of the
human through distortion elicits the grotesque, may be considered Garcilaso's pictorial analogues. In the Farnesina decoration,
Daphne's hair has become leaves, her wrists sprout branches,
and the lower part of her body, stretched and covered with
bark, still bears the shadow of a thigh. Veneziano uses a favorite
pose of Mannerist art, the *contrapposto*. Daphne's body is contorted in a gracefully bizarre *serpentina:* her left arm, bent over
her head, elongates into a tortuous branch, and her legs intertwine, twisting into involuted roots, curiously recalling Garcilaso's hybrid nymph. In addition to a disquieting quality, these
grotesque Mannerist Daphnes display a teasing, ludicrous element and so exhibit a clashing mixture of the comic and the disturbing not found in Garcilaso's grotesque Daphne. Conversely,
Garcilaso's design projects a violence not found in *maniera*.
Nonetheless, Garcilaso's Daphne belongs to the *maniera* pantheon of figures devoid of emotion, hollow in their torsions and rit-
ualistic gestures, because the poem concentrates on surface images. The emphasis on surfaces reveals Daphne's role as a
distant, recalcitrant beloved.

Having traced the evolution of Daphne's iconography, I
find that the Baroque and Renaissance representations of
Daphne are based on principles of figural design in which the

grotesque plays no role. And a brief look at Bernini's Baroque Daphne and at Antonio del Pollaiuolo's Renaissance version will show how Garcilaso's design lies between the two, bearing its Mannerist stamp.

Bernini's nymph is caught in a wave of flux and fear as she looks back at her pursuer (fig. 15). In keeping with the naturalism of the Baroque, a reaction against what the seventeenth century regarded as the "perverse artificiality" of Mannerism,[15] signs of the laurel cling to Daphne's body without destroying its anatomical correctness. Renaissance canons of harmony and proportion govern Pollaiuolo's treatment (fig. 16). Daphne, dressed in contemporary garb, is posed as a gracile "ballerina"; her arms are two bushy branches symmetrically extended over her head; her left leg, encased in roots, is anchored to the ground, and the right is extended in a mild, graceful arabesque. The figure is allowed to keep its harmonious integrity, permitting the artist to concentrate on Daphne's ideal, rational beauty. In both the Renaissance and the Baroque representations, the tree remains at the fringes of the body, sparing Daphne the deformation imposed by the Mannerists and Garcilaso.[16]

There is an important distinction to be made, however, between the role of distortion in Garcilaso and in the practitioners of *maniera*. For these Mannerists, the strange and the deformed become the norm, the means of displaying virtuosity and ingenuity; the bizarre becomes the source of an odd kind of beauty. For Garcilaso, distortion is not the norm but that which destroys the norm, the established canons of ideal beauty, and is thus an anomaly. And it is this classical bias, the notion of the distorted image as anomalous, that reveals the function of the grotesque element in Garcilaso.

Since Garcilaso's pictorial design belongs to a literary framework, it is more literary than pictorial, and as such its meaning must be sought in its relation to the poetic structure of which it is a part. As noted, the grotesque element serves to present with poignancy the loss of the courtly lady. But it is more. *For the grotesque image,* with its violation of nature and incongruous, disquieting distortion, signals a collapse of order and reveals a certain chaos, and so *functions as a thematic metaphor for the disruption of harmony in the world of love.*

When placed in the totality of Garcilaso's courtly poetry, the grotesque belongs to a series of negative, unnatural images (not all necessarily grotesque) that reflect this disharmony. While

the Daphne image is the best-developed example of distortion
clearly yielding the grotesque element, there is also a touch of
the grotesque in the metamorphosis of the cruel, obdurate Anaxarete into a marble statue, an admonition to an equally obdurate
beloved to reform. The woman's bones elongate and harden, the
flesh petrifies, and the entrails and blood dry up (*canción* V.86–
97). And in other erotic poems, the constant turmoil arising from
unrequited love and the lady's death leads to numerous unnatural images, such as the poet's conversion into a river (sonnet XI),
a wasteland generating thistles through a lover's tears (eclogue
I), a lover's sickness breeding a poisonous tree inside him (*canción* IV), the lady's death envisioned as the uprooting of a tree
(sonnet XXV).

In his use of unnatural images of metamorphosis in an
erotic context, Garcilaso is following tradition. We have but to
turn to Petrarch's canzone 23, "Nel dolce tempo de la prima
etade," which contains a series of emblematic images of transformation, in particular the poetic *persona*'s conversion into a laurel.
Both Petrarch and Garcilaso, in their designs, parallel pictorial
treatments of hybrids of their times. In Garcilaso there is a merg-
ing of forms in which one "grows" from the other in a spirit of
dissolution, as in the Mannerist renditions of Daphne. In Petrarch there is an assemblage of human and laurel akin to the
grotesques of his period, both in its composite form and in its
Christian function, for it shows the poet in incongruous union
with his vices, the secular snares of woman and poetic glory
symbolized by the laurel.

Garcilaso exerts a major influence on the development of
the mythological tradition in Spain—a repository of the fabulous
and the fantastic—and the grotesque, in his poem of Daphne, becomes a model for subsequent renditions. It is treated by both major
and minor poets, including Hurtado de Mendoza in his description of Myrrha's transformation in the *Fábula de Adonis* (1553),
Silvestre in his rendition of Daphne's change in the *Fábula de
Dafnes [sic] y Apolo* (1582), and the Marqués de Tarifa who as late
as 1631 bases his transformation of Myrrha on Garcilaso's design.

But the grotesque, a perfect vehicle for visions of disintegration, is not used extensively by any one poet in Golden Age
poetry until established traditions become the targets of burlesque writers. It is then that a poet like Quevedo accords the
grotesque a central place in his aesthetic. Whereas Garcilaso employs the grotesque in isolated cases at the service of his courtly

Figure 13. B. Peruzzi or Giulio Romano, fresco of Apollo and Daphne, Palazzo della Farnesina, Rome, 1510–12. Photo Alinari/Art Resource, New York.

Figure 14. Agostino Veneziano, copper engraving of Apollo and Daphne, c. 1515/18. Photo Warburg Institute.

Figure 15. Bernini, sculpture of Apollo and Daphne, Borguese Gallery, Rome, 1622–25. Photo Alinari/Art Resource, New York.

Figure 16. Antonio del Pollaiuolo, Apollo and Daphne, panel, National Gallery, London, undated.

verses, Quevedo, by contrast, makes it a key element in his poetics and uses it reductively to parody, among others, the courtly and mythological traditions by poking fun at their conventions. As we shall see in Quevedo's burlesque poetry, Daphne, no longer the cherished lady love, is reduced to a bat as she flees her lover, the sun.

We have observed aspects of the grotesque in the depiction of Daphne in Garcilaso as well as in his model Ovid, in the Mannerists, and briefly in Petrarch and Quevedo. Now, as we move from Daphne's disfiguration to Apollo's tears, we see that the contorted metamorphosis does not simply parallel but also prompts the unnatural gesture of the god, preserving the notion of disharmony as it extends to the lover in his grief.

For Apollo, the grieving Renaissance lover, the laurel tree has no meaning other than as a sign of the loss of the woman. By contrast, the laurel plays a significant role in Ovid. When the Ovidian Apollo realizes that, even after the transformation, Daphne is beyond his grasp, he consecrates the laurel as the eternal symbol of honor and victory. This solemn gesture appears on the surface as an opportunity to establish a union with the lost Daphne, but is in fact a means of saving face, of dignifying his exit from a foolish adventure.

Garcilaso never mentions the laurel as such but refers to it only as this tree *(este árbol)*. The bay is simply "Daphne transformed." The tree is all that remains of the beloved and what will forever remind the lover of the woman. It has the same value as the *dulces prendas* of sonnet X and Elissa's lock of hair treasured by the shepherd Nemoroso in the First Eclogue. The tree, the *prendas,* and the hair are tokens that bring forth the remembrance of the lost lady and, along with it, the pain and the weeping.

Garcilaso's lachrymose lover bears no resemblance to Ovid's deity, who appears both pompous and comic after his loss. The Spanish poet's Apollo has as his ancestor the Apollo of the *Canzoniere,* an anguished lover who seeks Daphne in vain: "per doglia insano, / che molto amata cosa non ritrove" ("mad with grief at not finding some much-loved thing," 43.7–8). Apollo's sacred laurel becomes a symbol of the recalcitrant Laura, and in the love-religion of the courtly Petrarch it is worshiped "come cosa santa" (228.14). Although in Garcilaso the laurel has no symbolic value, as a token of the lost lady it elicits a reverence similar to Petrarch's; Apollo's tears are like an offering placed on Daphne's arboreal shrine.

Petrarch's shedding of his tears on the laurel in "Amor co
la man destra il lato manco" (sonnet 228) is reminiscent of Apollo's gesture in Garcilaso's sonnet:

> Vomer di penna con sospir del fianco
> e 'l piover giù dalli occhi un dolce umore
> l'adornar sì, ch'al ciel n'andò l'odore,
> qual non so già se d'altre frondi unquanco.

> (My pen, a plow, with my laboring sighs, and the
> raining down from my eyes of a sweet liquid have
> so beautified it, that its fragrance has reached
> Heaven, so that I do not know if any leaves have
> ever equaled it.)

The rain of tears, the end product of the lover's amorous ma-
laise, nourishes the bay and causes its fragrance. These tears are
part of the emblematic image that defines the task of the courtly
lover, who bestows fame upon Laura by singing her praises in
verse. In Garcilaso, on the other hand, the tears dramatize the
lover's suffering as it appears in contrast to the blooming of the
bay. The more he weeps, the more the laurel grows, and so his
pain increases in an endless cycle.

As in Ovid and Petrarch, Garcilaso's Apollo emerges as an
exclusus amator, the shut-out lover who is denied access to his
obdurate lady. But this Renaissance Apollo stands closer to the
conventional, grieving *exclusus amator* of Graeco-Roman poetry
and to Petrarch's than to the pompous Ovidian deity who does
not give way to suffering when he is totally excluded by
Daphne's arboreal escape. Ovid's duped lover dons the sacred
laurel in a stubborn, haughty gesture to regain his badly bruised
dignity and is ready to go off to his next ill-fated amorous adventure; Garcilaso's deity abjectly accepts his defeat and stages a
watery vigil in the typical courtly attitude of the scorned yet
clinging lover.

Garcilaso's god is the inheritor of a legacy of servitude
dating back to ancient times that becomes the trademark of
Golden Age lovers. Like the classical elegiac *amator*, who docilely
submits to the commands of his *domina*, and the medieval courtly lover always unquestioningly obedient to his *midons*, Apollo
becomes a slave of love. Even after the loss of the beloved, he
does not break the shackles imposed by his lady. In his humility
and willing servitude, the once-mighty deity performs the ultimate duty of amatory ritual; with his tears he feeds the cause of

his misery. Like the galley-slave who is imprisoned by love and suffers "al remo condenado, / en la concha de Venus amarrado" (*canción* v.34–35), Apollo is bound to the bay and his affliction.

The hyperbole of Apollo's role as a mere "watering device" to his "vegetable love" is extreme but not comic. This tormented exaggeration is an accurate reflection of the lover's psychological condition, and his pain justifies the gesture. The scene would be comical had Garcilaso not written it in such earnest. This image in the hands of the irreverent Quevedo or Andrew Marvell would have yielded a picture certainly suffused with irony, if not outright burlesque.

Like so many Renaissance sonnets, Garcilaso's poem ends epigrammatically:

> que con llorarla crezca cada día
> la causa y la razón por que llorava!

> (that from his weeping each day should grow
> the cause and reason of his weeping!)

Here the poliptoton *(llorarla / llorava)*, a conceptist device so dear to *cancionero* poetry, reinforces the conceit that portrays the paradoxical position of the weeping god before the growing tree. But the ending is not only a climax of wit and ingenuity, as in the classical epigram, but a phonetic peak in which an explosion of cacophonous sounds echoes the psychological state of the lover at the moment of the intensification of his pain.

The cacophonous alliteration, whose main function is to heighten the meaning of the verses—the relentless growing of the tree as cause of the god's tears—also suggests the persistent wounding and pain incited by the continuous growth of the tree. There is a curious affinity between these two verses and John of the Cross' "un no sé qué que quedan balbuciendo" in the *Cántico espiritual*. In Saint John's line, the alliterative cacophony stresses onomatopoetically the stuttering of the creatures, who are unable to describe the ineffable—that is, God's grandeur. But the repetition of the harsh sounds also conveys, as in Garcilaso, the frustration and pain of the lover, in this case inflicted by the constant babble of the creatures.

The phonetic climax of Garcilaso's sonnet not only reflects Apollo's pain but also echoes Daphne's physical deformation, now conveyed in abstract language in contrast to the concrete representation of her actual metamorphosis. The word *causa*, which defines Apollo's role as the cause of Daphne's *daño* in line nine, now defines Daphne's role as the cause of Apollo's *mal ta-maño* in line twelve. A semantic-phonetic fusion emerges in which the harsh-sounding *causa*, as part of the sequence of cacophonous and in this sense deformed language, coincides with the deformed Daphne, that is, the tree. The reciprocal relation established by the term *causa* (Apollo as the cause of the tree; the tree as the cause of Apollo's tears) serves as background and reinforces the circular conceit of tears and growth. In the last two lines, the sound pattern itself is circular because of the poliptoton and alliterative [k]'s. *Que con llorarla* is echoed in *por que llorava,* and *crezca cada día* is echoed in *la causa y la razón,* thus establishing a circle of repeating sounds, A,B,B,A:

    A   B
que con llorarla / crezca cada día

    B   A
la causa y la razón / por que llorava!

As the sonnet ends epigrammatically, it leads us to a final area: the emblematic. The visual imagery and paradoxical wit of Garcilaso's sonnet link it to the emblematic tradition, a pictorially bizarre and "conceited" mode in which grotesque elements, often drawn from mythology, abound.[17] This sonnet is emblematic in that its pictorial images are explained aphoristically by means of a love message; loss breeds grief, grief breeds loss, eternally.

The emblematic tradition spurred by Andrea Alciati's *Emblematum liber* (1531) flourishes in the sixteenth century, and Apollo and Daphne are not excluded. The first of many emblems of the god and the nymph (Aneau, *Picta poesis,* 1552) presents a deformed Daphne, partially disfigured by the overcoming laurel, and an anxious Apollo, arm outstretched, reaching toward the nymph. Its moral is contained in the words: "Amor cum prudentia non convenit" ("Love and prudence do not agree").[18]

Garcilaso's emblematic scene does not convey a moral message as do Aneau's and so many of the Apollo and Daphne emblems, for, in portraying a lover's suffering, it is akin to many of the emblems of the profane *emblemata amatoria,* one of whose chief sources is Petrarch's *Canzoniere.* And, like so many of Petrarch's poetic images, Garcilaso's sonnet needs only a picture to become an emblem proper. The epigrammatic last lines, dealing with Apollo's loss, serve as motto to the design.

Ovid's story of Apollo and Daphne, removed from its religious context, is an irreverent, playful fantasy in which

Daphne's transformation—with its element of the grotesque—provides her with an escape from the lustful Olympian, who is etched as a duped, comic lover. The Roman's playful fantasy becomes earnest fantasy in Garcilaso, who creates a highly dramatic spectacle of Ovid's central scene. Fully within the courtly tradition, Garcilaso endows the thwarted love experience with pathos ultimately verging on bathos. Moreover, by inserting himself through the *vi*, he gives the experience a personal visionary authority. Garcilaso's closeness to his subject, as opposed to Ovid's ironic detachment, leads him to identify with the scorned lover, who becomes his alter ego.

In an age when examples of the grotesque are plentiful in the visual arts—in *maniera*, the ornamental grotesque, the emblematic tradition—Garcilaso uses the grotesque element in Ovid, intensifies it, and, with subtle mastery, integrates it into his private, courtly vision. The world of the Renaissance Garcilaso is one of idealized female beauty and nature, but it is also a world of extreme disquiet and disharmony. What better way to express the culmination of this disharmony, the beloved disappearing from the lover's grasp, than by a vision of idealized beauty distorted in a grotesque image? The grotesque also illuminates and circumscribes the lover in his defeat. Fully developed only once, in the sonnet of Apollo and Daphne, Garcilaso's hitherto unrecognized grotesque is of no little importance in the history of the grotesque in Spain. It leaves a sharp imprint on the mythological tradition. Moreover, Garcilaso's use of this mode, the first by a Spanish Renaissance poet, helps to distinguish its later use in Quevedo, prince of the grotesque, who employs it to burlesque his courtly and mythological figures.

5

Myth in Quevedo: The Serious and the Burlesque in the Apollo and Daphne Poems

In his poems about Apollo and Daphne, Francisco de Quevedo evokes two contradictory postures, the cosmic and the comic, the serious love story and the slapstick fable. While in a poem in *quintillas* (five eight-syllable-line stanzas), he gives us the celestial world of a grave courtier, in two sonnets he creates a stage for his linguistic extravagances and savage burlesque.[1] The courtly, in which erotic, cosmological, and Christian agons mingle, turns into the anticourtly, with its battle of vices between a miser and a prostitute. And in both serious and burlesque versions the grotesque plays a specific role: in the *quintillas*, it is one more aspect in a picture of cosmic convulsion; in the sonnets, it is the chief means of derision.

In his use of the serious and the comic, Quevedo reveals the topos of *spoudogeloion*, the mixture of jest and earnest inherited from the ancients. Homer treats the gods both majestically and in mockery, as in the familiar scene when Hephaestus surprises Aphrodite in the arms of Ares; Ovid in his "comedy of the gods" in the *Metamorphoses* can introduce a lofty Apollo, killer of dragons, and later deflate him with his ironic and farcical barbs. Similarly, Quevedo portrays a serious Apollo and Daphne in the *quintillas* while in the sonnets these figures become objects of ridicule.[2]

Quevedo often treats the same topic in both earnest and jest. The solemn ascetic and worshiper of ideal beauty can also be playful or attack with all the verbal wizardry of *conceptismo*, bringing out an amusing, if often sinister, armory of linguistic and imagistic monsters, vulgarisms, and flashy *germanía* (thieves' jargon). Thus, in dealing with religion, myth, love, Quevedo strikes a double posture. At one moment he praises; the next he darts around the table to write satire and burlesque (often with models in *Greek Anthology* lampoons and Latin satire) or simply to indulge in pure wit and fun. So his writing of lofty religious tracts does not prevent him from dealing irreverently with the sacred, his serious ballads on traditional themes have their comic counterparts in bantering ballads like the "Pavura de los condes de Carrión" ("The Fright of the Counts of Carrión"), and his glorious sonnets of idealized love to Lisi are matched by vicious verses mocking women and love. We see the double mask, for instance, in the corrosive "Rostro de blanca nieve, fondo en gra-jo" ("Snow-white face framed in crow-like blackness") where re-pulsive scatology mingles with and debases the courtly common-places, which, in serious moments, Quevedo delights in.

Quevedo's humorous use of myth is both a parody of a tradition (which in the Golden Age reveals every kind of mytho-logical contrivance) and a means of playing with the gods for comic effect as Ovid and Lucian had done before him. Since Quevedo mocks the tradition in which he indulges, the very sto-ry he elsewhere treats seriously, his comic excursions into myth emerge as self-parody. A revealing example of such parody—with a large dose of play—are his sonnets on Apollo and Daphne.

Quevedo's serious version of Apollo and Daphne is one of his early poems, published by Pedro Espinosa in the *Flores de poetas ilustres* (Valladolid, 1605).[3] Quevedo keeps only the barest outline of the Ovidian story, focusing on the chase and the transformation, endowing each with new form and meaning. Ovid himself was not a mere recorder of myths but an urbane poet who manipulated mythological material with a freedom of invention and imagination emulated, in turn, by Quevedo and many of his fellow poets. Ovid's Apollo carries the stamp of the erotic persona of his love poems, of that suffering creature with touches of the ludicrous, which has given the Augustan the du-bious title of debaser of elegiac erotic conventions. In like man-ner, Quevedo, also a love poet, creates an Apollo who resembles the lover of his amorous verses. So the Ovidian foolishness is cast out in favor of self-pity, inflated and tinged with pathos, making Phoebus-Apollo a figure fully at home in his courtly set-ting. Quevedo's Apollo, like Garcilaso's, is Petrarchan rather than Ovidian, and tears will be one of his identifiable marks. The rejected, despondent suitor is teamed with his counterpart, the cruel, disdainful lady of perfect beauty and chastity, and both carry out their own conventional roles in the erotic agon in

an atmosphere of pagan animism and Neoplatonic undercur-
rents.

The poem starts *in medias res* with the sun chasing
Daphne, beautiful as the dawn:

> Delante del Sol venía
> corriendo Dafne, doncella
> de extremada gallardía,
> y en ir delante tan bella
> nueva aurora parecía. (1–5)

> (Before the Sun came Daphne
> fleeing, a virgin
> of extreme gracefulness,
> so lovely moving before him
> she seemed like a new dawn.)

Apollo appears as Phoebus, his role as sun-god, which is the
key to the elaboration of solar and stellar imagery central to the
poem. Quevedo also establishes the atmosphere of animistic
reality that prevails throughout the poem by presenting the pursuit along the lines of a solar myth, of the Sun chasing Dawn.
Quevedo removes Apollo and Daphne from the ground—the
nymph, metaphorically—and sets the celestial tone for his cosmological explorations.

In her radiance, Daphne is a star—"corre la estrella," 27—
and, because of her resplendent beauty, the courtly Sol, in typical overpraise of his courtly beloved, calls her the sun and its
light:

> Si el Sol y luz aborreces,
> huye tú misma de ti. (44–45)

> (If you abhor the Sun and the light,
> flee from yourself.)

Again an element of solar myth appears as Daphne is linked to
the Night, who is running away from the Sun:

> si no fueras tan hermosa,
> por la Noche te tuviera. (49–50)

> (if you were not so beautiful,
> I would guess you were the Night.)

Only her beauty, shining in courtly splendor, saves her from ac-

tually becoming the Night. These associations of Daphne with
sun, star, and night place her metaphorically in a celestial landscape that is discordant because of the central, disruptive figure
of the lover, Sol, who, like all traditional lovers, burning and
teary, experiences love as a living death (43), his heart typically
imprisoned in the beloved (64). Once again we find Apollo and
Daphne in opposite poles in the erotic agon; the lover in his
fiery passion confronts the modest virgin, typically idealized in
her beauty.

The notion of Sol causing havoc rests on a familiar cosmological theory current in Quevedo's time. Ptolemaic and Neoplatonic, this traditional world view is based on a fixed system of
hierarchies revealing the interdependence and unity of all creation. The universe is an enormous sphere, with Earth at its center and the Primum Mobile at its outer rim. In the middle is the
region of the four elements—earth, water, air, and fire—which
make up man and everything inhabiting the Earth. Surrounding
this sublunar realm are the celestial spheres of the seven
planets—the Moon, Mercury, Venus, the Sun, Mars, Jupiter,
and Saturn—and the fixed stars. And beyond the created universe is the Empyrean, the abode of God and the blessed. Central to this cosmological vision is a ladder of creation stretching
from God to the lowest inanimate things. It traverses the spiritual world of the angels, the celestial spheres of the planets, and
the region of the four elements, to man, animals, and the inanimate. According to this world view, human affairs are intimately
linked with the events in the cosmos; human transgressions or
heavenly disorder bring about chaos in the whole of creation.[4]
By using this cosmology, Quevedo not only makes his poem fit
into current philosophical thought but also manages to create his
own mythological imagery, bringing originality to a theme elaborated again and again, often as a hackneyed convention.

By an anthropomorphic act the planet Sol, which illumines the universal sphere (48, 85), becomes the lover and descends to the sublunar world of the elements. But instead of fitting into the established order of Nature he becomes a man
ruled by earthly passion. Order collapses. The havoc of desire
leads to chaos; a river and wind run wild, a woman becomes a
tree. A parallel to what happens in Quevedo—when Sol comes
in disorder to the world below the moon—is Ulysses' speech on
degrees in Shakespeare's *Troilus and Cressida*, perhaps the best-
known statement of the interrelation of all spheres in the created
universe:

The heavens themselves, the planets, and this centre
Observe degree, priority, and place,
Insisture, course, proportion, season, form,
Office, and custom, in all line of order;
And therefore is the glorious planet Sol
In noble eminence enthron'd and spher'd
Amidst the other, whose med'cinable eye
Corrects the ill aspects of planets evil
And posts, like the commandment of a king,
Sans check, to good and bad. But when the planets
In evil mixture to disorder wander,
What plagues and what portents, what mutiny,
What raging of the sea, shaking of earth,
Commotion in the winds! (1.3.85–98)

As Quevedo's Sol "to disorder wander[s]," we see how air and water are disturbed and join Sol in cosmic convulsion:

El Sol corre por seguilla;
por huir corre la estrella;
corre el llanto por no vella;
corre el aire por oílla,
y el río por socorrella.[5] (26–30)

(The Sun runs in her pursuit;
the star runs to flee;
the tears run for they can't see her;
the wind runs to hear her,
and the river to help her.)

The chaos brought about by the god-turned-lover extends to the beloved as she disappears through metamorphosis into the laurel, a violation of nature that yields a grotesque. Jupiter effects the conversion[6] to save her from Sol, but her salvation, as in Ovid, is ambiguous, for her virginity is safeguarded at the expense of her body:

Sus plantas en sola una
de lauro se convirtieron;
los dos brazos le crecieron,
quejándose a la Fortuna
con el rüido que hicieron.
Escondióse en la corteza
la nieve del pecho helado,
y la flor de su belleza

dejó en la flor un traslado
que al lauro presta riqueza. (71–80)

(Her feet turned into a
single foot of laurel;
her two arms grew,
complaining to Fortune
with the noise they made.
    The snow of her frozen breasts
hid in the bark,
and the flower of her beauty
left its copy in the tree's flower,
lending richness to the laurel.)

Quevedo contrives a transformation that contains a faint echo of
Ovid's version as Daphne's beauty lingers on and becomes part
of the newly born laurel. Otherwise it is different from Ovid's
smooth conversion, which offers a protective citadel for the
nymph's virginity. The hybrid clash and the distortion of the human by the plant in Ovid are aspects that can also be found in
Quevedo's grotesque. But, in Quevedo, there is a heightening of
the sense of abnormality and alienation from order, which is
ideally suited to the theme of universal chaos and the collapse of
a world developed in the *quintillas*. In Ovid, a cosmology of migrating forms provides a background that mitigates the ominous
grotesquerie of dehumanization; the reader knows that the metamorphosis is the means by which the nymph acquires a new
"body" and so preserves her identity as a virgin. In Quevedo, as
in Garcilaso, the absence of the ancient cosmology intensifies the
grotesque effect. Furthermore, unlike Ovid's smooth rendition,
the *quintillas* contain an element of violence; as the maiden's
arms become branches of laurel, there is an explosion of sound
and a lamenting cry to Fortune as if in protest against the violation. The presence of Fortune fits perfectly into this world in
which the "center cannot hold," for in her fickle and restless
guise this figure is traditionally identified with "chance." Reign-
ing over the domain of haphazard and capricious forces, she
gives rise to adversity and disorder.[7]
    Daphne as the tree remains recalcitrant as she was in her
human form—an Ovidian motif—and air and water reappear to
serve as a teary, lamenting chorus to the poet's eulogy of the
woman who sacrificed her body to preserve her chastity. Sol is
left behind and not mentioned in the last three *quintillas*. As if

tainted by his appetite, he has been ostracized. Note that
there is no open condemnation of the god here; he simply fades
away.

The silence of Sol, the carrier of passion, permits Quevedo
a Christian resolution to the poem. And if the courtly poet appropriately fails to openly condemn the lover in his passion,
now the Christian moralist has nothing but praise for the beloved in her virtue. In Ovid, Daphne flees from the lover to retain her identity as a virgin huntress, to be like Diana, the chaste
goddess of the hunt whose father had bestowed upon her perpetual virginity. In Quevedo, pagan maidenhood becomes Christian purity; the Quevedian nymph runs to safeguard her *honestidad*. So at the end of the poem, Daphne, like Dante's Beatrice,
evolves from an object of sensual love to something of a saint as
the river kisses the "foot" of the tree characterized as *divino y
santo* (105). By using the term *pie* for the tree's roots, the gesture
is not only an act of homage but points to the tree as a monu-
ment, an arboreal statue of Daphne that recalls Petrarch's idol
sculpted in living laurel in the *Canzoniere* (30.27). This is an
expression of Petrarch's quasi-religious reverence for Laura who,
as the antitype of Daphne, is not only a woman of perfect beauty but also of perfect chastity.

There is, however, a stronger reminiscence here. The use
of the epithets divine and saintly, in praise of the virginal tree,
situates the poem in the tradition of Christian allegory of ancient
myth, which found moral and theological teaching behind the
"veil" of the classical fables. The Church Fathers had placed
Daphne among the purest of virgins—a notion that, as we have
seen, is developed by Ovid's medieval commentators, who make
the laurel a symbol of chastity worn by virgins in heaven as a reward for their virtue and even identify it as an emblem of the
Virgin Mary herself. The Golden Age welcomes this reconciliation of Graeco-Roman mythology (the *fingimiento de los poetas*)
with Christian values and exploits it to the fullest. The fusion of
the pagan and the Christian is of course dear to the young
Quevedo, a disciple of the Flemish Neostoic Justus Lipsius,
whose Christian exegesis of pagan texts influenced our poet as
evidenced in his *Anacreón castellano* and his translation of the
pseudo-Phocylides.[8] Later in the *Marco Bruto* (1644), Quevedo al-
legorizes the myth of Apollo and Daphne including the typical
explanation of the laurel as a reward for *honestidad*.[9]

The last lines of the poem restore a kind of order as

Daphne/tree becomes part of the natural world. Nature goes out of her way to protect her:

> Y viendo caso tan tierno,
> digno de renombre eterno,
> la reservó, en aquel llano,
> de sus rayos el verano,
> y de su yelo el invierno. (106–10)

> (And seeing this tender happening,
> worthy of eternal fame,
> summer protected her, on that plain,
> from its rays,
> and winter from its frost.)

In this passage *rayos* may refer both to the scorching rays of the sun and to lightning. The notion that the laurel will not be harmed by lightning (Pliny, *Natural History,* 15.40.135) and that it will always retain its evergreen freshness go back to ancient lore. Later elaborated by medieval writers, these notions pass on into Renaissance mythography. In Ovid it is the lover Apollo himself who, in his paean to Daphne, promises the maiden the eternal evergreen youth of the laurel. Here, however, Quevedo reserves the final apotheosis for Nature since it would not seem fitting that Apollo, who had disrupted its order, be assigned to restore it. In a final act of redemption, Nature singles out for a special reward one whose quest for purity had led to a violation of her natural integrity. Combining pagan ideas of Nature and Christian hope, Quevedo saves Daphne, her life and chastity, as a saintly tree.

In the sublunar world of the four elements, Daphne represents elemental earth, for in becoming the tree, the nymph is not only forever encased in eternal Mother Earth but, in a sense, is part of that Earth. In human form Daphne is identified metaphorically with fire and water in celebration of her beauty; Sol converts her golden hair into fiery rays (81–85), and her white breasts are like snow (77), which is a sign of her fairness and her cold, passionless posture. But in becoming the laurel, the nymph joins the earth—in ancient myth her mother was Gaea the Earth—and leaves behind her body, which had brought her into the realms of water and fire. In her transformation, she excludes the other elements forever, those in herself and those external to her, especially Sol who is associated with fire, with water—

when he is transformed in elemental subversion as his rays of
light and fire become fountains of water (tears) after Daphne's
transformation (89–90)—and with air as he becomes all movement and competes with the wind while running after the maid-
en (19–20). In this war of the elements—of Daphne/earth against
fire, air, and water—the maiden shuns those elements above the
earth and remains silent and triumphant in her leafy fortress. As
the laurel, even Sol cannot touch her since summer shields her
from his rays in a final exclusion.

The structure of Quevedo's poem rests upon three planes
of opposites revealing three distinct agons: the *courtly* (the typical erotic battle between the "cruel" beloved and the faithful, yet
scorned lover; the fire of passion v. the ice of the distant beloved); the *cosmological* (Sun v. Night; elemental fire v. elemental
earth); and the *Christian* (vice v. virtue; passion v. chastity). The
warring opposites manifest themselves as dramatic images of a
huge, convulsive, topsy-turvy battle in which the elements are
thrown into disarray, Daphne turns into a laurel, and Sol's fire
becomes water. Frank Warnke has pointed out that "the sense of
life as the conflict of opposites supplies a clear spiritual basis for
the seventeenth-century preoccupation with the drama: on an
unconscious level, presumably, the agon of fictional characters
reenacts, as did that of the ancient Greeks, the universal agon of
the cosmos."[10] Dressed in their cosmic guises, Quevedo's characters reenact this all-embracing agon, openly in their case, unlike
the characters of the stage who reenact it subliminally. But like
characters in a drama, Quevedo's agonistic figures are part of
that excessive preoccupation with the theme of conflict that appears in so many modes and guises in the seventeenth century—in its poetry of meditation, in Saint-Amant, in John Donne,
and of course in so many of Quevedo's works.

In the cosmic conflict of the *quintillas*, Apollo and Daphne
stand for primeval forces of nature, imagery that belongs to a
primitive mode of thought. And these battling figures, who
played their poetic, demythologized roles in Ovid, in Petrarch,
in Garcilaso and, to a point, in Quevedo also, regain a measure
of their mythical presence. Like the archetypal, functional figures
of ancient myth who point beyond themselves to a higher reality, Quevedo's Apollo and Daphne address profound, metaphysical preoccupations. The cosmic conflict, however, would be regarded simply as an artifice, a construct designed to bring
newness to a tired theme, if it were not for the fact that Queve-

do's persistent elaboration of the topic of a chaotic world—of a world upside-down—corresponds not only to an aesthetic impulse but to a metaphysical posture as well. So the poem—a blend of ancient myth and contemporary cosmological and Christian thought—is an emblem of what Quevedo believed existence to be: constant strife, the "turbio río" of his moral poems. In a much-quoted letter, Quevedo speaks of life as universal discord, in words that perfectly define the turmoil in the *quintillas* and in much of his work, a network of clashing polarities:

> Nadie jamás fue tan obedecida del mundo como la
> discordia: perpetuamente reina en los elementos,
> sin que pueda tener tregua su guerra; no consiente
> un instante de paz a nuestros humores; si crees a
> los astrólogos, todo el cielo es una discordia
> resplandeciente: no hay estrella que no se oponga
> a otra, y todas militan con aspectos contrarios;
> con ella vivimos, della somos compuestos, a ella
> estamos sujetos por naturaleza.[11]

> (No one was ever so obeyed by the world as was discord:
> it reigns perpetually in the elements, in a war that
> finds no truce; it does not allow our
> humors a moment of peace; if you believe astrologers,
> all heaven is a resplendent discord: there is no star
> that is not against another, and each one fights in
> opposing manner; we live with discord, we are composed
> of it, we are bound to it by nature.)

But there is more. Even though they are few, we find definite elements of order in Quevedo's agonistic metaphysics, and one turns up in the mysterious workings of divine Providence. In the letter quoted above, Quevedo speaks of providential order amidst the chaos: "Mucho tiene de providencia esta disensión, que compone, sustenta y vivifica" ("This strife has much of providence, which reconciles, sustains and gives life.") In the *quintillas*, order occurs in typical Quevedian fashion; our poet devotes little time to it and, when order comes, it is providential. It is thrust abruptly at the poem's end, and it seems almost as a palinodic afterthought. This order is provided by Nature, which acts, we may say, as an agent of Providence, playing the role assigned to it by Quevedo in one of his *Sentencias:* "Nos sirve la naturaleza para nuestra conservación de madre, como de ángel custodio . . . en lo temporal" ("Nature—like a mother—helps us in our preservation in temporal matters, playing the role of a guardian angel").[12]

In an age in which myth is largely regarded as a literary convention, myth in Quevedo curiously and ironically fulfills something of its original function: to explain the mysteries of existence. In this case, Quevedo depicts life as constant chaos in which order appears at the last moment, in the guise of an act of Providence.

But if the courtly and Christian poet sees myth with perfect seriousness,[13] the insolent debaser subjects it to devastating burlesque, that familiar irreverence with which Quevedo treats most things sacred or profane. The mythological burlesque is a popular mode that, in Spain, appears as the mythological tradition reaches its peak at the end of the sixteenth century. Even though old practices continue to be repeated and re-elaborated in numerous variations—and at times with happy strokes of originality, as in Quevedo's serious Apollo and Daphne—more and more writers turn to parody, bringing with it new, unexpected scenes to the world of mythology. It is a commonplace to speak of the mythological burlesque simply as an attack against the abuses of the tradition, a debunking by those who were growing tired of it. But the mythological burlesque, with its clever, nimble humor, is less a revolt against old formulas than a means of holding on to these formulas—at times "stretching" them, at times negating them—to create novel effects. Furthermore, the fact that many of the poets who treat myth seriously also poke fun at it—Quevedo, Góngora, Faria e Sousa—speaks eloquently for these self-conscious artists who can detach themselves from their material not only ridiculing the fables but using them as a springboard for their aesthetic games. And so the mythological burlesque, with its distortions of shapes and contortions of language, provides an ideal workshop for the ingenious tricks of the *conceptista* writer. This is the case with Quevedo, for whom the parody of myth is a welcome opportunity not only to degrade the gods with caustic, deforming humor but to display his amazing wit.

In his humorous treatment of myth, Quevedo is in good company. Antiquity did not always treat its gods with respect, for it subjected these hallowed figures to merciless comedy. Myth, seen with serious philosophical piety by Aeschylus, Pin-

dar, or Virgil, did not fare so well in the critical minds and skeptical urbanity of Ovid or Lucian. Homer's frequent mockery of
the Olympians plants the seed for future comedy, a fact that did
not make it any easier for his apologists to defend him against
attacks of impiety and immorality. The burlesque of myth in the
phlyax vases shows how widespread this practice was in ancient
Greece; Aristophanes, as we know, took great liberties with the
gods. In the Roman world, Ovid provides the best "comedy of
the gods" in the *Metamorphoses,* where the Olympians are subjected to his subtle wit, detached irony, and occasional farce as
in his portrayal of the foolish Apollo. Ovid's stories become a
storehouse of myth for sixteenth- and seventeenth-century writers eager for material to display their classical erudition. But
when these writers choose to humor the ancient tales, their comic treatment is more Rabelaisian than Ovidian. In Quevedo, as in
so many of his counterparts in continental and English travesties, ironic subtlety gives way to crassness, the mock-heroic to
low burlesque.

Quevedo mocks mythical characters often, and the planetary gods—especially Jupiter and Apollo—bear the brunt of his
crude and perverse humor. These are the best-known and might-
iest gods and Quevedo, a skillful marksman, knows that in comedy as in tragedy the higher they rise, the more spectacular the
fall. The planetary divinities become lowly players in a *jácara*
("Mojagón, preso, celebra la hermosura de su Iza" "Jailed, Mojagón celebrates the beauty of his Iza," 3.860); Apollo and Jupiter
are ready targets in a ballad on love and jealousy ("Efectos del
amor y los celos" "The effects of love and jealousy," 3.768); Jupiter's metamorphoses, the god's clever ploys in his sexual adventures—which Ovid had treated with malicious but mild humor—are now reduced to a "¡Hucho-ho!"[14] and "avechucho"
("ugly bird"),[15] the laughable animalizations of an overdevel-
oped libido. The burlesque of the gods, however, culminates
with *La hora de todos,* a parody reminiscent of Lucian's *Dialogues
of the Gods.* But Lucian's lighthearted mockery of the Olympians
is worlds apart from Quevedo's vulgar farce of ruffianesque and
foulmouthed buffoons belonging to a smelly underworld.[16]
Phoebus-Apollo appears here in a ridiculously gruesome costume. He is a brass-faced, tinsel-bearded musician, a death-
bringing planet, and a comically inefficient lover, as Fortune reminds him of his failure with Daphne: "ya te he visto yo . . .
correr tras una mozuela que, siendo sol, te dejó a escuras" ("I

have already seen you . . . running after a young girl who left
you in darkness even though you are the sun").[17] Quevedo details their adventure in the burlesque sonnets, which are our
concern here.

Quevedo subverts Ovid's tale doubly: in his early poem in
quintillas, he exaggerates the sentimental aspects of Apollo and
yields to courtly seriousness; in his comic sonnets, he exaggerates the playful and the result is degrading caricature. The Ovidian half-fool becomes not only a total fool but a clown as well.
And not even Daphne, who had been spared Ovid's ironic
barbs, escapes Quevedo's barbarous digs. The grotesque, which
in the *quintillas* appears as a function of universal disorder, is
used in the sonnets as a tool of the burlesque, as a dehumaniz-
ing, deforming device to demean and to ridicule. There is also
an element of play in Quevedo's comic grotesque. The master of
language and gratuitous wit cannot hide for long behind the
mask of the parodist; Quevedo's distortions dazzle by their sheer
visual and linguistic ingenuity, calling attention to themselves as
aesthetic play. So in the sonnets, the grotesque emerges both as
an instrument of parody and as a literary game, an occasion for
elaborating clever details—a familiar combination in Quevedo
also found in his nongrotesque schemes. The salient feature in
Quevedo's comic grotesque is the clash of incongruous elements,
the mingling of the human and the nonhuman, which is also the
case in the grotesque of the *quintillas*. But unlike the *quintillas*,
where the disquiet of the grotesque occurs without amusement,
the sonnets contain ready laughter, a reductive humor that mingles with feelings of revulsion and disgust.[18]

In Quevedo's sonnets of Apollo and Daphne, the real target of the parody is not the Ovidian tale *per se* (even though
Ovid is the original model and must be taken as a reference) but
the serious versions that, from Garcilaso on, convert the ancient
characters into courtly figures in courtly landscapes. And so in
the sonnets, the antimythological and the anti-Petrarchan merge,
as in the many burlesques of ancient tales of love. Quevedo's
poem in *quintillas*, one of many serious courtly versions, breeds
its parodic counterpart in the obvious self-mockery of the sonnets:

> Bermejazo platero de las cumbres,
> a cuya luz se espulga la canalla,
> la ninfa Dafne, que se afufa y calla,

si la quieres gozar, paga y no alumbres.
Si quieres ahorrar de pesadumbres,
ojo del cielo, trata de compralla:
en confites gastó Marte la malla,
y la espada en pasteles y en azumbres.
Volvióse en bolsa Júpiter severo;
levantóse las faldas la doncella
por recogerle en lluvia de dinero.
Astucia fue de alguna dueña estrella,
que de estrella sin dueña no lo infiero:
Febo, pues eres Sol, sírvete de ella.[19] (2.536)

(Redheaded silversmith of the heights
in whose light the rabble picks its fleas,
if you want to possess the nymph Daphne,
who scrams without a word, pay her and don't light up.
If you want to save yourself trouble,
eye of the heavens, try to buy her;
Mars sold his coat of mail for sweets,
and his sword for pastries and jugs.
Severe Jupiter turned himself into a purse;
the maiden raised her skirt
to catch him in a shower of money.
That was the cunning of some duenna star,
for I can't attribute it to a star without a duenna:
Phoebus, since you're the sun, make use of her.)

Quevedo deforms and belittles the ancient figures imagistically through caricature and linguistically through a taunting,
conceptual language sprinkled with *germanismos*. His stage of
fools is the low world of hustlers and prostitutes, where love is a
matter of money and cunning. The poet assumes the role of a
teacher of love, providing Apollo with a wicked message on the
art of seduction—pay if you want to love, advice that rests on
one of Quevedo's satirical commonplaces: to women, love and
money are synonymous. The topic of *dinero* and *dinerismo* (the
total supremacy of money) plays a dominant role in Quevedo,
whose unmasking of the evils of money ranges from the mildly
satirical, as in his early *letrilla*, "Poderoso caballero es Don Dinero" ("A Powerful Gentleman is Sir Money"), to the darkly
ominous, as in the *Sueño de la Muerte* (*Dream of Death*), where Dinero appears as a demonic monster.[20] But in the Apollo sonnet
(and later in the Daphne), Quevedo the moralist, concerned with

exposing the folly and vice of a depraved society, is pushed into
the background, leaving the way open to the outrageous humor-
ist of time-honored literary traditions. Quevedo places the god
and the nymph in a corrupt underworld and then invents a
shameless voice to toy perversely with them.

The Apollo sonnet starts off with light images springing
from the central figure of the sun-god, as in the *quintillas*. But
this first address to the deity as *bermejazo platero de las cumbres*
("redheaded silversmith of the heights")—the *rubicundo Apolo* of
nobler contexts—immediately suggests that we are far from the
splendor of courtly idealism. In this line Quevedo dresses Apollo
for comedy, since *bermejazo*, an allusion to the color and size of
the astral body and the red-gold hair of the youthful god in anthropomorphic getup, carries a moral slur. In popular supersti-
tion, used extensively in Golden Age letters, red or blond hair is
a sign of treachery and deceit.[21] In Quevedo, Judas is always *bermejo.*[22] The courtly wooer has become a crafty seducer but, as it
turns out, not a very resourceful one. In its derogatory function,
the superlative adjective deflates not only Sol but also the nomi-
nal phrase *platero de las cumbres,* which describes the god's lumi-
nosity as he shines from imperious heights. The lofty words,
which might find an equally lofty place in any gongorist poem,
are here ridiculous, particularly because of their preciosity which
jars harshly with the degrading adjective. In the second line,
Sol's degradation continues by implication, for the mighty planet
does not shine on worthy things but rather on the dregs of society.

This last scene spills over into the realm of the grotesque,
for Quevedo not only makes Sol reveal the *canalla* ("rabble")
scornfully in all the sordid aspects of its fallen state but animal-
izes it since he is punning on the word, finding a dog in its first
syllable *can*. The human merges with the animal, yielding a humorously disgusting image; doglike, the dirty rabble picks its
fleas in the sunlight. The comic distortion of the *canalla,* in nasty,
inflated caricature, sets the tone for the perverted world of the
sonnet. Dámaso Alonso calls the scene "fondo goyesco, dos si-
glos antes que Goya, capricho dibujado en once sílabas" ("a go-
yesque background, two centuries before Goya, a *capricho* drawn
in eleven syllables").[23] And yet, even if the grotesque disposes
of its victim (the proper function of all successful satiric and parodic grotesques), we can only respond with fascination to Quevedo's fanciful contortions, to the lines that destroy but also

draw admiration for their wild ingenuity. This is the "play-urge" in Quevedo, here and in his best grotesques, such as the batlike Daphne and the predatory, mechanized Apollo, both of whom we will meet later on.

Daphne, like Apollo, emerges as a lowly presence. The nymph is introduced in the third line immediately after the *canalla*, and the reader feels that she participates in the *canalla*'s degradation and grotesquerie.[24] This association is brought about in a subtle way. We know that Daphne is herself part of the rabble, for the term *ninfa*, a reference that in ancient times defined her maidenhood, is a *germanismo* meaning prostitute, and so as we read the lines "a cuya luz se espulga la canalla, / la ninfa Dafne, que se afufa y calla" ("in whose light the rabble picks its fleas, / the nymph Daphne, who scrams without a word") the fallen virgin becomes one with the flea-picking *canalla*. And, curiously, these lines are also connected by the internal rhyme of *se espulga* and *se afufa*, which in their humorous mockery reinforce the link between the *canalla* and Daphne, this time phonetically. Daphne is a figure fit for one of Quevedo's *jácaras*. While she silently escapes—an Ovidian reminiscence—two *germanismos* denote her low station: *afufarse* ("to scram") and the above-mentioned *ninfa* (prostitute). The two terms are linked not only as part of a common jargon but by the pejorative sounds *fu-fa* which, linked to the *af* of *Dafne*, further degrade the woman. This repetition of cacophonous sounds in order to demean is a typical Quevedian technique, especially in his excremental poems. (Like the combination *fu-fa*, the rhyme *-alla/-ella* throughout the sonnet is irreverent and belittling, for it parodies a prevalent rhyme in the *quintillas*, bringing with it an implicit mockery.) A play on words in the fourth line carries Quevedo's message to Apollo, the astral seducer: *paga y no alumbres* ("pay her and don't light up"). One would have expected *apaga y no alumbres* ("put out the light and don't light up"). By saying *paga*, Quevedo suggests lewdly that money is the answer; deal with the woman on her own ground, that is, in the dark.

The second quatrain conveys the message by playing on the antithetical economic terms *ahorrar–comprar* ("to save"–"to buy"), which go back to *pagar* ("to pay") as the only means of catching the elusive, if easy, prey. In line six, Quevedo returns to the sky imagery of the beginning, this time degrading Phoebus by association in a takeoff on the well-known scatological *frase hecha* (set phrase) by maliciously calling the giver of light who sees all *ojo del cielo*—"anus of the heavens."[25] In this quick lexical parody, the poet gathers all his impatience and contempt for the god who should know better.[26] This obscene debunking of the god is especially irreverent since Quevedo uses the heavens, Apollo's domain, in the abusive phrase.

In the next lines the argument continues, now backed by ancient authority: by Ovid, the skilled teacher of love, and by his gods, whose erotic adventures the witty sensualist recounts in the *Metamorphoses* and uses as exempla in the *Ars amatoria*. Quevedo, no less informed than Ovid in the classical art of persuasion, introduces two cunning and successful lovers; Mars and Jupiter, planetary divinities like Phoebus, are models to copy in the sun-god's attempts at seduction. By selling his war-god accoutrements, Mars buys Venus *confites, pasteles,* and *azumbres* ("sweets," "pastries," and "jugs") to bribe and seduce her. This recalls *La hora de todos,* where Quevedo has the love-goddess, portrayed as a boor and a glutton, gorging herself on cakes and candy probably given her by Mars: "estaba sepultando debajo de la nariz a puñados rosquillas y confites" ("she was burying under her nose by the handful doughnuts and sweets").[27] The second model, Jupiter, supreme among the gods and obviously a lover of greater means, becomes a shower of money which Danae quickly gathers in her skirts. (The gold of the original myth has been substituted by money, stressing the buying of the woman.) The once innocent maiden here raises her skirts in a clever image of both female greed and indelicate immodesty as she exposes herself to Jove. In this tercet, Quevedo downgrades not only Danae but Jupiter as well, for the reference to the solemn deity transformed into a *bolsa* ("purse") subtly ridicules him.

The sonnet ends in a clever, complex epigrammatic turn, a play on *dueña* ("duenna") and *estrella* ("star"), to convince Phoebus that cunning is the only answer. The duplicity that Quevedo wants Apollo to assume is fittingly expressed in duplicitous language. In a note to this tercet in his edition of Quevedo's poetry, Florencio Janer observes that in Golden Age poetry and theater it is common to give the name *Dueña Estrella* to widows who supervised unmarried girls.[28] If we accept this connection between the two words, Quevedo's meaning is clear. The successful erotic adventures of Mars and Jupiter were brought about by a Duenna Star, not by a star without a duenna. Thus Phoebus the Sun, the king of the stars, must use the duenna (and her cunning) in order to get his hands on the maiden Daphne.

The poem to Apollo just examined is the first of a two-part sequence in which the second is the sonnet to Daphne. Both poems should be read together, for they constitute a unit: Quevedo's apostrophe to Apollo is a counsel on how to catch the elusive Daphne; the apostrophe to Daphne offers a warning on Apollo's intentions and tells of his defeat:

> "Tras vos, un alquimista va corriendo,
> Dafne, que llaman Sol, ¿y vos, tan cruda?
> Vos os volvéis murciégalo sin duda,
> pues vais del Sol y de la luz huyendo.
>
> "El os quiere gozar, a lo que entiendo,
> si os coge en esta selva tosca y ruda:
> su aljaba suena, está su bolsa muda;
> el perro, pues no ladra, está muriendo.
>
> "Buhonero de signos y planetas,
> viene haciendo ademanes y figuras,
> cargado de bochornos y cometas."
>
> Esto la dije; y en cortezas duras
> de laurel se ingirió contra sus tretas,
> y, en escabeche, el Sol se quedó a escuras. (2.537)

> ("An alchemist is running after you, Daphne,
> who is called the Sun, and you so rough
> and raw? You turn into a bat undoubtedly,
> for you flee the Sun and the light.
>
> "He wants to possess you, from what I see,
> if he catches you in this coarse forest:
> his quiver's ringing, his pouch is mute;
> the dog, since he's not barking, is dying.
>
> "A peddler of signs and planets,
> he's making gestures and poses,
> laden with stifling heat and comets."
>
> All this I said to her; and to foil his tricks,
> she grafted herself into hard laurel bark,
> and, marinated, the Sun was left in darkness.)

Here again the light imagery is used to degrade. The god becomes an alchemist, the sun whose light turns things to "gold." The king of the celestial sphere "produces" the king of metals, "the sum of all metalic virtues" and, alchemically, a mixture of the elements in perfect proportion.[29] But alchemy, a pseudoscience popular during Quevedo's times, had become a butt of jokes and, in Quevedo himself, a frequent target of satire.[30] The treacherous *platero* ("silversmith") yields to the ludicrous alchemist.

Daphne, *cruda* in her recalcitrant escape, flees from Sol and his light. Quevedo's amusing play on the word *cruda* brings two notions together: the woman's cruel courtly rigor and the fact that she remains "uncooked," that is, untouched not only by Sol's "roasting" heat but by the lusty alchemist's oven.[31] The image of the nymph escaping from Sol, which produced an encomium in the *quintillas*, is here a cynical attack. The night imagery gives way to a creature of the night; Daphne is a bat, an animal given to comic treatment and popular in the grotesque. The fantastic atmosphere of the ancient tale permits the construction of this clever, ugly distortion in which the human takes on animal qualities—comical and nightmarish—bringing the poem into the realm of the grotesque and of black humor as well. Here Quevedo is indulging in a device used frequently in mythological burlesque, a creation of a ridiculous transformation where no transformation existed in the original myth. Quevedo's contemporaries in England often use this same trick. For instance, in Thomas Nashe's burlesque of Hero and Leander in his *Prayse of the Red Herring* (1599), the lovers are transformed into a fish called "ling" and a "Cadwallader Herring."[32] We may remember Quevedo's own reference to the swimmer of the Hellespont in his "Hero y Leandro en paños menores" ("Hero and Leander in Underwear") as *aprendiz de rana* ("frog apprentice") and *pescado* ("fish").

The second quatrain makes Apollo's less-than-honorable intentions clear, stressed by the verb *coger* ("to catch") with its obvious sexual connotations. Apollo had not heeded Quevedo's advice and now, spitefully, the poet reveals to Daphne the god's plan for her in the rugged landscape of Thessaly. Quevedo tells the girl of Apollo's threatening "ringing quiver," with its veiled phallic implications, a reference both to the sound of the god of archery as he runs with his accoutrements and to his sexual excitement. But Quevedo tells Daphne more—something that will keep the nymph running for sure: the god's money pouch is silent; no money is forthcoming. The antithesis of the "ring" of sex and the "silence" of money is a combination that in Quevedo speaks of instant failure.

The notion that Apollo is not paying manifests itself once
again in the dog image: "el perro, pues no ladra, está muriendo"
("the dog, since he's not barking, is dying"). The animal imagery of Apollo as a dog derives from Ovid. The Augustan uses the
image to humor the god's urgencies as a victim of *furor*, the elegiac *topos* of the madness of passion, which makes a frenzied
Apollo run like a Gallic hound after the virgin, who in turn is
pictured as a hare. Like Ovid, Quevedo uses this animalization
to degrade Phoebus in his sexual rapacity. But here there is an
added meaning. In Golden Age texts, references to a dead dog
frequently allude to not paying a prostitute for her services, as in
Tirso's *El burlador de Sevilla* (II. 206) and Quevedo's poem "Que
no me quieren bien todas, confieso" ("I confess, not all women
love me well").[33] In our sonnet, this clever animal image not
only defines Apollo's stinginess but brings into focus the basic
conflict of the god and the nymph in their amusing, dislocated
relationship. The battle of virtue and vice in the *quintillas* becomes here a battle of vices: the lusty god who is not paying and
the prostitute who will not relent unless she is paid. If Daphne's
reasons for running are known only by implication, they are
made explicit in the ballad, "Encarece la hermosura de una
moza" ("Praises the beauty of a girl"), where the god is again a
miser and the maiden is a Quevedian "ninfa de daca y toma"
("a nymph who gives and takes")—a phrase referring to
a whore:

> Si la luz trujo arrastrando,
> como otros suelen la soga,
> tras Dafne el Sol, cuadrillero
> con más saetas que joyas;
> si la corrió como liebre,
> y se corrió como zorra
> de que la dijese: "Aguarda,"
> y no la dijese: "Toma."[34] (2.682, 169–76)

> (If the Sun, a bowman with more
> arrows than jewels, came after Daphne,
> dragging light as others drag a cord;
> if he ran after her as if she were a hare,
> and she ran off like a fox
> because he said: "Wait,"
> rather than: "Take.")

These transparent creatures, flat in their single-minded-
ness, are characteristic creations of Quevedo's satirical and burlesque machinery. Like so many of Quevedo's comic characters—such as Pablos in the *Buscón* and the many figures that
inhabit the *Sueños*—they are drawn in quick strokes, exaggerated
gestures and physical details, which, if successful in conveying
their foibles, fail to give them real substance and psychological
complexity. But far from being a weakness, this two-dimen-
sionality points to Quevedo's remarkable virtuosity as a carica-
turist.[35] And Apollo and Daphne are two of his happiest creations, belonging as they do to his répertoire of types. Daphne
enters his gallery of dehumanized, filthy, greedy women—*don-
cellas* in name only. And Apollo, in his urgent chase and later in
his farcical "dance" of the first tercet, emerges as a Quevedian
lecher: that frenetic *fantoche* ("puppet") who, in the words of
Amédée Mas, has surrendered himself to the demon of the
flesh.[36] The comic distortion of the once sentimental lover of the
quintillas, who is converted into a sexual predator, follows a
common practice in anti-Petrarchan literature. In the mockery of
the traditional Petrarchan wooer, sensual love, which had coex-
isted in uneasy tension with idealized emotions and sublimated
passion, gives way to uncontrollable lust and sexual perversion.
And so it is in Quevedo's own jeering of love and the lover. In
the *Poema heroico de las necedades y locuras de Orlando (Heroic Poem
of the Foolishness and Madness of Orlando),* for instance, Quevedo
gives us Ferragut—another one of his lusty lovers—in terms
similar to those in which he portrays Apollo. Ferragut runs after
Angélica in a mad, comic pursuit that, like Phoebus chasing
Daphne, combines both frenzy and canine animalization:

> Tales cosas, corriendo por los cerros,
> iba gritando, y de uno en otro prado;
> tras él, en varias tropas, corren perros:
> iba de todas suertes emperrado. (3.875, canto 2, 561–64)

> (Such things he shouted as he ran through the
> hills, and from meadow to meadow;
> after him ran dogs in several packs:
> he went off dog-maddened in every way.)

The association of Apollo—king of the stars—with a dog
recalls an image from Greek and Roman letters that Quevedo,
the ostentatious classicist, may have had in mind. Sirius, the

dog-star (Sirius in Greek means "the scorcher"), is the brightest and "hottest" star in the heavens; in classical texts, it is a source of turmoil and causes people to flee. As we know, turmoil and escape characterize the relation between Apollo and Daphne.

The first tercet presents that burst of convulsive energy alluded to above and which is so often used by Quevedo for comic effect. The solar god appears in slapstick as a clownish street vendor peddling his celestial wares of signs and planets, perhaps in an effort to impress Daphne: "buhonero de signos y planetas, / viene haciendo ademanes y figuras" ("a peddler of signs and planets, / he's making gestures and poses"). Ovid's Apollo, on the other hand, had spoken of his noble birth and lofty position as a deity. The god's strange, mechanical contortions render him grotesque. He appears as a lifeless doll put into motion by a cruel puppeteer. (Apollo's puppetlike character will be discussed below.) The image also pokes fun at Phoebus in his connection with astrology, which, like alchemy, was a frequent target of Quevedo's satire.[37] But this gesticulating buffoon—whose fumbling run is mimicked in the awkward repetition of the conjunction *y*—bears the marks of his "trade" as a depraved seducer, for he carries *bochornos y cometas* ("stifling heat and comets"). The word *bochornos* not only points to the god's moral depravity but also refers to the sultry heat that Apollo, as the sun, creates; so it is a tie to the theme of the dog-star and the god's frustration. *Cometas* also has a double meaning: it suggests a link to Apollo as astral deity, but in *germanía* it means arrow, carrying us back to the quiver image and its sexual connotations. The juxtaposition of *bochornos* and *cometas* is a mingling of the abstract and the concrete which is so characteristic of Quevedo's humor. In this grotesque portrayal of a clown Quevedo has totally pulled the rug from under Apollo. All that is left for him is his fall, which is not long in coming.

As Quevedo ends his speech to Daphne, the girl tricks the miserly trickster by "grafting" herself into the laurel's rigid bark, out of the god's reach: "en cortezas duras / de laurel se ingirió contra sus tretas." The jilted god stays behind comically, but fittingly, as part of an *escabeche* ("a marinade"), for laurel leaves are an ingredient used in this culinary sauce.[38]

In these disorderly vignettes that are Quevedo's sonnets, Apollo and Daphne are drawn with quite different brushes, harsh as each may be. The nymph is held up to ridicule, touched by a repulsive animality; we see the fallen virgin associated with the doglike rabble scratching itself, and we see her fleeing with bat wings. Quevedo's grotesque of Daphne belongs to a long line of grotesques so popular in medieval times and so masterfully conceived in works such as Bosch's phantasmagorias, where the mixture of human and animal is a graphic portrayal of man's ignoble place in the chaotic world of sin. And if Daphne is endowed with a monstrous, fantastic air, Apollo, on the other hand, is presented to us wearing a dunce cap. It is upon this fool that our attention is focused, for Daphne is chiefly a foil against which the god's comicity is revealed. The mockery of the astral seducer rests largely on two popular traits in Quevedo's many caricatures of fools: inadequacy and puppetry. Apollo is a fool because he cannot perform. In the underworld of the poem, Phoebus is a failed *pícaro*. He bungles his erotic caper because he is an artless rogue; he lacks the deftness of the successful *pícaro*, where rapacity and cunning exist in delicate balance, constantly reinforcing each other. The god is a trickster with no tricks in his bag, and so we see him only as the clumsy lover.

Apollo also emerges as a puppet, possessed by that mechanized rigidity that Bergson finds at the root of the comic and that is so characteristic of Quevedo's burlesque characters, those hollow figures moving under the impulse of their own blind, petty concerns. There is a touch of this automatism in Ovid's Apollo. Driven by love as a malady that destroys reason and overrides the will, the god becomes laughable in the chase and after the transformation, when he embraces the tree and kisses it as if it were Daphne. But Ovid's Apollo—not the total fool like Quevedo's—"awakens" from his erotic madness and becomes the god again and, somewhat awkwardly, tries to regain his solemnity through his paean to Daphne. Quevedo's Apollo, in a similarly undignified Dionysiac frenzy, is caught in a whirl of lust but, in the hands of a less benevolent master, falls right "in the soup," perhaps drowning, and if not in a foul pool of urine like Rabelais' Parisians, at least in tasty *escabeche*. This is farce at its wildest.

Ovid's half-fool is given a half-solution at the end of the story; by consecrating the laurel, at least Apollo has the sacred wreath as a consolation for his loss as he leaves the "stage." Ovid, the storyteller, keeps his hero alive for another day. Quevedo's total fool, by contrast, suffers total defeat symbolized by darkness. The light of the beginning, as the radiant Sol in hopeful, predatory pursuit follows Daphne, contrasts markedly with this darkness. By means of the popular *chiaroscuro* of Baroque art and letters, Quevedo dramatizes the comically sad predicament of the solar deity; there is no shred of hope for the god. Quevedo "turns the light off" and all is over.

In the sonnets, Apollo and Daphne are figures placed in a background of silence—actors without voices moving comically on a silent stage (except perhaps for the faint sound of the god's quiver). This silence permits Quevedo to shape his characters at will, to present them in the most ridiculous light possible; the ancient figures appear not only helpless in their comicity but a bit stupid as well. And contrasting with this silence is the sound of the poet's voice in the foreground, advising and cautioning, sure and masterful, like that of a perverse Pantocrator. Though the foolish Apollo escapes his advice, Daphne pays close attention and, in her transformation, ultimately serves as his weapon of revenge against the god who would not listen.

In Quevedo's handling of the mythological poem, one of the most derivative of genres, we find a masterful combination of convention and originality, of rhetorical commonplaces and striking invention. Quevedo treats the myth of Apollo and Daphne as a poetic fiction as Ovid his model had done before him. The Augustan couches the legend in the erotic conventions of Roman elegy, creating a tale of jilted love both serious and playful. In similar fashion, Quevedo, appropriating few but significant details from Ovid, uses the love traditions of his day for his story. But unlike Ovid, Quevedo, a poet of double masks, separates the earnest from the jest by writing a turbulent serious version in *quintillas* that contrasts sharply with his burlesque treatment in the sonnets. Following in Garcilaso's footsteps, he encases his tale in a courtly frame, pitting the idealized beloved against the sentimental teary lover. But his imaginative vision carries him beyond the erotic into the realms of the cosmological and the Christian, and the discordant clashes in these realms ultimately mirror his metaphysical broodings. The theme of convulsion and the world-upside-down in the *quintillas* extends to the burlesque, when the ancient characters are projected in insolent, deformed inversion. But here parody and wit carry the day in a comedy of erotic frenzy and madness: a splendid virginal nymph turns into a dirty, animalized whore, and Apollo— robbed of his solemnity and seriousness, traits due him by virtue of his cult—is a lusting Dionysian and a fool. The elements of humor in Ovid's mock-heroic treatment of the god become, in Quevedo, a vaudeville burlesque in which all his verbal flair and grotesque imagination produce these two unworthy figures. Of course, lurking behind the grotesque, behind the fallen, romantic sun-god and the maiden-become-prostitute, are hints of the sordidness and folly of the human condition that were never far from the elegant savagery of Quevedo's pen.

From Ovid to Quevedo we have seen how radically the Apollo and Daphne myth is altered to suit the intentions of writers of such different casts, revealing their aesthetic and intellectual values and those of their age. In its journey or transformation, the myth proves endlessly adaptable. It is used for aesthetic purposes as well as to convey something far beyond the immediate narration. At these latter moments the myth speaks of the mysteries of existence or a self's relation to its world. The tale splendidly serves the purposes of the bantering Ovid, who creates an amusing story of unrequited love. Yet, serious behind the playful mask of his erotic agon, Ovid offers a political statement against Augustus in his portrayal of a grotesque, comical Apollo. The myth serves equally well the stern allegorizers of the Middle Ages, with their moral and sacred battles in which grotesque distortions portray the fall into sin; playful grotesques peek through in illustrations, brief moments of freedom from rigid codes. Petrarch, using the grotesque sparingly, fits the tale of Apollo and Daphne in his tortured courtly universe, which is further encumbered by preoccupations with salvation; failure is a constant presence in his erotic and moral agons. Whereas in Garcilaso courtly conduct dictates that the scorned lover and exquisite, modest woman enter an anguished struggle—the grotesque in Daphne's transformation paralleling Apollo's grief which is itself harsh and distorted—in the sonnets of the cantankerous Quevedo the lovers are placed at the center of a lowly anticourtly world of conflicting vices. Quevedo converts Ovid's rapacious Apollo into a fully grotesque aberration, and of course Daphne enters the wild, deformed play. The grotesque is again used to turn the myth back upon itself, the object of ridicule now being the courtly tradition that had so fruitfully carried the myth along since Petrarch's times. Quevedo, by his outrageous comedy and scatological visions, not only provides the ultimate example of the myth's unlimited shapes but permits us to broaden our view to appreciate the ways in which the transformation myth of Apollo and Daphne was itself transformed by his predecessors.

Quevedo's Revisions of His Daphne Sonnet

Quevedo's Daphne sonnet, examined in chapter 5, was first published in 1648 in González de Salas' *El Parnaso español*. According to José Manuel Blecua, it is a revision of an earlier obscene version that appears in a manuscript now owned by the Biblioteca Provincial at Evora.[1] Blecua argues, rightly I believe, that the extraordinary correction of the entire first tercet proves that the Evora sonnet (hereafter cited as *A*) is the primitive version of the sonnet in the *Parnaso* (hereafter cited as *B*).[2] The fact that there are two versions of the sonnet invites speculations on Quevedo's motives for the changes: was it external censorship, self-imposed censorship, or were aesthetic criteria the basis for his revisions?

Two rigorous editors of Quevedo's poetry, Blecua and James O. Crosby, have observed that the poet skillfully reworked many of his texts. They offer substantial evidence to prove that Quevedo, far from his common reputation of writing quick, unrevised poems, was a meticulous artist who labored over his drafts, revealing in the process the complexities of his dazzling craft.[3] Of course, we can only speculate about Quevedo's reasons for revising his poetic texts, particularly when these revisions rid a poem of sexually "scandalous" images and obscene language. Living in seventeenth-century theocratic Spain placed an enormous burden on its writers, and more so on one as profane and irreverent as Quevedo who, especially for his *Sueños*, was an easy target of the Inquisition. In some cases Quevedo may have made changes in his works to please the ecclesiastical censors, those fearful guardians of the faith and morals, or to ease a troubled conscience.

Quevedo's early version *(A)* of the Daphne sonnet utilizes grotesque images, some of which belong to what Mikhail Bakh-

tin calls "grotesque realism."[4] As we shall see, the touches of
sexual grotesquerie in the revised version *(B)*—the veiled scatological image of Apollo as *ojo del cielo* ("anus of the heavens")
and the phallic references hidden in the god's jiggling quiver
and his comets—are but remnants of Quevedo's explicit reference to genital organs in the early poem, instances of carnival
humor.

My purpose here is twofold. I will show that while *A* is
an early version of *B*, it is more than a mere *step* in reaching a
definitive redaction; *A* makes a statement of its own and
emerges in theme and imagery as a strikingly unique poem. Sec-
ondly, I will examine the possible reasons why Quevedo revised
his original sonnet *(A)* so extensively as to create a new poem
(B)—the one selected by González de Salas for his anthology.

Version *A* reads as follows:

> "Tras vos, un boquirrubio va corriendo,
> Dafne, que llaman Sol, ¿y vos, tan cruda?
> Morciégalo os queréis volver sin duda,
> pues vais del Sol tan sin cesar huyendo.
>
> "El empreñaros quiere, a lo que entiendo,
> si os coge en esta selva tosca y ruda;
> Júpiter, el cachondo, le da ayuda,
> y el dios maestro de esgrima, el brazo horrendo.
>
> "Si sus flechas teméis con tantas tretas,
> con carne os lo ha de hacer: que son locuras
> pensar que os lo ha de hacer con las saetas."
>
> Esto la dije yo en las espesuras,
> y al punto en lauro convirtió las tetas,
> y, arrecho, el pobre Sol se quedó a escuras. (2.537)

> ("A red-mouthed guy is running after you, Daphne,
> who is called the Sun, and you so rough
> and raw? You wish to turn into a bat undoubtedly,
> for you flee endlessly from the Sun.
>
> "He wants to get you pregnant, from what I see,
> if he catches you in this coarse forest;
> Jupiter, the lecher, helps him out,
> and the master god of fencing lends him his horrible arm.
>
> "If with all your tricks you fear his arrows,
> he'll do it to you with meat: for it is madness
> to think he will do it to you with the arrows."
>
> All this I said to her in the thick of the woods,

and instantly her tits turned into laurel,
and, erect, the poor Sun was left in darkness.)

In Ovid, the chase, the peak of the erotic agon, is embroidered with mock-heroic elements, such as Apollo's use of lofty
words to woo Daphne on the run, and touches of farce and caricature when the god, through a clever simile, is identified with a
dog pursuing a defenseless hare. Quevedo exaggerates the comedy and transforms it into low burlesque—much more outrageous than version *B* examined in chapter 5.

The first quatrain presents the lover as a *boquirrubio*, an allusion both to the color of the sun and to a weakness of character. The word is used by Golden Age writers to portray an inex-
perienced, naive and awkward lover in his first attempts at
seduction. According to the *Diccionario de Autoridades*, the term
also refers to a simpleton, someone easy to trick. Both meanings
perfectly define Phoebus who foolishly chooses running as a
means to reach Daphne, his first love, and who is easily thwarted by the transformation. The escaping nymph, like Sol, is also
ridiculed. Daphne is called *cruda*, meaning cruel in the courtly
sense and uncooked, that is, untouched by Sol's pursuing heat.
With malicious humor, Quevedo implies that the nymph's raw
meat has eluded the fiery cook. Furthermore, as she runs away
from Sol, Daphne is identified, in Quevedo's grotesque imagination, with a bat, a comical and nightmarish rodent of darkness.
In the second quatrain, the nasty *empreñaros* ("to get you pregnant") serves as a prelude for coarser things to come. The god's
sole purpose is to ravish the girl, and two powerful and successful lovers, libidinous Jupiter and the mighty war-god Mars—lust
and strength, sure weapons for Phoebus' rape—aid him in his
attempt. The upshot is that even though Apollo is a weak, inept
lover, with the help of his planetary cohorts, he becomes a lusty
warrior, a fearsome foe as the violent *brazo horrendo* ("horrible
arm") suggests. Here Quevedo uses an ancient *topos,* that of love
as warfare and the lover as a soldier, a commonplace in the erotic doctrine of Roman elegy (for example, Ovid's *Amores,* 1.9),
which later passes into courtly canons. Quevedo exaggerates the
topic and makes the love encounter a ridiculous travesty.

In the tercets we meet Quevedo, the ultimate vulgarian,
in two sinister, grotesque touches that mock the fears of the virgin and bring in elements of black humor; it is meat, not arrows,
that will carry out the deed ("con carne os lo ha de hacer: que
son locuras / pensar que os lo ha de hacer con las saetas"). The

thought is ludicrously vicious and is followed by a lighter but no less perverse image when the nymph's breasts become laurel ("y al punto en lauro convirtió las tetas").[5] Apollo is left *arrecho* ("erect") in the dark, a reference to the sexual arousal of the jilted god as he is left behind, comically helpless and excluded from the girl—a fitting last obscenity in a poor lecher's journey to defeat.

Version *A* is another example of Quevedo as the clever artificer of "dirty" literature, rivaled only perhaps by François Rabelais and Jonathan Swift. Quevedo is close both to Rabelais' carnivalesque scatological visions and to Swift, whose excremental imagery is a powerful instrument in his destructive satirical sketches.[6] In his satire, Quevedo uses obscenity to ridicule folly and unmask disguised vices, while in his burlesque he uses it to wound and to insult, revelling in mockery and play. Evidently *A* is an example of the latter. It is a playful, if perverse, burlesque. Its object is solely to poke fun and vilify two mythological figures who in other moments are lofty and revered (even in Quevedo himself).

Compared with *A*, *B* contains very different language and imagery; Quevedo "cleanses" *A* of its obscenities and produces a new poem. The term *boquirrubio* of *A* gives way to *alquimista*, a humorous reference to the alchemical power of the sun, whose light turns all things to "gold." Quevedo keeps *A*'s malicious abuse of Daphne by again calling her *cruda*—cruel and uncooked. But here the humor is reinforced by the presence of the god turned alchemist, for the nymph escapes not only Sol's heat but his oven. The comic degradation of the maiden continues as in version *A*, when she is likened to a bat running away from Sol. But the phrase *tan sin cesar* of the fourth line of *A*, in *B* becomes *y de la luz*, stressing the girl's flight from the light rather than the urgency of her escape. The grotesque and exquisitely perverse image of Daphne as a bat, a creature of the night, is strengthened in *B* by the explicit reference to the act of shunning the light created by Sol, the glittering, diurnal magician. Moreover, *A* expresses Daphne's wish to be transformed into a bat ("Morciégalo os queréis volver sin duda"), whereas *B* speaks of Daphne as actually being transformed ("Vos os volvéis murciégalo sin duda"). So, while *A* maliciously exposes the nymph's inability to transform herself to escape her threatening pursuer, *B* is a cynical belittling of Daphne as she flees her luminous lover in grotesque costume.

In the second quatrain, *B*, like *A*, reveals Apollo's plan for the huntress. But the lines that in the early version emphasize the fury of Apollo's erotic quest become in *B* a portrait of a total fool, predatory and miserly. The god wants seduction with an empty pouch, a disclosure that spells disaster for the unsuspecting lover. In the tercets there are more drastic changes. While the early version presents images of a cruel, fiendish humor, *B* offers a picture of a ludicrous buffoon who collapses at the end in farcical defeat. The first tercet is a splendid slapstick, grotesque vision of the god: Sol as a clownish street vendor of signs and planets, his astrological hardware, and as a puppet-like fool in his convulsive, mechanical contortions. The explicit relation of arrows and sex in lines 9–11 of *A* has become in *B* a part of Quevedo's games of *dilogía*—his skillful equivocations—in the veiled phallic connotations of the term *cometas* (both the astral bodies that inhabit the domain of Phoebus-Apollo, the king of stars, and his arrows as the god of archery) and of the jiggling quiver of line 7. The overly clever cacophony of "teméis con tantas tretas" and the unpoetic repetition of "os lo ha de hacer" in *A* have been eliminated in *B* and replaced by lines that create a scale of interconnected sounds corresponding to interconnected meanings, leading to the image of the astrological, lascivious clown. The entire tercet offers a series of pulsating internal rhymes:

> "Buhonero de signos y planetas,
>
> viene haciendo ademanes y figuras,
>
> cargado de bochornos y cometas."

> ("A peddler of signs and planets,
> he's making gestures and poses,
> laden with stifling heat and comets.")

The sequence of three stressed *y*'s on the eighth syllable of each line of the tercet and the internal rhymes of *buhonero/bochornos* and *viene/haciendo* intensify the balanced repetition of sounds.

In the last tercet, the obscenities of *A* give way to a brilliant farce. Daphne dupes the miser by "grafting" herself into the safety of the laurel, whose rigid bark (*cortezas duras*) parallels the recalcitrance of the unbending beloved. Luminous, clumsy Sol receives an appropriate punishment; he ends up in darkness, that is, in failure, floating in *escabeche*, a sauce whose staple is none other than laurel leaves.

It is abundantly clear that each sonnet is written with its own distinctive voice; each creates its own set of images to belittle and destroy. *A*, with gruesome delight, portrays lechery and fear; *B*, on the other hand, gives a picture of foolish stinginess, pettiness, and trickery.

Why the reworking? Why did Quevedo decide to turn *A* into *B*? The answer is not simple nor clear-cut. It must ultimately remain speculative, and our speculations must be offered in a roundabout way. *A*'s imagery and language, its profanities, clowning, references to genital organs—what Mikhail Bakhtin in his discussion of "grotesque realism" calls the "bodily lower stratum"—place the sonnet in the tradition of carnival laughter, the folk humor of the marketplace.[7] In Bakhtin's words, this laughter "asserts and denies," "buries and revives" (12). It is mocking and deriding but at the same time liberating. The wit and mockery act to free the spirit; obscene railing and wanton vitality open the door to a special kind of release. And this is the release we find in version *A*. In the Middle Ages, clerics and theologians indulged in the carnival spirit as "relaxation from pious seriousness," as seen, for instance, in the so-called "Monkish Pranks" (*Joca monacorum*).[8] Quevedo's indulgence in carnival laughter may be for him a moment of liberation, a "relaxation" from his serious work—his solemn ascetic and religious tracts, his serious courtly verses—perhaps an affirmation of his freedom from the moral strictures of a theocratic state, and even from his own self-imposed moral constraints.[9]

We must recognize, however, that the joyful gaiety that is a part of carnival laughter truly conceived as such is often absent in Quevedo. Such gaiety is undercut by perversity, cynicism, and black humor as in the notorious "Rostro de blanca nieve, fondo en grajo" ("Snow-white face framed in crow-like blackness") or "La vida empieza en lágrimas y caca" ("Life starts in tears and shit"). But much of Quevedo's comic imagery is neither somber nor dark, and this is quite evident in works such as the *Gracias y desgracias del ojo del culo (Graces and Disgraces of the Asshole)* with its "joyful" participation in obscene imagery for its own sake. And even though the festive gaiety is less evident in *A* than in the infamous *Gracias y desgracias*, it is equally present, especially in the rollicking rhyme *tretas*, *saetas*, and *tetas* ("tricks," "arrows," and "tits") of the tercets and in the wild image of the sexually aroused Apollo, like the men with huge phalluses in ancient *phlyax* vases (including Apollo himself) or in Au-

brey Beardsley's hilarious illustrations of Aristophanes' *Lysistrata*.
Quevedo's obscene abuse of his mythological figures is the key
to the realm of "merrymaking." And Freud's notion of the festive spirit is also true for Quevedo's own festive comedy: "the
liberty to do what is as a rule prohibited."[10]

If *A* is an act of rebellion and release from restraints, then
B—in its strategy of containment—is a reminder, a "corrective"
to Quevedo's own unbridled energies and, in a sense, an act of
penance for his license, an act of contrition, real or simulated. In
moving from *A* to *B*, Quevedo passes from Rabelaisian freedom
into official precincts, putting on the mask of "civilization," accepting what can or cannot be *said*. This is Quevedo perhaps
giving in to censorship. Let us recall that the changes in the
Sueños and the "humble" prologue for the *Juguetes de la niñez*
(Childhood Toys) (1631) show that Quevedo could not ignore the
ecclesiastical censors.[11] Quevedo was revising his poetry for publication shortly before his death,[12] and, since he had been frequently attacked for his malicious pen, he may have included *A*
among those items he was reworking and perhaps laundering
for his book.[13] The reluctance to print anything shocking in
Counter Reformation Spain is born out by González de Salas'
Parnaso, for the good editor made corrections to remove offensive material from Quevedo's poems for his posthumous edition.[14] Some of Quevedo's more explicitly obscene sonnets in
manuscript (such as *A*) did not see the light of print in the *Parnaso* (perhaps because González de Salas never saw them—an
unlikely possibility—or because he did not want to expose them
to the scrutiny of Quevedo's prudish critics).[15] By curtailing his
own freedom in creating *B*, Quevedo indeed may have given in
to censorship.

But what if Quevedo the moralist had his own qualms
about the implications of this freedom, of the suspension of
rules, as he participated in what lies outside the bounds of morality? In this case, Quevedo's revisions of *A* would emerge as
an act of catharsis as troubling images and words are expurgat-
ed. But whether to please the censors or appease his conscience,
Quevedo delivers a better poem in *B*. Not that ridding a poem of
"offensive" material in itself makes for a better poem. But in *A*
Quevedo relies on obscenities for much of the comedy and the
result is an uproarious, "easy" comedy; in *B*, on the other hand,
he must rely on more complex linguistic and imagistic games
and, in the process, taps his abundant poetic genius.

This brings us to a last point: speculations about Queve-do's possible aesthetic motives for his revisions. Since we know that Quevedo carefully polished and improved his poems, as re-vealed in the extant *autógrafos,* and since in this case *B* is clearly stylistically superior to *A,* we can infer that there were literary motives for the extensive changes. *B* is a much richer poem, a mosaic of subtle allusions and equivocal terms that show Queve-do at the peak of his form. In moving from *A* to *B,* Quevedo has left behind the notorious obscenities, the crude joke with its harsh language, to offer in its place a nasty but sophisticated put-down, a linguistic foray conceived in his inimitably intricate *conceptismo.*

There may be yet one more literary explanation for the re-visions—one of poetic design. In González de Salas' edition, the sonnet to Daphne *(B)* has a companion sonnet to Apollo, and both make up a "two-poem-sequence." Quevedo may have wanted to turn *A* into *B* in order to have a Daphne poem that would be a counterpart, in theme and mood, to his Apollo son-net. Both *B* and the Apollo sonnet are nasty, but in their clever farce they are less perverse than *A.* Quevedo's sonnet to the god is advice on how to catch the elusive Daphne (a maiden-become-prostitute): pay and you will succeed, words that Apollo will ig-nore. In the Daphne sonnet that immediately follows, the poet, obviously miffed by Apollo's reluctance to heed his advice and as a punishment to the god, tells the maiden of Phoebus' plans for her: love without money. The result as we have seen is a clownish tightwad jilted by an unwilling prostitute. After the poem of advice comes a poem of warning and comic chastise-ment. Version *A* would not have worked in this "two-sonnet-se-quence." Its ludicrously grim vision of the attempted rape of an obviously frightened, innocent virgin by a violent Sol would have made no sense at all. *A* is primarily a cruel taunting of Daphne: Quevedo wants to scare the daylights out of her and then laugh at her expense. Furthermore, the characterization of Jupiter and Mars as comrades-in-rape in *A* would have clashed with their portrayal in the Apollo sonnet as accommodating hus-tlers who buy their ready and willing mistresses.

What I have presented above as Quevedo's possible liter-ary concerns in revising his Daphne sonnet also conveniently conform to the pressures of Inquisition censorship, since the sex-ual obscenities are eliminated in the process. To what extent Quevedo was actually worried about the *Santo Oficio* we can only guess. Clearly, it is unlikely that version *A*, obscene as it was, could have been published in Quevedo's day, and indeed it was not; some three hundred years were to pass before it would appear in print. In the revised sonnet, we have an extraordinary new poem, whatever the cause that initiated the revisions— ignoble censorship, self-censorship, aesthetic motives, or all three. But we should not forget the original version, whose typically obscene and cruel bias, an explosion of Quevedo's obsessions, makes it a paradigm of the untamed Quevedo who suffered the many blades of censorship.

Notes

Introduction

1 "Hymn to Apollo," in *Hymns and Epigrams*, ed. and trans. A. W. Mair (Loeb Classical Library, 1955), 51ff. The translation is a revised version of Mair's.

2 Histoire des idées et critique littéraire, vol. 92 (Genève: Droz, 1968).

3 Studien der Bibliothek Warburg, vol. 23 (Leipzig: Teubner, 1932).

4 On the notion of transformation in Renaissance theories and practice of imitation, see, especially, G. W. Pigman III, "Versions of Imitation in the Renaissance," *Renaissance Quarterly* 33 (1980): 1–32; Thomas M. Greene, *The Light in Troy: Imitation and Discovery in Renaissance Poetry* (New Haven: Yale University Press, 1982); Nancy S. Struever, *The Language of History in the Renaissance: Rhetoric and Historical Consciousness in Florentine Humanism* (Princeton: Princeton University Press, 1970); A. J. Smith, "Theory and Practice in Renaissance Poetry: Two Kinds of Imitation," *Bulletin of the John Rylands Library* 47 (1964): 212–43.

5 *Le familiari*, ed. Vittorio Rossi and Umberto Bosco, 4 vols. (Florence: Sansoni, 1933–42), 1:44. The translation is adapted from Pigman's ("Versions of Imitation," 7).

6 *Mythology and the Renaissance Tradition in English Poetry* (1932; reprint, New York: Norton, 1963), xiii.

7 On the ornamental grotesque, see Nicole Dacos, *La Découverte de la Domus Aurea et la formation des grotesques à la Renaissance*, Studies of the Warburg Institute, vol. 31 (London: Warburg Institute, 1969); H. P. L'Orange, *Domus Aurea, der Sonnenpalast* (Oslo: Serta Eitremiana, 1942); Samuel Ball Platner, *A Topographical Dictionary of Ancient Rome* (London: Oxford University Press, H. Milford, 1929); Ernest Nash, *Pictorial Dictionary of Ancient Rome*, 2 vols. (New York and Washington: Frederick A. Praeger, 1961), with an excellent bibliography; and Axel Boëthius, *The Golden House of Nero. Some Aspects of Roman Architecture* (Ann Arbor: University of Michigan Press, 1960).

8 In the well known *De la pintura antigua* (first Portuguese edition, 1548) by Francisco de Holanda, "Michelangelo"—in a fictitious discussion on art—presents his conception of the grotesque: a means to delight the senses through variety and invention, a popular notion in the art world of his times. I have consulted the reprint of the 1563 Spanish translation by Manuel Denis (Madrid: Jaime Ratés, 1921), 188–89. Elsewhere, Michelangelo himself speaks in defense of unnatural and monstrous incongruity as a tool for decoration:

"One may rightly decorate better when one places in painting some monstrosity (for the diversion and relaxation of the senses and the attention of mortal eyes . . .)." Quoted in Robert J. Clements, *Michelangelo's Theory of Art* (London: Routledge & Kegan Paul, 1963), 217. Giorgio Vasari applauds Michelangelo's architectural style for the same reason that he admires the grotesque ornamentation, its originality in its departure from "measure, order, and rule." Vasari gives an account of Michelangelo's life and works in *Le vite*, ed. Gaetano Milanesi (Florence: Sansoni, 1906), 7: 135–404.

9 *Le vite*, 6:551–52 and 3:461–62.

10 *De architectura*, ed. and trans. Frank Granger (Loeb Classical Library, 1955–56), 2:105. I have made alterations in Granger's version.

11 L. P. Wilkinson, *Ovid Recalled* (Cambridge: Cambridge University Press, 1955), 160.

12 Georges Lafaye, *Les Métamorphoses d'Ovide et leurs modèles grecs*, Bibliothèque de la faculté des Lettres, vol. 19 (Paris: F. Alcan, 1904), 20–21.

13 The terms "paralysis of language" and "non-thing" are used by Geoffrey Harpham in his discussion of the grotesque form in his recent book, *On the Grotesque: Strategies of Contradiction in Art and Literature* (Princeton: Princeton University Press, 1982), 4, 6. E. H. Gombrich had already wrestled with this notion of the failure of language in defining the grotesque: "There are no names in our language, no categories in our thought, to come to grips with this elusive dream-imagery in which 'all things are mixed.' " See *The Sense of Order* (Ithaca: Cornell University Press, 1979), 256.

14 *The Sense of Beauty* (1896; reprint, New York: Dover, 1955), 4.64, 257.

15 *The Grotesque in Art and Literature*, trans. U. Weisstein (Bloomington: Indiana University Press, 1963), 184–86.

16 *The Ludicrous Demon: Aspects of the Grotesque in German Post–Romantic Prose* (Berkeley: University of California Press, 1963), 8.

17 For further thoughts on the grotesque, see Arthur Clayborough, *The Grotesque in English Literature* (1965; reprint, Oxford: Clarendon, 1967); Michael Steig, "Defining the Grotesque: An Attempt at Synthesis," *Journal of Aesthetics and Art Criticism* 29 (1970): 253–60; Philip Thomson, *The Grotesque* (London: Methuen, 1972); and, especially, Geoffrey Harpham, "The Grotesque: First Principles," *Journal of Aesthetics and Art Criticism* 34 (1976): 461–68.

18 Hermann Fränkel, *Ovid: A Poet between Two Worlds* (Berkeley and Los Angeles: University of California Press, 1945), 220 n. 72.

19 *Homo Ludens. A Study of the Play-Element in Culture* (Boston: Beacon, 1964), 129ff., 136ff.

20 *Ovid Recalled*, 160–63.

21 "Ovid's *Metamorphoses*: Greek Myth in Augustan Rome," *Studies in Philology* 68 (1971): 371–94 and *Landscape in Ovid's Metamorphoses: A Study in the Transformations of a Literary Symbol*, Hermes Einzelschriften, no. 23 (Wiesbaden: F. Steiner, 1969).

22 See *Rabelais and His World*, trans. Hélène Iswolsky (Cambridge: MIT Press, 1968).

23   Suppose you'd been asked to come for a private view
      Of a painting wherein the artist had chosen to join
      To a human head the neck of a horse, and gone on
      To collect some odds and ends of arms and legs
      And plaster the surface with feathers of differing colors,
      So that what began as a lovely woman at the top
      Tapered off into a slimy, discolored fish—

Could you keep from laughing, my friends? Believe me, dear Pisos,
Paintings like these look a lot like the book of a writer
Whose weird conceptions are just like a sick man's dreams,
So that neither the head nor the foot can be made to apply
To a single uniform shape.

In *The Satires and Epistles of Horace,* trans. Smith Palmer Bovie (Chicago: University of Chicago Press, 1959), 271. This passage has been often misread as a condemnation of the grotesque by Horace. But what Horace the critic offers here is a cautionary word to poets who should write homogeneous poems and keep from indulging in ridiculous mixtures. Horace the poet was no stranger to the grotesque. For instance, in Ode 2.20 he describes his transformation into a swan, a grotesque which is later imitated by Petrarch in his canzone 23, "Nel dolce tempo de la prima etade."

24 Cited in Neil Rhodes, *Elizabethan Grotesque* (London: Routledge & Kegan Paul, 1980), 7.

25 Antonio Gallego Morell, ed., *Garcilaso de la Vega y sus comentaristas* (Madrid: Gredos, 1972), 349 n. 93.

26 It has become increasingly apparent that critics who write on the grotesque often assign to it a response that belongs exclusively to the kind of grotesque they are discussing. Wolfgang Kayser, who deals with the Romantic and post-Romantic grotesque, finds the sinister and ominous even in the ornamental grotesque—and when he speaks of laughter, it is a "satanic" laughter *(The Grotesque in Art and Literature).* Mikhail Bakhtin's response to the grotesque is a gay, festive laughter since he treats a grotesque that belongs to folk, carnival humor *(Rabelais and His World).* And Vasari, who writes extensively on the decorative grotesque, finds only play in Bruegel's disturbing designs (Rhodes, *Elizabethan Grotesque,* 167 n. 16).

27 For details on Apollo's origin, appellatives, functions, and attributes, see Lewis R. Farnell, *The Cults of the Greek States,* 5 vols. (Oxford: Clarendon, 1896–1909), 4:98–306; Ludwig Preller, *Griechische Mythologie* (Berlin: Weidmann, 1860), 1:182–228; Paul Decharme, *Mythologie de la Grèce antique* (Paris: Garnier, 1879); Wilamowitz-Moellendorff, *Der Glaube der Hellenen,* 2 vols. (Berlin: Weidmann, 1931–32), 2:26–42 and passim.

28 Pausanias, *Description of Greece,* trans. W. H. S. Jones (Loeb Classical Library, 1961), 4:393. All references to Pausanias will come from this edition.

29 On Daphne's original character, see Joseph Fontenrose, *Orion: The Myth of the Hunter and the Huntress,* University of California Publications in Classical Studies, vol. 23 (Berkeley: University of California Press, 1981), 50–51.

30 See Wilhelm Vollgraff, *Nikander und Ovid* (Groningen: J. B. Wolters, 1909), 64.

31 In his commentary to Book I of the *Metamorphoses* (Heidelberg: Carl Winter, 1969), Franz Bömer suggests that Ovid is the first to deal with the Thessalian version of the myth with its Peneus-Tempe-Daphne-Apollo-Delphi connections (1:144–45). Bömer regards as inconclusive the evidence that cites Nicander's *Alexipharmaka* as an earlier treatment of the account. For further details on the versions of the myth with additional ancient sources, see *Realencyclopädie der classischen Altertumswissenschaft,* s. v. "Daphne," 4:2136–40; Brooks Otis, *Ovid as an Epic Poet* (Cambridge: Cambridge University Press, 1966), 350–53; Fontenrose, *Orion,* 48–68; Yves Giraud, *La Fable de Daphné,* 28–39; Hugo Magnus, "Ovids *Metamorphosen* in doppelter Fassung?" *Hermes* 40 (1905): 191–239.

There is also a Syrian version of the myth. However, this is a foundation legend which accounts for the origin of Daphne, a suburb near the city of Anti-
och on the Orontes. According to the story, Seleucus Nicator was hunting
when his horse uprooted an arrow with the inscription φο'ιβου. He draws the
conclusion that this is the place of the metamorphosis of Daphne, the daughter of the river Ladon, and the location where Phoebus-Apollo let his arrows
drop out of sorrow over the loss of the nymph. Seleucus founds the suburb
and builds a sanctuary there in honor of the god.

32 Farnell, *The Cults of the Greek States*, 4:124. My account of Apollo and the laurel
   is largely based on Farnell (4:188, 284–86). For details on the role of the laurel
   in Apollo's cult and ritual, see M. B. Ogle, "Laurel in Ancient Religion and
   Folklore," *American Journal of Philology* 31 (1910): 287–311 and P. Amandry, *La
   Mantique apollinienne à Delphes: Essai sur le fonctionnement de l'oracle* (Paris: E. de
   Boccard, 1950), 126–29, with abundant ancient sources.

33 *Hesiod. The Homeric Hymns and Homerica,* trans. Hugh G. Evelyn-White (Loeb
   Classical Library, 1964), 353.

34 *Myth, Ritual and Religion* (London: Longmans & Green, 1913), 2:226. In a more
   recent study Joseph Campbell, following the Jungian concept of the arche-
   types of the collective unconscious, interprets the myth in the context of the
   voyage of the mythical hero. See, *The Hero with a Thousand Faces* (1949; reprint,
   Cleveland and New York: World Publishing, 1970). Campbell sees Daphne as
   one who refuses the call to "adventure" (embodied in the figure of Apollo),
   for the maiden is unwilling to break the bond that ties her to her parent and
   seek a new world orientation. The metamorphosis is seen by him as a "dull
   and unrewarding finish." It represents the "impotence to put off the infantile
   ego, with its sphere of emotional relationships and ideals. . . . [Daphne] is
   bound in by the walls of childhood; the father and the mother stand as
   threshold guardians, and the timorous soul fearful of some punishment fails
   to make the passage through the door and come to birth in the world without" (62). It seems to me that Campbell's explanation is excessive. He utilizes
   Ovid's version to explain Daphne's story, and it has to be kept in mind that
   the Augustan poet is not a mythographer nor a faithful "recorder" of myths.
   The *Metamorphoses* abounds in fictional situations, and a case in point is Apollo's plea to the fleeing nymph which Campbell regards as "mythical."

1 *Ovid's* Metamorphoses

1 On the notion of play in Ovid, see Charles Altieri, "Ovid and the New Mythologists," *Novel: A Forum on Fiction* 7 (1973): 31–40 and Charles Segal,
  "Ovid's *Metamorphoses*: Greek Myth in Augustan Rome," *Studies in Philology* 68
  (1971): 371–94.

2 On this *topos*, see E. R. Curtius, *European Literature and the Latin Middle Ages*,
  trans. Willard R. Trask, 2d ed. (New York: Harper & Row, 1963), 417–35.

3 *Homo Ludens: A Study of the Play Element in Culture* (Boston: Beacon, 1964), 5.

4 In some Ovidian manuscripts, Daphne invokes the aid of Gaea, a detail that
  has given rise to the so-called "double-recension" controversy. In his edition
  of the *Metamorphoses* (Loeb Classical Library, 1966–68), F. J. Miller notes that
  the reference to Earth appeared as a result of an emendation (1:40 n. 1). Hugo
  Magnus ("Ovids *Metamorphosen* in doppelter Fassung?" *Hermes* 40 [1905]: 191–
  239) cites several versions of the verses and argues convincingly that the

words that introduce Earth are a result of a post–Ovidian interpolation. Less convincing are the arguments of Wilhelm Vollgraff (*Nikander und Ovid* [Groningen: J. B. Wolters, 1909], 69–90) and P. J. Enk ("*Metamorphoses* Ovidii duplici recensione," in *Ovidiana*, ed. N. I. Herescu [Paris: Les Belles Lettres, 1958], 324–29), who contend that Ovid himself introduces Gaea. Enk suggests that nothing prevents us from assuming that both Ovid and Hyginus, who includes both Peneus and Gaea in his version, drew from a common Greek source.

5 *Ovid as an Epic Poet* (Cambridge: Cambridge University Press, 1966), 102.

6 Certainly this is not the first time that Apollo has been subjected to such degradation. For instance, both Tibullus (2.3.11–28) and Ovid (*Ars amatoria*. 2.239–40) utilize the Apollo-Admetus story as *exemplum* to depict love's slavery. Among other things, Apollo pastured the cattle and lived in a humble hut, all in the name of love. On this question, see Frank O. Copley, "*Servitium amoris* in the Roman Elegists," *Transactions of the American Philological Association* 78 (1947): 292–93.

7 On the relation between *Amores* 1.1 and Apollo's encounter with Cupid, and its background in Callimachus' theophany in the *Aetia*, see W. S. M. Nicoll, "Cupid, Apollo, and Daphne (Ovid, *Met*. 1.452 ff.)," *Classical Quarterly* n. s., 30 (1980): 174–82.

8 Georg Luck, *The Latin Love Elegy* (London: Methuen, 1959), 152.

9 References to the Latin text of the *Metamorphoses* will come from the edition of M. Haupt, O. Korn, J. Müller, and R. Ehwald; rev. M. von Albrecht (Zurich and Dublin: Weidmann, 1966). English translations are from F. J. Miller (cited in note 4). I have made slight changes in Miller's translations.

10 For a study of this *topos*, see Archibald W. Allen, "Elegy and the Classical Attitude toward Love: Propertius I.1," *Yale Classical Studies* 11 (1950): 255–77. Allen defines the elegists' concept of love as a "violent passion, a fault which destroys the reason and perverts the will, but a power which the lover is helpless to control and from which he can find no release" (264). For the tradition of this figure, see J. L. Lowes, "The Loveres Maladye of Hereos," *Modern Philology* 11 (1914): 491–546.

11 Allen, "Elegy and the Classical Attitude toward Love," points out that in Latin love elegy the term *miser* has an almost technical meaning, for it defines the lover as the victim of a violent and irrational passion (259–60). Cf. Propertius 1.1.1, Catullus 76.19, and Ovid, *Amores* 1.1.25 and 1.4.59.

12 Charles Segal ("Ovid's *Metamorphoses*: Greek Myth in Augustan Rome," 391) and Brooks Otis (*Ovid as an Epic Poet*, 104) read too much seriousness here. Apollo's fear that Daphne will fall or scratch herself has less to do with solicitude (Otis) or gallantry (Segal) than with a means to have the nymph stop her flight.

13 On the relation of Ovid's wit and the rhetorical tradition in Apollo's plea to Daphne, see Nicolas P. Gross, "Rhetorical Wit and Amatory Persuasion in Ovid," *Classical Journal* 74 (1979): 305–7. Gross rightly notes that the wavering between Apollo's authoritarian divinity and his role as suppliant renders the god amusing. On the failure of Apollo's use of speech, see B. R. Fredericks, "Divine Wit vs. Divine Folly: Mercury and Apollo in *Metamorphoses* 1–2," *Classical Journal* 72 (1977): 244–49.

14 Hugh Parry, "Ovid's *Metamorphoses*: Violence in a Pastoral Landscape," *Transactions of the American Philological Association* 95 (1964): 270–72.

15 Cf. *Amores* 1.2.19, 29; *Met.* 2.873; *Ars amatoria* 1.125; *Heroides* 8.82.

16 L. P. Wilkinson, *Ovid Recalled* (Cambridge: Cambridge University Press, 1955), 125.

17 For a discussion of Ovid's parody of epic conventions in Apollo and Daphne, see Adolf Primmer, "Mythos und Natur in Ovids 'Apollo und Daphne,' " *Wiener Studien* 10 (1976): 210–20. Primmer, however, does not touch on the epic hunt as a parallel to Apollo's pursuit of Daphne. While it is true that Ovid treats epic elements humorously in the tale, he is not so much parodying Virgil and Homer, as Primmer suggests, as playfully treating the established epic values to taunt the true object of his comedy, the divine Apollo.

18 Mikhail Bakhtin, *Rabelais and His World*, trans. Hélène Iswolsky (Cambridge: MIT Press, 1968), 6.

19 Albin Lesky, *A History of Greek Literature*, trans. James Willis and Cornelis de Heer (London: Methuen, 1966), 234.

20 On Old and Middle Comedy in Greece, see Margarete Bieber, *The History of the Greek and Roman Theater*, 2d ed., rev. and enl. (Princeton: Princeton University Press, 1971), 36–53, with an extensive bibliography.

21 On the extant fragments of the *phlyakes*, see G. Kaibel, *Comicorum graecorum fragmenta* (Berlin: Weidmann, 1958), 183–97 and Alessandro Olivieri, *Frammenti della commedia greca e del mimo nella Sicilia e nella Magna Grecia*, 2d ed. (Naples: Libreria Scientifica Editrice, 1946). For further details on the *phlyakes* and *phlyax* vases, see Bieber, *Greek and Roman Theater*, 129–46 and *Die Denkmäler zum Theaterwesen im Altertum* (Berlin and Leipzig: Vereinigung Wissenschaftlicher Verleger, 1920), 138–53; Allardyce Nicoll, *Masks, Mimes and Miracles* (London: George G. Harrap, 1931), 50–65; A. D. Trendall, *Paestan Pottery: A Study of the Red-Figured Vases of Paestum* (London: Macmillan, 1936) and *Phlyax Vases*, Institute of Classical Studies no. 19, 2d ed., rev. and enl. (London: University of London, Institute of Classical Studies, 1967), with a good bibliography; and Arthur Pickard-Cambridge, *The Dramatic Festivals of Athens* (Oxford: Clarendon, 1953), 235ff.

22 On this vase, see Bieber, *Greek and Roman Theater*, 131; Trendall, *Paestan Pottery*, 37–38; and G. Karl Galinsky, *The Herakles Theme* (Oxford: Basil Blackwell, 1972), 95–96.

23 Thomas Wright, *A History of Caricature and Grotesque in Literature and Art* (1865; reprint, New York: Frederick Ungar, 1968), 18–19 and Champfleury, *Histoire de la caricature antique* (Paris: F. Dentu, 1879), 187–88. As is the case with many of the *phlyax* vases, the scene on the Apulia vase has been the object of differing interpretations. Bieber, *Greek and Roman Theater*, 135, interprets the scene as the journey of Cheiron to "a watering place seeking a cure among the nymphs for his gout or arthritis. . . . A servant named Xanthias pulls him onto the stage by the head, while another servant pushes him forcibly from behind." Achilles, student of Cheiron, is the young man standing at the right hand side, and the nymphs are the "ugly old ladies" looking on from above. Bieber leaves out of her analysis the cap, the bag and the bow, for which she apparently finds no explanation. Ettore Romagnoli in his *Nel regno di Dioniso* (Bologna: Nicola Zanichelli, 1953) finds the scene less clear to interpret. According to him, it simply shows two servants (one called Santia) helping an old man up the steps, and looking on are two nymphs and a young man (27).

24 T. B. L. Webster ("South Italian Vases and Attic Drama," *Classical Quarterly* 42 [1948]: 22), speculates that the scene on this vase may show either Hermes or

Apollo giving Ion to the Pythia in Eubulus' *Ion,* and that the old man may be Zeus or Xuthus.

25 Huizinga, *Homo Ludens,* 13.

26 To my knowledge, there is no extant example of a comic Apollo on the Roman stage. There is plenty of evidence, however, of the travesties of other mythological figures; the best known is Plautus' burlesque of Zeus and Alcmena in his *Amphitruo.* On Roman comedies, farces, and mimes see, especially, William Beare, *The Roman Stage,* 3d ed. (London: Methuen, 1964); Bieber, *Greek and Roman Theater,* 147–60, 227–53; Nicoll, *Masks, Mimes and Miracles,* 65–134; and George D. Duckworth, *The Nature of Roman Comedy* (Princeton: Princeton University Press, 1952).

27 On carnival laughter, see Mikhail Bakhtin, *Rabelais and His World* and C. L. Barber, *Shakespeare's Festive Comedy* (Princeton: Princeton University Press, 1959).

28 See, especially, Otis, *Ovid as an Epic Poet,* 323ff.; Charles Segal, "Myth and Philosophy in the *Metamorphoses:* Ovid's Augustanism and the Augustan Conclusion of Book XV," *American Journal of Philology* 90 (1969): 257–92 and "Ovid's *Metamorphoses:* Greek Myth in Augustan Rome," 392–93; G. Karl Galinsky, "The Cipus Episode in Ovid's *Metamorphoses* (15.565–621)," *Transactions of the American Philological Association* 98 (1967): 181–91. On anti-Augustan elements in the *Tristia,* see R. Marache, "La Révolte d'Ovide exilé contre Auguste," in *Ovidiana,* 412–19.

29 The phrase is Cedric H. Whitman's in *Aristophanes and the Comic Hero* (1964; reprint, Cambridge: Harvard University Press, 1971), 10.

30 On Callimachus' lighthearted humor, see Bruno Snell, "Art and Play in Callimachus," in *The Discovery of the Mind,* trans. T. G. Rosenmeyer (Oxford: Basil Blackwell, 1953), 264–80.

31 Not all of Ovid's comedy is based, however, on this type of incongruity between solemnity and lowly behavior. Examples are Ovid's play of masks to show the silly liar and, as we shall see later, Apollo kissing the laurel in comic rigidity, followed by his humorously feeble (and unsuccessful) attempt to escape Ovid's comic world through his solemn paean.

32 Hermann Fränkel has touched on this topic in *Ovid: A Poet between Two Worlds* (Berkeley and Los Angeles: Univ. of California Press, 1945), 78, 99. For further details on the theme of metamorphosis and identity, see Simone Viarre, *L'Image et la pensée dans les Métamorphoses d'Ovide* (Paris: Presses Universitaires de France, 1964), 298–302 and passim, and G. Karl Galinsky, *Ovid's Metamorphoses: An Introduction to the Basic Aspects* (Berkeley and Los Angeles: University of California Press, 1975), 45–51.

33 *Ovid Recalled,* 160.

34 Ovid often speaks of mythology as fiction. Cf. *Tristia* 2.64, 3.8.1–2, and 4.7.11–20; *Am.* 3.12.21–42, 3.4.13–18. It is equally doubtful that Ovid's educated contemporaries believed in the literal truth of the mythical legends.

35 *Ovid: A Poet between Two Worlds,* 110. Fränkel suggests further that the "rationalizing spirit" of Pythagoras' speech contradicts the mythological stories, which are "not to be believed." But this explanation is somewhat misleading, for the changes that Pythagoras speaks about do not contradict those in the *Metamorphoses.* Pythagoras' notions and the tales of transformation never quite really "meet," except for one fleeting moment as will be seen next. For an excellent discussion of the relation between myth and philosophy in Ovid, see

Douglas Little, "The Speech of Pythagoras in *Metamorphoses* 15 and the Structure of the *Metamorphoses*," *Hermes* 98 (1970): 340–60. Little expounds on Fränkel's position.

36 Charles Segal has touched on this connection between Pythagoras' speech and the transformations in "Myth and Philosophy in the *Metamorphoses*," 284–88.

37 "Ovid's *Metamorphoses*: Greek Myth in Augustan Rome," 384, 393.

38 On this ambivalent aspect of the grotesque, see Geoffrey Harpham, *On the Grotesque: Strategies of Contradiction in Art and Literature* (Princeton: Princeton University Press, 1982), 71–72 and passim.

39 Philip Thomson, *The Grotesque* (London: Methuen, 1972), 64.

40 On the laurel and laurel wreath as Augustus' "personal badge of honor," see G. Karl Galinsky, "The Cipus Episode in Ovid's *Metamorphoses*," 185–86, with bibliography, especially, F. Bömer (*P. Ovidius Naso. Die Fasten: Kommentar* [Heidelberg: C. Winter, 1957], 2: 151–52) who documents literary and epigraphic sources. Galinsky offers an interesting analysis of Ovid's use of the laurel to effect a veiled mockery of Augustan ideals in the Cipus story.

41 On this theme in classical poetry, see Frank O. Copley, *Exclusus amator: A Study in Latin Love Poetry* (Madison: American Philological Association, 1956); Elizabeth H. Haight, *The Symbolism of the House Door in Classical Poetry* (New York: Longmans & Green, 1950); and J. C. Yardley, "The Elegiac Paraclausithyron," *Eranos* 76 (1978): 19–34.

42 See, for instance, W. H. Friedrich, "Der Kosmos Ovids," in *Festschrift Franz Dornseiff* (Leipzig: Bibliographisches Institut, 1953), 97ff.

43 *A Poet between Two Worlds*, 99.

2   *Ovid's Medieval Commentators*

1 L. P. Wilkinson, *Ovid Recalled* (Cambridge: Cambridge University Press, 1955), 367.

2 See Dorothy M. Robathan, "Ovid in the Middle Ages," in *Ovid*, ed. J. W. Binns (London and Boston: Routledge, 1973), 191.

3 *Ovid and the Renascence in Spain*, University of California Publications in Modern Philology, vol. 4, no. 1 (Berkeley: University of California Press, 1913), 10. E. R. Curtius suggests that while "Virgil remained the backbone of Latin studies," Ovid's *Fasti* and *Ex Ponto* were merely tolerated and his erotic poetry and the *Metamorphoses* were rejected. See *European Literature and the Latin Middle Ages*, trans. Willard R. Trask, 2d ed. (New York: Harper & Row, 1963), 36, 49.

4 Cited in Hans Liebeschütz, *Fulgentius metaforalis, ein Beitrag zur Geschichte der antiken Mythologie im Mittelalter*, Studien der Bibliothek Warburg, vol. 4 (Leipzig: Teubner, 1926), 21 n. 34.

5 Lester K. Born, "Ovid and Allegory," *Speculum* 9 (1934): 370. On the fate of Ovid in the Middle Ages see, especially, Giovanni Pansa, *Ovidio nel medioevo e nella tradizione popolare* (Sulmona: U. Caroselli, 1924); Karl Bartsch, *Albrecht von Halberstadt und Ovid im Mittelalter* 1861; reprint; Amsterdam: Editions Rodopi, 1965); Franco Munari, *Ovid im Mittelalter* (Zurich: Artemis, 1960); E. K. Rand, *Ovid and His Influence* (New York: Plimpton Press, 1928); and Liebeschütz's introduction to the *Fulgentius metaforalis*, an excellent analysis of the medieval mythographical tradition. The literature on the subject is extensive.

6 See *Vorlesungen und Abhandlungen,* 3 vols. (München: C. H. Beck, 1909–20), 2:115.

7 See Jean Pépin, *Mythe et allégorie. Les Origines grecques et les contestations judéo-chrétiennes,* 2d ed. (Paris: Etudes Augustiniennes, 1976), 97–98. See also Paul Decharme, *La Critique des traditions religieuses chez les Grecs* (Paris: Alphonse Picard, 1904), 273–75.

8 I have consulted Félix Buffière, translation from the Greek, *Héraclite: Allégories d'Homère* (Paris: Les Belles Lettres, 1962). On the pseudo-Heraclitus, see Félix Buffière, *Les Mythes d'Homère et la pensée grecque* (Paris: Les Belles Lettres, 1956) and Pépin, *Mythe et allégorie,* 159–67.

9 Curtius, *European Literature and the Latin Middle Ages,* 203. On the *topos* of the poet as sage, see 203–27.

10 J. D. Cooke, "Euhemerism: A Mediaeval Interpretation of Classical Paganism," *Speculum* 2 (1927): 396. See also Paul Alphandéry, "L'Evhémérisme et les débuts de l'histoire des religions au moyen âge," *Revue de l'histoire des religions* 109 (1934): 5–27.

11 Jean Seznec, *The Survival of the Pagan Gods,* trans. Barbara F. Sessions (1953; reprint, New York: Harper & Row, 1961), 12. Seznec also notes that in the *Tusculan Disputations* (I.12–13) Cicero seems to admit the euhemeristic explanation of the gods (12 n. 5).

12 *Servianorum in Vergilii carmina commentariorum,* 3 vols., ed. Edward Kennard Rand et al. (Lancaster, Pa.: American Philological Association, 1946–65). References to the commentary, written c. 395/410, will come from this edition. On Servius' allegorical method, see J. W. Jones, "Allegorical Interpretation in Servius," *Classical Journal* 56 (1961): 217–26.

13 I have consulted Thomas Muncker's edition (Amsterdam: Joannis à Someren, 1681). All references to Fulgentius will come from this edition. For studies on Fulgentius (c. 480/550), see Max L. W. Laistner, "Fulgentius in the Carolingian Age," in *The Intellectual Heritage of the Early Middle Ages,* ed. Chester G. Starr (1957; reprint, New York: Octagon Books, 1966), 202–15, and Domenico Comparetti, *Virgilio nel medio evo,* ed. Giorgio Pasquali (Florence: "La Nuova Italia" Editrice, 1955).

14 The text of Macrobius to be used throughout is James Willis's edition, vol. 1 (Leipzig: Teubner, 1963). For a study of Macrobius, see Pierre Courcelle, *Late Latin Writers and Their Greek Sources,* trans. Harry E. Wedeck (Cambridge: Harvard University Press, 1969), 13–47. This is a translation of *Les Lettres grecques en occident de Macrobe à Cassiodore* (Paris, 1948). Courcelle places the date of composition of the *Saturnalia* around 395 (13 n. 3).

15 Edited by James Willis (Leipzig: Teubner, 1983). The traditional view places the treaty between 410 and 439. On Martianus, see Pierre Courcelle, *Late Latin Writers,* 211–19; on the date of this work, see 211 n. 19.

16 *Etymologiarum sive originum libri xx,* 2 vols., ed. W. M. Lindsay (Oxford: Clarendon, 1911).

17 Rabanus Maurus' ninth century work appears in Migne, *Patrologia latina* 111. 9–614.

18 This work has been edited by Cora E. Lutz, *Commentum in Martianum Capellam,* 2 vols. (Leiden: E. J. Brill, 1962–65). There are two other extant Carolingian commentaries on Martianus: Dunchad, *Glossae in Martianum,* ed. Cora E. Lutz (Lancaster, Pa.: American Philological Association, 1944) and Johannes Scotus, *Annotationes in Marcianum,* ed. Cora E. Lutz (Cambridge, Mass.: Me-

diaeval Academy of America, 1939). On the commentaries, see Cora E. Lutz, "The Commentary of Remigius of Auxerre on Martianus Capella," *Mediaeval Studies* 19 (1957): 137–56 and M. L. W. Laistner, "Martianus Capella and His Ninth Century Commentators," *Bulletin of the John Rylands Library* 9 (1925): 130–38.

19 The Vatican mythographers have been edited by Georg Heinrich Bode, *Scriptores rerum mythicarum Latini tres,* 2 vols. (Cellis: E. H. C. Schulze, 1834). For details on manuscripts, authorship, and date of these treatises, see Kathleen O. Elliott and J. P. Elder, "A Critical Edition of the Vatican Mythographers," *Transactions of the American Philological Association* 78 (1947): 189–207. On the sources of the third Vatican mythographer, the chief source of mythographical information up to the fourteenth century, see Robert Raschke, *De Alberico mythologo,* Breslauer Philologische Abhandlungen, vol. 45 (Breslau: M. & H. Marcus, 1913), 1–164. Raschke (72–88) notes that the third Vatican mythographer draws on several sources for his allegorization of Apollo: Fulgentius, Remigius' commentary on Martianus Capella, Servius, Statius' *Thebaid,* and the *Saturnalia* and *Comm. in Somnium Scipionis* by Macrobius.

20 D. C. Allen, *Mysteriously Meant* (Baltimore: Johns Hopkins University Press, 1970), 3–5. See also Gerard L. Ellspermann, *The Attitude of the Early Christian Latin Writers towards Pagan Literature and Learning,* C. U. A. Patristic Studies, vol. 82 (Washington, D.C.: Catholic University of America Press, 1949).

21 Migne, *Patrologia graeca* 9.410.

22 Cited in Curtius, *European Literature,* 219. For further details on the attitude of the Church Fathers toward classical learning, see Ellspermann, *Early Christian Latin Writers;* Jean Pépin, *Mythe et allégorie,* 260–474; and Henry Chadwick, *Early Christian Thought and the Classical Tradition* (New York: Oxford University Press, 1966).

23 *Allegorical Imagery: Some Mediaeval Books and Their Posterity* (Princeton: Princeton University Press, 1966), 304.

24 Edited by Fausto Guisalberti, "Arnolfo d'Orléans, un cultore di Ovidio nel secolo XII," *Memorie del Reale Istituto Lombardo di Scienze e Lettere* 24 (15 della serie III), fasc. 4 (1932): 157–234, with notes and a fine introduction. The title of the treatise is Guisalberti's as well as the division into books and chapters. Guisalberti is helpful in pointing out some of Arnulf's sources. Translations are mine.

25 "Arnolfo d'Orléans," 181. On the "accessus" in medieval literature, including Arnulf's, see Fausto Guisalberti, "Mediaeval Biographies of Ovid," *Journal of the Warburg and Courtauld Institutes* 9 (1946): 10–59.

26 An exception is Paule Demats, *Fabula: Trois études de mythographie antique et médiévale* (Genève: Droz, 1973).

27 For details on the Pythian combat, see Joseph Fontenrose, *Python: A Study of Delphic Myth and Its Origins* (Berkeley and Los Angeles: University of California Press, 1959), 13–22.

28 "Arnolfo d'Orléans," 202 n. 8.

29 Lewis R. Farnell, *The Cult of the Greek States,* 5 vols. (Oxford: Clarendon, 1896–1909), 4:242. I am indebted to Farnell for my discussion of the relation of Apollo with truth and wisdom.

30 W. S. M. Nicoll, "Cupid, Apollo, and Daphne (Ovid, *Met.* 1.452ff.)," *Classical Quarterly,* n.s., 30 (1980): 181.

31 Prudentius, ed. and trans. H. J. Thomson, 2 vols. (Loeb Classical Library,

1949–53), 1:274–343. For details on the *Psychomachia,* see C. S. Lewis, *The Allegory of Love* (1936; reprint, New York: Oxford University Press, 1958), 66–73 and Adolf Katzenellenbogen, *Allegories of the Virtues and Vices in Medieval Art,* trans. J. P. Crick, Studies of the Warburg Institute, vol. 10 (London: Warburg Institute, 1939), 1–13. See also Angus Fletcher, *Allegory: The Theory of a Symbolic Mode* (1964; reprint, Ithaca: Cornell University Press, 1970), 157–61. Fletcher calls this moral battle the "primary symbol of Christian allegory." For details see, especially, 199–205.

32 *Homo Ludens: A Study of the Play Element in Culture* (Boston: Beacon, 1964), 116.

33 Edited by Fausto Guisalberti, *Integumenta Ovidii, poemetto inedito del secolo XIII* (Messina-Milano: Giuseppe Principato, 1933), with notes and a helpful introduction. On the manuscripts of this commentary, see Lester K. Born, "The Manuscripts of the *Integumenta* on the *Metamorphoses* of Ovid by John of Garland," *Transactions of the American Philological Association* 60 (1929): 179–99 and Guisalberti, 8–12, 32–33. On John of Garland and his works, see Louis John Paetow, *Morale scolarium of John of Garland* (Berkeley: University of California Press, 1927), 77–145. Translation is mine.

34 I have consulted Fausto Guisalberti's edition, "Giovanni del Virgilio, espositore delle *Metamorfosi,*" *Il Giornale Dantesco* 34 (1933): 3–110. For details on Giovanni's commentary, see Philip H. Wicksteed and Edmund G. Gardner, *Dante and Giovanni del Virgilio* (Westminster: A. Constable, 1902).

35 Edited by C. de Boer in Verhandelingen der Koninklijke Akademie van Wetenschappen, vols. 15–43 (Amsterdam: Johannes Müller, 1915–38). The myth of Apollo and Daphne appears in volume 15. For details on authorship, date, and general characteristics, see Joseph Engels, *Etudes sur l'Ovide moralisé* (Groningen: J. B. Wolters, 1945), 46–84. Engels also includes a short study of the first book, 87–142. There is a prose rendition of the *Ovide moralisé* called the *Ovide moralisé en prose* (1466–67), edited by C. de Boer in Verhandelingen der Koninklijke Nederlandse Akademie van Wetenschappen, vol. 61 (Amsterdam: Noord-Hollandsche, 1954). This work is an abridged version of the original with glosses from numerous sources. For details, see de Boer's introduction, 5–14. Ernest Langlois has described the manuscript (Vat. Reg. 1686) in "Une Rédaction en prose de l'*Ovide moralisé,*" *Bibliothèque de l'Ecole des Chartes* 62 (1901): 251 no. 1. My translations of the *Ovide moralisé* have benefited from suggestions by Alan Knight, Caroline Eckhardt, and Robert Lima.

36 See de Boer's introduction, 15:21–27 and Engels, *Etudes sur l'Ovide moralisé,* 69–71.

37 See "Blind Cupid," in *Studies in Iconology* (1939; reprint, New York: Harper & Row, 1967), 98–128.

38 For details on this canon of beauty, see M. B. Ogle, "The Classical Origin and Tradition of Literary Conceits," *American Journal of Philology* 34 (1913): 125–52.

39 On these playful grotesques, see Geoffrey Harpham, *On the Grotesque: Strategies of Contradiction in Art and Literature* (Princeton: Princeton University Press, 1982), 75, 82.

40 Cited in E. H. Gombrich, *The Sense of Order* (Ithaca: Cornell University Press, 1979), 255.

41 Philo discards the claim of the Greek Homeric and Hesiodic exegetes that mythology contains philosophical truths that may be elicited by allegory. But, as H. A. Wolfson suggests, "what he denies to mythology he claims for the divinely revealed Hebrew Scripture." See *Philo: Foundations of Religious Philosophy*

in Judaism, Christianity, and Islam, 2 vols. (1947; reprint, Cambridge: Harvard University Press, 1948), 1:133. For details on Philo's interpretations and his borrowings from the twofold method of Greek allegory, see Wolfson, *The Philosophy of the Church Fathers* (1956; reprint, Cambridge: Harvard University Press, 1970), vol. 1, *Faith, Trinity, Incarnation,* 30–38.

42 See H. A. Wolfson, *The Church Fathers,* 1:24. For details on Paul's typology, see Samuel Amsler, "La Typologie de l'Ancien Testament chez Saint Paul," *Revue de Théologie et de Philosophie* 37 (1949): 114–28. On the typology of the Fathers see, especially, Jean Daniélou, *Origène* (Paris: La Table Ronde, 1949) and *From Shadows to Reality: Studies in the Biblical Typology of the Fathers,* trans. D. W. Hibberd (London: Burns & Oates, 1960); R. M. Grant, *The Letter and the Spirit* (London: S.P.C.K., 1957), 58–104; and R. P. C. Hanson, *Allegory and Event* (London: S.C.M. Press, 1959).

43 For details on Adamic typology in Paul, see Jean Daniélou, *From Shadows to Reality,* 18–21.

44 The Stoic tradition, with its commonplace of Apollo as the sun, provides the Minorite with the point of departure for his physical explanation: Apollo is the all-illuminating sun whose "amorous" rays, along with the moisture of the banks of the river Peneus, make the laurels there grow and multiply (3065–74). The euhemeristic interpretation explains the tale as an unhappy story of modesty and love. Daphne is a rich, young, and noble maiden who wants to lead a chaste life. After having tried in vain to tempt her, Apollo pursues the maiden who flees to safeguard her honor. The chase brings death to the virgin, and she is buried under a laurel. Hence, the legend of Daphne's metamorphosis into the tree (3075–3108). The Minorite's moral allegory follows familiar steps. Daphne stands for the virtue of chastity (3111–15), and she flees her lover to escape corruption. (This latter detail is present in patristic writings. Clement of Alexandria speaks of Daphne as the only one of Apollo's loves to escape "the prophet and his corruption." See *The Exhortation to the Greeks,* trans. G. W. Butterworth [Loeb Classical Library, 1960], 67.) The metamorphosis into the laurel signifies her emancipation from the temptations of the flesh. The monstrous Python signifies evil (2651–52), which is conquered by Apollo, who symbolizes wisdom. Whereas the allegorical explanation of Daphne closely follows the literal meaning of the text, the Minorite's interpretation of Apollo reverses and negates what the poem tells. For despite the damaging display of the god's intellectual and moral downfall, he becomes the symbol of wisdom. It is evident, however, that in this allegorization the commentator is merely imitating tradition. He seems to draw from John of Garland for his explanation:

> C'est Phebus, que l'Integument,
> Selonc la paienne creence,
> Apele dieu de sapience,
> Qui tout enseigne et endouctrine. (3126–29)

> (Following pagan belief,
> The Integument calls Phoebus
> The god of wisdom,
> Who teaches and indoctrinates all.)

However, Fausto Guisalberti in his introduction to the *Integumenta* (13–14) has pointed out that the commentator must have used as his source a fourteenth-century codex with glosses in which it was customary to introduce an allegory with the expression *Integumentum de*. So it is possible that the Minorite drew upon a marginal commentary which included John of Garland's interpretation as well as others.

45 Erich Auerbach, "Typological Symbolism in Medieval Literature," *Yale French Studies* 9 (1952): 6. See also G. W. H. Lampe and K. J. Woollcombe, *Essays on Typology*, Studies in Biblical Theology, no. 22 (Naperville, Ill.: Alec. R. Allenson, 1957) and Auerbach, "Figura," in *Scenes from the Drama of European Literature* (New York: Meridian, 1959), 11–76.

46 Auerbach, "Typological Symbolism," 5.

47 Hugo Rahner, *Greek Myths and Christian Mystery*, trans. Brian Battershaw (New York: Harper & Row, 1963), 97. For additional details on Christian solar imagery, cf. F. J. Dölger, *Sol salutis. Gebet und Gesang im christlichen Altertum* (Münster: Aschendorff, 1925).

48 Scripture contains numerous references to the healing powers of Christ. See, for instance, Matt. 4:23, Luke 5:17, and John 4:47.

49 For details on this question, see Wolfson, *Church Fathers*, 1:245–49.

50 The Minorite does not employ the terms Christological, mystical, or eschatological. But since his interpretations follow familiar lines of Biblical exegesis, they can be easily recognized and labeled with traditional terms as I have done. The threefold typological terminology was drawn from Jean Daniélou's analysis of Origen's typological method regarding the fall of Jericho in *From Shadows to Reality*, 277.

51 In I Cor. 9:24–25, Saint Paul evokes the crown bestowed upon the triumphant Christian: "Know you not that they that run in the race, all run indeed, but one receiveth the prize? So run that you may obtain. / And every one that striveth for the mastery, refraineth himself from all things: and they indeed that they may receive a corruptible crown, but we an incorruptible one."

52 For a discussion of Orpheus-Christus in early Christianity, see John B. Friedman, *Orpheus in the Middle Ages* (Cambridge: Harvard University Press, 1970), 38–85.

53 *Orpheus in the Middle Ages*, 220 n. 34.

54 Quoted in Rahner, *Greek Myths and Christian Mystery*, 122. On the use of pagan imagery by early Christians, see also Harald Hagendahl, "Pagan Mythology and Poetry Applied to Christian Beliefs," in *Latin Fathers and the Classics*, Studia Graeca et Latina Gothoburgensia, vol. 6 (Göteborg: Elanders Boktryckeri Aktiebolag, 1958), 382–95.

55 On the theme of sacred and profane love, see M. C. D'Arcy, *The Mind and Heart of Love, Lion and Unicorn: A Study in Eros and Agape*, (1947; reprint, New York: Meridian, 1956) and Mario Praz, "Profane and Sacred Love," in *Studies in Seventeenth-Century Imagery* (Roma: Edizioni di Storia e Letteratura, 1964), 83–168.

56 "Art and Play in Callimachus," in *The Discovery of the Mind*, trans. T. G. Rosenmeyer (Oxford: Basil Blackwell, 1953), 276.

57 "The Joseph Scenes on the Maximianus Throne," in *Late Antique, Early Christian and Mediaeval Art* (New York: Braziller, 1979), 43.

58 Beryl Smalley, *English Friars and Antiquity in the Early Fourteenth Century* (Oxford: Basil Blackwell, 1960), 261.

59 *De formis figurisque deorum* has been edited by Joseph Engels, *Reductorium mo-*

rale, liber XV: Ovidius moralizatus, cap. i., De formis figurisque deorum (Utrecht: Rijksuniversiteit. Instituut voor Laat Latijn, 1966). Bersuire's moralization of Ovid's tales has been edited by Fausto Guisalberti, *L'Ovidius moralizatus di Pierre Bersuire*, Studj Romanzi, vol. 23 (Roma: Presso la Società, 1933). Guisalberti publishes only portions of the treatise. The *Ovidius moralizatus* has been attributed at various times to Thomas Waleys, Robert Holkot, and John Ridevall, among others. But Barthélemy Hauréau, in his conclusive study on the matter, assigns it to Pierre Bersuire. See "Mémoire sur un commentaire des *Métamorphoses d'Ovide,*" *Mémoires de l'Académie des Inscriptions et Belles-Lettres* 30 (1883): 45–55. There is a French rendition of *De formis figurisque deorum* which has been edited by Jeannette van't Sant with the title *Le Commentaire de Copenhague de l'Ovide moralisé* (Amsterdam: H. J. Paris, 1929). For a helpful list of studies on Bersuire, see Joseph Engels, "Berchoriana I: Notice bibliographique sur Pierre Bersuire," *Vivarium* 86 (1964): 62–112. Translations from Bersuire are mine.

60 Nicola Festa (Firenze: G. C. Sansoni, 1926), 58. The translation is by Thomas G. Bergin and Alice S. Wilson (New Haven: Yale University Press, 1977), 47.

61 Ernest H. Wilkins has given a short point by point comparative analysis of the representation of Apollo in Petrarch and Bersuire in order to show the close correspondence that exists between the two. See "Descriptions of Pagan Divinities from Petrarch to Chaucer," *Speculum* 32 (1957): 516. It is evident, however, that aside from the use of the same attributes (Bersuire adds the crow and the tripod), Apollo's image and its meaning in the *Ovidius moralizatus* are quite different from those in the *Africa*.

62 *The Consolation of Philosophy*, trans. Richard Green (New York: Bobbs-Merrill, 1962), 4.3, 82–83.

63 D. W. Robertson, Jr., *A Preface to Chaucer* (Princeton: Princeton University Press, 1962), 155.

64 See Allardyce Nicoll, *Masks, Mimes and Miracles* (London: George G. Harrap, 1931), 187–92.

65 On Schöngauer's grotesque, see Geoffrey Harpham, *On the Grotesque*, 4–5.

66 The actual words of the Vulgate are: "Super aspidem et basiliscum ambulabis: et conculcabis leonem et draconem" ("You will walk upon the asp and the basilisk: and you shall trample under foot the lion and the dragon").

67 For details concerning this motif, see Katzenellenbogen, *Allegories of the Vices and Virtues in Medieval Art*, 14–21.

68 See, for instance, the third Vatican mythographer (8.1) and Remigius I.19.11.

69 For details on these illustrated texts, see Erwin Panofsky and Fritz Saxl, "Classical Mythology in Mediaeval Art," *Metropolitan Museum Studies* 4 (1933): 242–45.

70 Liebeschütz, *Fulgentius metaforalis*, fig. 5.

71 On the crisis of the fourteenth century, see, especially, Barbara W. Tuchman, *A Distant Mirror: The Calamitous 14th Century* (New York: Knopf, 1978).

72 See Guisalberti, *L'Ovidius moralizatus*, 102–4.

73 This treatise (Vatican Library, Cod. Reg. 1290) has been edited by Hans Liebeschütz in his edition of the *Fulgentius metaforalis*, 117–28, with illustrations. For a comparison of this work with those of other mythographers, see Liebeschütz, 58–64. See also Erwin Panofsky, *Renaissance and Renascences in Western Art* (New York: Harper & Row, 1960), 79–81 n. 2. On the question of sources,

see Raschke, *De Alberico mythologo,* 138–64; on Apollo, see 141–42. Raschke wrongly attributes the work to Alberic, the third Vatican mythographer.

74 Seznec, *The Survival of the Pagan Gods,* 176.

75 Two of the most important manuals of mythography after Bersuire's are Boccaccio's *Genealogia deorum gentilium* and Thomas Walsingham's *De archana deorum.* I do not treat them in detail because Boccaccio's exposition of Apollo and Daphne does not touch on the themes of love, agon, and the grotesque, and Walsingham's work is but an exhaustive compilation of what was previously said by the mythographers and Ovidian commentators. They exert enough influence, however, to warrant a few comments. Boccaccio's *Genealogia,* written sometime between 1363 and 1373—obviously before *L'Epître d'Othéa* by Christine de Pisan, who uses it as a model—is not a commentary of Ovid. The first thirteen books deal with ancient myth as a whole; the last two are a defense of poetry. Boccaccio's work is in essence an encyclopedia, and its purpose in treating myth is not to instruct but to collect and save the ancient and medieval legacy concerning mythological lore, with its historical, cosmological, moral, and even religious truths, for the student of classical poetry and history. Boccaccio's short exposition of the myth of Apollo and Daphne deals with a physical explanation (Daphne-humidity, Apollo-sun) and a discussion of the laurel as a symbol of glory and fame. See Vincenzo Romano's edition (Bari: Gius. Laterza, 1951), 1:363–64. On Boccaccio's *Genealogia,* see Charles G. Osgood, *Boccaccio on Poetry* (1930; reprint, New York: Liberal Arts Press, 1956); Ernest H. Wilkins, "The Genealogy of the Editions of the *Genealogia deorum,*" *Modern Philology* 17 (1919): 425–38; and Cornelia C. Coulter, "The Genealogy of the Gods," in *Vassar Medieval Studies,* ed. Christabel Forsyth Fiske (New Haven: Yale University Press, 1923), 317–41. Like Boccaccio's *Genealogia,* the purpose of Walsingham's treatise, which was written in the early fifteenth century, is not to edify. It is a manual for poets and students of classical poetry, a huge compendium of mythographical information on the iconography and the nature of the gods, with all the allegorical baggage bequeathed to him by mythographers and commentators. His exposition of Apollo and his attributes—Python, Cupid, and Daphne—in book one (chapters 8, 20, 33, and 34) is drawn almost word for word from the third Vatican mythographer and Bersuire's *Ovidius moralizatus.* Unlike Bersuire, however, Walsingham concentrates on physical and moral interpretations, excluding the religious. He also quotes from Ovid at length, showing his humanistic interests. *De archana deorum* has been edited by Robert A. van Kluyve (Durham: Duke University Press, 1968), with a helpful introduction.

76 The miniatures of this manuscript (no. 9392) have been reproduced in J. van den Gheyn, *Epître d'Othéa. . . . Reproduction des 100 miniatures du manuscrit 9392 de Jean Miélot* (Brussels: Vromant, 1913).

77 *Allegorical Imagery,* 34.

78 There is no edition of the French text. I quote from Stephen Scrope's translation, edited by Curt F. Bühler (London: Oxford University Press, 1970), 20. George F. Warner has also edited Scrope's translation (London: J. B. Nichols, 1904). There is another English translation ascribed to Anthony Babyngton and edited by James D. Gordon, *The Epistle of Othéa to Hector: A 'Lytil Bibell of Knyghthod'* (Diss., University of Pennsylvania, 1940). On Christine's *Epître,* see P. G. C. Campbell, *L'Epître d'Othéa: Etude sur les sources de Christine de Pisan*

(Paris: Librairie Ancienne Honoré Champion, 1924); Marie-Josèphe Pinet, *Christine de Pisan, 1364–1430: Etude biographique et littéraire* (1927; reprint, Genève: Slatkine Reprints, 1974), 272–80; and Rosemond Tuve, *Allegorical Imagery*, 33–45, 285–311. For a recent bibliography on Christine, see Angus J. Kennedy, *Christine de Pizan: A Bibliographical Guide* (London: Grant & Cutler, 1984).
79 *The Waning of the Middle Ages* (New York: Doubleday, 1954), 152.

3 Petrarch's Canzoniere

1 Erwin Panoksfy, *Studies in Iconology* (1939; reprint, New York: Harper & Row, 1967), 100. The polarity of the sacred and the profane, *Caritas* and *cupiditas*, is defined by Saint Augustine in the *De doctrina christiana* as the enjoyment of God for his own sake, all else being subordinated to Him, and the enjoyment of things worldly without reference to God ("Caritatem voco motum animi ad fruendum deo propter ipsum et se atque proximo propter deum; cupiditatem autem motum animi ad fruendum se et proximo et quolibet corpore non propter deum"). See *De doctrina christiana*, ed. William M. Green, vol. 80 of the *Corpus Scriptorum Ecclesiasticorum Latinorum* (Vienna: Hoelder-Pichler-Tempsky, 1963), 89.
2 *Secretum*, ed. Enrico Carrara, in *Prose* (Milano: Riccardo Ricciardi, 1955), 130–32. All subsequent references to this work will come from this edition.
3 On Petrarch's "poetics of fragmentation," see Giuseppe Mazzotta, "The *Canzoniere* and the Language of the Self," *Studies in Philology* 75 (1978): 271–96.
4 There are several works that deal with the myth in Petrarch's *Canzoniere*. Ugo Dotti, "Petrarca: il mito dafneo," *Convivium* 37 (1969): 9–23, comments briefly on the role of Daphne's hair, her escape, and her transformation in Petrarch's contemplative lyrics, with their images of elusive beauty, human frailty, and the passing of time. Carlo Calcaterra, "Giovene donna sotto un verde lauro," in *Nella selva del Petrarca* (Bologna: Licino Cappelli, 1942), concentrates on the contrast between two types of inspiration, Christian and pagan ("l'ispirazione apollinea"), the first no less literary than the second. Calcaterra discusses the ramifications of these inspirations, including the dual role of the woman: Laura-Daphne, the ideal image that leads to the laurel of poetic glory, and Laura, the guide to heaven. Marga Cottino-Jones concentrates mainly on the element of transformation in her study, "The Myth of Apollo and Daphne in Petrarch's *Canzoniere*: The Dynamics and Literary Function of Transformation," in *Francis Petrarch, Six Centuries Later: A Symposium*, ed. Aldo Scaglione, North Carolina Studies in the Romance Languages and Literatures, Symposia 3 (Chapel Hill: Department of Romance Languages, 1975), 152–76. I have two objections to this carefully reasoned article. Laura is not "transformed symbolically into Daphne" as Cottino-Jones suggests (160). Daphne is a *figura*, a type of Laura, and as such a prefiguration of the Petrarchan beloved. This is why Petrarch can speak of Daphne as if she *were* actually Laura, which he would not be able to do if the nymph were just a symbol of the woman. By the same token, Petrarch's poetic persona is not a projection of Apollo (160). On the contrary, Apollo is a projection of the poetic persona. Both are lovers and poets, but Petrarch transforms Apollo into "his" kind of lover and "his" kind of poet. P. R. J. Hainsworth, "The Myth of Daphne in the *Rerum vulgarium fragmenta*," *Italian Studies* 34 (1979): 28–44, regards the tale as a unifying motif

in the *Canzoniere* and uses it to interpret some of the more elusive aspects of the work. Yves Giraud mentions a few familiar parallels between the Ovidian tale and Petrarch. See *La Fable de Daphné,* Histoire des ideés et critique littéraire, vol. 92 (Genève: Droz, 1968), 141–49.

5 Introduction to his edition and translation of Petrarch's Canzoniere, *Petrarch's Lyric Poems* (Cambridge: Harvard University Press, 1976), 26–33.

6 This portion of the Coronation Oration comes from E. H. Wilkins's translation of the Latin text in *Studies in the Life and Works of Petrarch* (Cambridge, Mass.: Mediaeval Academy of America, 1955), 307.

7 *Studies in Seventeenth-Century Imagery* (Roma: Edizioni di Storia e Letteratura, 1964), 13, 23. See also Mario Praz, "Petrarca e gli emblematisti," in *Ricerche anglo-italiane* (Roma: Edizioni di Storia e Letteratura, 1944), 303–19.

8 All citations and translations from Petrarch's *Canzoniere* will come from Robert M. Durling, *Petrarch's Lyric Poems.*

9 *Secretum,* 106,132.

10 On this paradoxical combination, see Joan M. Ferrante, *"Cortes'Amor* in Medieval Texts," *Speculum* 55 (1980): 687. On courtly love, an elusive and controversial notion, see in addition to Ferrante's study, Moshé Lazar, *Amour courtois et fin'amors dans la littérature du XIIe siècle* (Paris: C. Klincksieck, 1964); Roger Boase, *The Origin and Meaning of Courtly Love* (Manchester: Manchester University Press, 1977); and Edmund Reiss, *"Fin'Amors:* Its History and Meaning in Medieval Literature," *Medieval and Renaissance Studies,* no. 8 (1979): 74–99. The literature on the subject is of course enormous.

11 *Studies in Iconology,* 109.

12 Giuseppe Mazzotta, "The *Canzoniere* and the Language of the Self," 276.

13 Erich Auerbach, "Typological Symbolism in Medieval Literature," *Yale French Studies* 9 (1952): 9–10.

14 "The Fig Tree and the Laurel: Petrarch's Poetics," *Diacritics* 5 (1975): 37.

15 On Petrarch's idolatry, see Freccero, "Fig Tree and Laurel"; Robert Durling, "Petrarch's 'Giovene donna sotto un verde lauro,' " *MLN* 86 (1971), 1–20; and Kenelm Foster, "Beatrice or Medusa: The Penitential Element in Petrarch's 'Canzoniere,' " in *Italian Studies Presented to E. R. Vincent* (Cambridge: W. Heffer, 1962), 41–56.

16 Robert Durling, "Petrarch's 'Giovene donna sotto un verde lauro,' " 3, regards the diamond as an emblem of "Laura's beauty and of her virtue, permanent, unassailable." This may be true and there is ample reason to think so since Petrarch uses diamond references in this manner elsewhere in the *Canzoniere.* But the diamond is also used to describe the cruelty of the woman, and this is my reading of the diamond image here. Of course, it could be both—beauty and virtue, and coldness—another one of Petrarch's ambiguous emblems.

17 On Petrarch's use of paronomasia, see François Rigolot, "Nature and Function of Paronomasia in the *Canzoniere,*" *Italian Quarterly* 18 (1974): 29–36.

18 On the "scattering" of the woman's image, see Nancy J. Vickers, "Diana Described: Scattered Woman and Scattered Rhyme," *Critical Inquiry* 8 (1981): 265–79.

19 For recent studies on canzone 23, see Dennis Dutschke, *Francesco Petrarca: Canzone XXIII from First to Final Version* (Ravenna: Longo, 1977), and Albert J. Rivero, "Petrarch's 'Nel dolce tempo de la prima etade,' " *MLN* 94 (1979): 92–112.

20 For notions of ecstasy and mysticism, I have relied on the following studies: R. C. Zaehner, *Mysticism, Sacred and Profane* (Oxford: Clarendon, 1957); Marghanita Laski, *Ecstasy. A Study of Some Secular and Religious Experiences* (Bloomington: Indiana University Press, 1961); and Willis Barnstone, *The Poetics of Ecstasy* (New York: Holmes & Meier, 1983).

21 *St. John of the Cross: The Dark Night of the Soul,* trans. Kurt F. Reinhardt (New York: Ungar, 1957), 1.2.5, 34.

22 *A Preface to Chaucer* (Princeton: Princeton University Press, 1962), 154.

23 *The Waning of the Middle Ages* (New York: Doubleday, 1954), 155.

24 Quoted in Freccero, "The Fig Tree and the Laurel," 35.

25 These words are Charles Segal's in his description of Ovid's use of setting in *Landscape in Ovid's Metamorphoses: A Study in the Transformations of a Literary Symbol,* Hermes Einzelschriften, no. 23 (Weisbaden: F. Steiner, 1969), 6. I am indebted to this study for my discussion of Ovid's landscape. It should be noted that in Ovid we often find a concreteness in the landscape lacking in Petrarch.

26 The landscape of the *Canzoniere* is chiefly the region of Vaucluse, near the Sorgue (supposedly Laura was born on a low hill between Vaucluse and Avignon). In some poems it is the forest of Ardennes or the Rhone region in Provençe. Nevertheless, the historical setting as Petrarch designs it, with its verdant valleys and slopes, bears close resemblance to the Vale of Tempe, the setting of Ovid's tale of Daphne and Apollo. Ovid does not describe the Tempe itself in much detail. He mentions Daphne's woods and at the beginning of the Io story mentions the wooded slopes and the "roar" of Peneus, whose waters sprinkle the top of the trees (569–73). But Tempe, as Curtius suggests, is in ancient literature the generic name for a variety of pleasances, "a cool wooded valley between steep slopes." See *European Literature and the Latin Middle Ages,* trans. Willard R. Trask (New York: Harper & Row, 1963), 199. The Tempe motif is very popular and passes into later literary traditions through such diverse sources as the elder Pliny's *Natural History* and Theocritus' famous pleasance in a wild wood depicted in his idyll *The Dioscuri.* Theocritus does not identify the landscape as Tempe, but it bears the identifiable marks. Petrarch may have become familiar with it from these or intermediary sources. In his *Natural History* (trans. H. Rackham [Loeb Classical Library, 1942] 2:141), Pliny offers a description of Tempe that could pass for Petrarch's Vaucluse if we substitute the Sorgue for the Peneus:

> Gently sloping hills rising beyond human sight on either hand, while the valley between is verdant with a grove of trees. Along it glides the Peneus, glittering with pebbles and adorned with grassy banks, melodious with the choral song of birds (4.8.31).

The fact that Petrarch makes Vaucluse like Tempe is significant. Just as Daphne and Laura become one in figural relation, mythical past and "historical" present mingling freely in our imagination, so do the two landscapes, Tempe (the birthplace of Daphne) and Vaucluse (the birthplace of Laura) unite by sharing common characteristics. They are paradoxically themselves and each other. The figural relation between Daphne and Laura is one way of achieving an illusion of atemporality; the handling of the landscape is another. Vaucluse, by its "contamination" with Tempe—both a literary *topos* and a setting for mythical "happenings"—becomes a place devoid of historicity and the witness of borrowed mythical fantasies—the miraculous transformations, the mythical figures, Laura herself becoming Daphne or a nymph or "other goddess" who sits on the bank of the Sorgue: "Or in forma di ninfa o d'altra diva / che del più chiaro fondo di Sorga esca / et pongasi a sedere in su la riva" (sonnet 281).

27 In Durling, *Petrarch's Lyric Poems*, note on 58.
28 *Landscape in Ovid's Metamorphoses*, 25.
29 "The *Canzoniere* and the Language of the Self," 272.

4 Garcilaso's Apollo and Daphne

1 On myth in the Golden Age, including details on translations of Ovid's *Metamorphoses* and mythographical texts, see Rudolph Schevill, *Ovid and the Renascence in Spain*, University of California Publications in Modern Philology, vol. 4, no. 1 (Berkeley: University of California Press, 1913) and José María de Cossío, *Fábulas mitológicas en España* (Madrid: Espasa Calpe, 1952). For further thoughts on mythology in the Renaissance see, especially, Douglas Bush, *Mythology and the Renaissance Tradition in English Poetry* (1932; reprint, New York: Norton, 1963) and Jean Seznec, *The Survival of the Pagan Gods*, trans. Barbara F. Sessions (1953; reprint, New York: Harper & Row, 1961).

2 Golden Age commentators and modern source critics point to Ovid as Garcilaso's model for Daphne's transformation. El Brocense also cites as a possible model Petrarch's conversion into the laurel in his canzone "Nel dolce tempo de la prima etade" (23). See Antonio Gallego Morell, ed., *Garcilaso de la Vega y sus comentaristas* (Madrid: Gredos, 1972), 268 n. 15. It is evident, however, that this is not correct, for Petrarch's design is completely different from Garcilaso's in language, imagery, tone, and event. Eugenio Mele ("In margine alle poesie di Garcilaso," *Bulletin Hispanique* 32 [1930]: 240) notes that even though the quatrains of Garcilaso's sonnet are based on Ovid, the tercets are independent from both the *Metamorphoses* and Petrarch. But as will be seen later, the tercets do share certain qualities with Petrarch.

3 *Obras completas con comentario*, ed. Elias L. Rivers (Madrid: Castalia, 1981), 101–2. All references to Garcilaso's poetry will come from this edition. The translation of the sonnet is based on a translation by Willis Barnstone. The translation of the Third Eclogue (161–68) is mine.

4 Ovid makes no reference to the color of Daphne's hair. It is Petrarch who utilizes the conceit to glorify the beauty of the nymph, a *figura* of Laura—the "aspra e superba nemica" of the poet:

> Apollo, s'ancor vive il bel desio
> che t'infiammava a le tesaliche onde,
> et se non ài l'amate chiome bionde,
> volgendo gli anni, già poste in oblio. (34.1–4)

> (Apollo, if the sweet desire is still alive
> that inflamed you beside the Thessalian waves,
> and if you have not forgotten, with the turning
> of the years, those beloved blond locks.)

In sonnet 348 Laura's hair makes both sun and gold appear less fair ("più bei capelli / che facean l'oro e 'l sol parer men belli"), an image that Garcilaso seems to echo in his sonnet. All references and translations from Petrarch's poems will come from Robert Durling, *Petrarch's Lyric Poems* (Cambridge: Harvard University Press, 1976).

5 For some thoughts on the symmetrical structure of the sonnet, see A. Cayol, "Un soneto de Garcilaso," *Garcilaso* no. 33 (1946): 12–13.

6 "A mi me parece sólo sirve este verbo de sustentar el verso. Pero puede tolerarse por causa de elegancia, y ser figura, como en el 6 de Virg[ilio], que sobra el pronombre" (Gallego Morell, ed., *Garcilaso de la Vega y sus comentaristas*, 349 n. 92).

7 In his article on Racine's "récit de Théramène," Leo Spitzer notes that the verb *voir* serves to introduce an intermediary between brutal reality and the reader. In effect, the verb *voir* functions in Racine's play like the verb *ver* in Garcilaso's sonnet. See "The 'récit de Théramène,' " in *Linguistics and Literary History: Essays in Stylistics* (1948; reprint, Princeton: Princeton University Press, 1974), 107.

8 Jean Hagstrum, *William Blake: Poet and Painter* (Chicago and London: University of Chicago Press, 1964), 8. On the tradition of "ut pictura poesis," see Rensselaer W. Lee, "*Ut pictura poesis:* The Humanistic Theory of Painting," *Art Bulletin* 22 (1940): 197–269 and Jean Hagstrum, *The Sister Arts: The Tradition of Literary Pictorialism and English Poetry from Dryden to Gray* (Chicago: University of Chicago Press, 1958). On visual aspects in Garcilaso, see Karl-Ludwig Selig, "Garcilaso and the Visual Arts: Remarks on Some Aspects of Visualization," in *Interpretation und Vergleich: Festschrift für Walter Pabst* (Berlin: E. Schmidt, 1972), 302–9. On ecphrasis in Garcilaso and in the Golden Age, see Alan K. G. Paterson, "Ecphrasis in Garcilaso's 'Egloga Tercera,' " *Modern Language Review* 72 (1977): 73–92 and Emilie Bergmann, *Art Inscribed: Essays on Ekphrasis in Spanish Golden Age Poetry*, Harvard Studies in Romance Languages, vol. 35 (Cambridge: Harvard University Press, 1979).

9 The weaving of the tapestries is accompanied by a pictorial vocabulary—led by the names of the Greek painters Apelles and Thimanthes—which underscores both the artifice of the nymph's embroidered stories and Garcilaso's contrived, stylized pastoral world. On the pictorial qualities of the eclogue, see Leo Spitzer, "Garcilaso, Third Eclogue, Lines 265–271," *Hispanic Review* 20 (1952): 243–48 and Elias L. Rivers, "The Pastoral Paradox of Natural Art," *MLN* 77 (1962): 130–44.

10 Other changes in the eclogue worth noting include the substitution of *sendos* for *luengos* and *s'estendían* for *bolvían*. These changes were perhaps introduced for reasons of euphony. The first substitution creates a smoother line by removing the awkward internal rhyme of *luengos-bueltos*; the second substitution avoids the strident alliteration of *bolvían-blancos*. To yield the alternate rhyme in lines 163–64, Garcilaso changes slightly the golden hair hyperbole and introduces an abrupt enjambment, breaking the rhythmic progress of transformation so evident in the sonnet: "y los cabellos, que vencer solían / al oro fino, en hojas se tornavan." The resulting fragmentation of line 164, unlike the sonnet, stylistically captures the destruction of that trait that makes the virgin one with ideal beauty, her golden hair. For further details on stylistic changes, see Alberto Blecua, *En el texto de Garcilaso* (Madrid: Insula, 1970), 52–53.

11 Not all critics agree that *degollada*, the adjective used by Garcilaso to describe Elissa, means decapitated. On the controversy, see Alberto Porqueras-Mayo, "La ninfa degollada de Garcilaso (Egloga III, versos 225–232)," in *Actas del Ter-*

cer Congreso Internacional de Hispanistas (México: Colegio de México, 1970), 715–24, and Enrique Martínez-López, "Sobre 'aquella bestialidad' de Garcilaso (égl. III.230)," *PMLA* 87 (1972): 12–25, who argues persuasively for decapitated.

12 Wylie Sypher, *Four Stages of Renaissance Style* (Garden City, N.Y.: Doubleday, 1955); Roy Daniells, *Milton, Mannerism and Baroque* (Toronto: University of Toronto Press, 1963); Arnold Hauser, *Mannerism: The Crisis of the Renaissance and the Origin of Modern Art* (New York: Knopf, 1965). Equally unsatisfactory is the approach of E. R. Curtius, *European Literature and the Latin Middle Ages*, trans. Willard R. Trask (New York: Harper & Row, 1963), 273–301, who conceives of Mannerism as the anticlassical strains (rhetorical excesses, verbal ornamentation, and affectations) present throughout literary history. But as Rosemond Tuve aptly notes, Curtius provides no criterion, for all literature uses these stylistic devices and "for a hundred reasons." See "Baroque and Mannerist Milton?" in *Milton Studies in Honor of Harris Francis Fletcher* (Urbana: University of Illinois Press, 1961), 211. Curtius's method leads to the excesses of his disciple, Gustav René Hocke (*Manierismus in der Literatur* [Hamburg: Rowohlt, 1959] and *Die Welt als Labyrinth* [Hamburg: Rowohlt, 1957]), who turns Mannerism into a grab bag for all that fragments and distorts the "normal." Helmut Hatzfeld, also following Curtius, calls Garcilaso a Mannerist for his habit of "overdoing metaphor." See "Literary Mannerism and Baroque in Spain and France," *Comparative Literature Studies* 7 (1970), 419–36. I will not cite further studies on literary Mannerism. On the controversy, approaches, and bibliography, I refer the reader to James Mirollo (who coins the term "Angst-mannerism"), "The Mannered and the Mannerist in Late Renaissance Literature," in *The Meaning of Mannerism,* eds. Franklin W. Robinson and Stephen G. Nichols, Jr. (Hanover, N.H.: University Press of New England, 1972), 7–24 and his recent book, *Mannerism and Renaissance Poetry* (New Haven: Yale University Press, 1984). See also Branimir Anzulovic, "Mannerism in Literature: A Review of Research," *Yearbook of Comparative and General Literature* 23 (1974): 54–66.

13 The term *maniera* is used here to refer to the second phase of Mannerism; the first phase comprises the tormented visions and spiritual intensity of the early Mannerism of artists such as Pontormo and Rosso. The *maniera* style emerges about 1520 and is in full bloom in the 1530s. However, precedents of *maniera* are found earlier in Giulio Romano, Peruzzi, Polidoro, and Perino del Vaga. On anticipations of *maniera*, see, for instance, F. Antal, "Observations on Girolamo da Carpi," *Art Bulletin* 34 (1952): 85 n. 25 and Walter Friedlaender, *Mannerism and Anti-Mannerism in Italian Painting* (1957; reprint, New York: Schocken, 1973), 19. I believe that to these early anticipations belong the two Mannerist Daphnes that will be discussed later. On the question of Mannerism, an aesthetic still subject to much controversy, see, especially, S. J. Freedberg, *Painting of the High Renaissance in Rome and Florence,* 2 vols. (Cambridge: Harvard University Press, 1961); Giuliano Briganti, *Italian Mannerism*, trans. Margaret Kunzle (Leipzig: Thomas & Hudson, 1962); John Shearman, *Mannerism* (Baltimore: Penguin, 1967); Craig Hugh Smyth, *Mannerism and Maniera* (Locust Valley, N.Y.: J. J. Augustin, 1963); E. H. Gombrich, *The Story of Art* (1950; reprint, Oxford: Phaidon, 1972), 277–83, 299–300. Garcilaso had ample opportunity to come into contact with the Mannerist sensibility. In 1529 he made the first of his many voyages to Italy and in 1532 was appointed to a post in the Viceroyship at Naples. On Garcilaso's travels in Italy, see E. Fer-

nández de Navarrete, *Colección de documentos inéditos para la historia de España,* vol. 16 (Madrid, 1850). It is significant that in 1519, while a guard at the court in Valladolid, Garcilaso came into contact with a Spanish brand of Mannerism in the art of Alonso Berruguete, who was at that time royal painter to Charles V and who had played a role in the development of early Florentine Mannerism. Berruguete's Mannerist creations are, however, very far from Italian *maniera.* In their intense energy and religious frenzy, his contorted, elongated figures—especially those of the altarpiece of S. Benito el Real—display the realism of the late Gothic sculpture of Spain. See C. R. Post, *A History of Spanish Painting,* Harvard-Radcliffe Fine Arts Series, vol. 14 (Cambridge: Harvard University Press, 1966), 20, 24.

14 For a discussion of this Mannerist Daphne, see Wolfgang Stechow, *Apollo und Daphne,* Studien der Bibliothek Warburg, vol. 23 (Leipzig: Teubner, 1932), 22. Stechow, however, does not discuss the grotesque elements in this fresco or those of any of the other Mannerist Daphnes in his study, including Veneziano's Daphne (23), which will be treated next. He deals instead with the question of antique models, the "transitory" aspects of the pursuit and metamorphosis, and the Peneus figure. Other Mannerist Daphnes discussed and reproduced in Stechow are those of Barthel Beham (plate 11, fig. 25), Jacopo Caraglio, after Perino del Vaga (plate 14, fig. 29) and Karel van Mander (plate 27, fig. 54).

15 John Rupert Martin, *Baroque* (New York: Harper & Row, 1977), 39.

16 On Bernini, see Howard Hibbard, *Bernini* (1965; reprint, New York: Penguin, 1976). On Pollaiuolo, see Frederick Hartt, *History of Italian Renaissance Art* (New York: Harry N. Abrams, 1969), 270–76.

17 On the emblematic tradition, see Mario Praz, *Studies in Seventeenth-Century Imagery* (Rome: Edizioni di Storia e Letteratura, 1964); Robert Clements, *Picta Poesis: Literary and Humanistic Theory in Renaissance Emblem Books* (Rome: Edizioni di Storia e Letteratura, 1960); and Rosemary Freeman, *English Emblem Books* (London: Chatto & Windus, 1948). On emblem literature in Spain, see Giuseppina Ledda, *Contributo allo studio della letteratura emblematica in Spagna (1549–1613)* (Pisa: Università di Pisa, 1970).

18 On Barthélemy Aneau's emblem, see Arthur Henkel and Albrecht Schöne, *Emblemata* (Stuttgart: Metzler, 1967), 1742. Aneau's grotesque Daphne serves as a model for Bernard Salomon's design in the well-known *Métamorphose figurée* (Lyon, 1557), which in turn becomes the period's most copied engraving of the nymph, appearing in emblem books and both Latin editions and translations of Ovid's *Metamorphoses.* A copy by Virgil Solis appears in the Anvers edition (1595) of Jorge de Bustamante's Spanish prose version of the *Metamorphoses.* For details on Daphne's iconography in emblem books, including Aneau's, see Yves Giraud, *La Fable de Daphné,* Histoire des idées et critique littéraire, vol. 92 (Genève: Droz, 1968), 191–96, 252–55. On illustrations of Ovid's *Metamorphoses,* where there are all degrees and manners of distortion imposed on Daphne, see, especially, 171–76, 256–57. See also M. D. Henkel, "Illustrierte Ausgaben von Ovids *Metamorphosen* im XV., XVI. und XVII. Jahrhundert," *Vorträge der Bibliothek Warburg* 6 (1926–27): 58–144.

5 Myth in Quevedo

1 These poems have received scant critical attention. José María de Cossío, in his *Fábulas mitológicas en España* (Madrid: Espasa Calpe, 1952), writes briefly on the *quintillas* (251–53) and Dámaso Alonso, in his *Poesía española* (Madrid: Gre-

dos, 1971), devotes a few lines to one of the sonnets (529–30). Alessandro Martinengo offers a few comments on Quevedo's treatment of myth, a topic yet to be explored fully, in his "La mitologia classica come repertorio stilistico dei concettisti ispanoamericani," *Studi di Letteratura Ispano-Americana* (Milan) 1 (1967): 78–84.

2 On the *topos* of jest and earnest, see E. R. Curtius, *European Literature and the Latin Middle Ages*, trans. Willard R. Trask (New York: Harper & Row, 1953), 417–35. Since the term *spoudogeloion* is commonly applied to a mixture of the serious and the comic in the same work, it would seem that it could not be properly used for Quevedo's treatment of Apollo and Daphne, where jest and earnest exist in different contexts. But it seems to me that if Quevedo's writings are considered as an organic whole, the term perfectly defines the constant shift (not only in his treatment of myth but of other subjects as well) between taunting prank and stern moral, amusing scatology and solemn philosophy, satiric irreverence and brooding eros. (Of course, in works such as the *Buscón* and the *Sueños*, the serious and the comic mingle. Moreover, we must remember that satire, that literary form of which Quevedo is a master, has long been recognized as a combination of earnest and jest—the Horatian *ridendo dicere verum*.)

3 José Manuel Blecua notes that the poem was written before September 20, 1603, which is the date of the *dedicatoria* of the *Flores*. See *Obra poética*, 4 vols. (Madrid: Castalia, 1969–81), 1:409. All quotes from Quevedo's poetry will come from this collection. The *quintillas* appear in 1.209. Translations from Quevedo are mine unless otherwise indicated.

4 On this cosmological picture, see Theodore Spencer, *Shakespeare and the Nature of Man* (New York: Macmillan, 1942), 5–10 and E. M. W. Tillyard, *The Elizabethan World Picture* (New York: Vintage Books, n.d.).

5 There is an element of latent humor in the easy rhyme *-illa-ella*. Quevedo's irrepressible spirit of play is felt even in the most serious moments, as in this scene.

6 In Ovid's *Metamorphoses*, the transformation is brought about by Daphne's father, the river-god Peneus, a notion that comes from the Thessalian version of the tale. Quevedo opts for Jupiter who transforms the maiden into the laurel in the Laconian version. Quevedo may have seen this version in one of the many mythographical texts available to him. He uses Jupiter for the transformation because he attributes another role to Peneus: the river represents the element of water, which plays a key part in the scene of cosmic convulsion and, as will be seen later, in the apotheosis of Daphne/laurel.

7 See Howard R. Patch, *The Goddess Fortuna in Mediaeval Literature* (Cambridge: Harvard University Press, 1927), 4.

8 See Raimundo Lida, "La 'España defendida' y la síntesis pagano-cristiana" and "De Quevedo, Lipsio y los escalígeros," in *Letras hispánicas* (Mexico: Fondo de Cultura Económica, 1958), 142–48, 157–62. See also Henry Ettinghausen, *Francisco de Quevedo and the Neostoic Movement* (Oxford: Oxford University Press, 1972), with reference to the useful studies of the *Anacreón castellano* and Quevedo's translation of the pseudo-Phocylides by S. Bénichou-Roubaud and D. G. Castanien (15). In subsequent writings, Quevedo continues the christianization of pagan texts, as in his reconciliation of ancient schools of thought and Christian morality in his *Doctrina estoica* and the *Defensa de Epicuro* (see Ettinghausen, 26–56). Quevedo's admiration for the pagans is such that, as Ettinghausen has shown, even when he apparently attempts to break with the classics as in the *Virtud militante*, he fails to do so (92–108).

9 See *Obras en prosa*, vol. 1 of *Obras completas*, ed. Felicidad Buendía (Madrid: Aguilar, 1961), 835.

10 *Versions of Baroque* (New Haven: Yale University Press, 1972), 92.

11 *Epistolario completo*, ed. Luis Astrana Marín (Madrid: Instituto Editorial Reus, 1946), 423.

12 *Obras completas en prosa*, ed. Luis Astrana Marín (Madrid: Aguilar, 1945), *Sentencia 733*, p. 953. Nature as an agent of Providence is a popular concept in the Golden Age. Otis Green has treated the topic in some detail in his *Spain and the Western Tradition* (Madison: University of Wisconsin Press, 1968), 2:97–104; on the topic in Quevedo, see 101–2. Green considers Quevedo's well-known letter quoted in my text as an example of the *topos* "concord in discord" so familiar to Golden Age readers. On this commonplace, see 52–63.

13 The *quintillas* are the only full serious treatment of Apollo and Daphne in Quevedo's extant poetry. There are, however, numerous allusions to the god and the nymph in his love and moral poetry, in the *túmulos* and *elogios*, and in the *Heráclito cristiano*, where Quevedo speaks of "la hermosa lumbre del lozano Apolo" ("the handsome glow of the luxuriant Apollo," 1.33)—a splendor which, as will be seen shortly, becomes a target of ridicule in our poet's typical about-face.

14 "Hucho-ho" is a call used in falconry by a hunter who is luring back the falcon that has escaped (Covarrubias). Quevedo uses "Hucho-ho" to identify the bull into which Jupiter transformed himself to woo Europa: "Convirtióse en '¡Hucho-ho!' / el mismo dios por Europa" (2.682, 221–22). Quevedo seems to be making an analogy between the hunter who hunts game with falcon (or who seeks to recover a falcon) and Jupiter the bull hunting down his erotic prey, Europa (who, according to this analogy, may also represent the lost falcon). Jupiter is analogous to the falconer, and Europa is analogous to the prey or the lost falcon. "Hucho-ho" carries the notion of seeking something intensely, an idea made explicit in 2.675, 11–15, where Quevedo again associates "Hucho-ho" with a bull. I thank James O. Crosby for the explanation of "Hucho-ho."

15 This is a reference to Jupiter's transformation into a swan, which Quevedo calls *ganso* ("goose"), in order to seduce Leda (2.682, 205–8):

> Habló por boca de ganso
> a Leda, y con la tramoya
> de plumas blancas y pico,
> dios avechucho, engañola.

> (He spoke through the mouth of a goose
> to Leda, and with his trappings
> of white feathers and beak,
> god and ugly bird, deceived her.)

16 Quevedo's gods are closer to Alessandro Tassoni's in *La secchia rapita* (1622), ed. Giovanni Ziccardi (Torino: Unione Tipografico Editrice Torinese, 1968). Even though Tassoni's Olympians are not as crude as Quevedo's, they are essentially petty (Juno cannot attend the council of the gods because she must wash her hair) and vulgar (Saturn starts his address to the gods by breaking wind).

17 *La hora de todos y la Fortuna con seso*, ed. Luisa López-Grigera (Madrid: Castalia, 1975), 70.

18 On the grotesque in Quevedo, see James Iffland, *Quevedo and the Grotesque,* 2 vols. (London: Tamesis, 1978–82).

19 There is no exact date for this sonnet or for the Daphne sonnet that will be analyzed later. They were first published in the first printed edition of Quevedo's poetry, *El parnaso español,* ed. José Antonio González de Salas (Madrid, 1648), 427b, 428a. The translations of the sonnets are by Elias L. Rivers, *Renaissance and Baroque Poetry of Spain* (New York: Dell, 1966), 289–90. I have made a few changes in Rivers's translations.

20 Cf. Raimundo Lida, "Sueños y discursos: el predicador y sus máscaras," in *Homenaje a Julio Caro Baroja* (Madrid: Centro de Investigaciones Sociológicas, 1978), 676–77. On the topic of money in Quevedo, see Emilio Alarcos García, "El dinero en las obras de Quevedo" (Discurso de apertura del curso 1942–43, Universidad de Valladolid).

21 M. Herrero-García, "Los rasgos físicos y el carácter según los textos españoles del siglo XVII," *Revista de Filología Española* 12 (1925): 158. See also T. W. Keeble, "Some Mythological Figures in Golden Age Satire and Burlesque," *Bulletin of Spanish Studies* 25 (1948): 238–39. Red hair as a sign of treachery is an ancient notion. According to the *Physiognomica* (67, 811b, and 812a) of Pseudo-Aristotle, "red hair and a red complexion signify a foxy rascal." See Margarete Bieber, *The History of the Greek and Roman Theater,* 2d ed., rev. and enl. (Princeton: Princeton University Press, 1971), 102.

22 See Blecua, *Obra poética,* 2.717, 21–24; 3.856, 145–48. The infamous Dómine Cabra in the *Buscón* is also *bermejo.* Red or blond hair abounds in the *Sueños.* See Felipe Maldonado's edition (Madrid: Castalia, 1982), 114 n. 13, with a reference to the numerous phrases concerning this topic in Correas' *Vocabulario.*

23 *Poesía española,* 530.

24 Dirt is one of Quevedo's favorite means of degrading women, especially the courtly beloved, whose luminous beauty becomes an ideal target. When in his portrayal of Hero, Quevedo speaks his two repugnant lines "las uñas con cejas / de rascar la caspa" ("her nails with eyebrows / from scratching her dandruff," Blecua, 3.771, 35–36), there is little left that could destroy this once radiant woman so thoroughly.

25 Quevedo's "ojo del cielo" is a play on "ojo del culo," the common Spanish obscene term for anus.

26 Emilio Alarcos García has studied in detail Quevedo's parody of phrases in "Quevedo y la parodia idiomática," *Archivum* 5 (1955): 23–36.

27 López-Grigera, ed., 224.

28 Biblioteca de Autores Españoles, vol. 69 (Madrid: Rivadeneyra, 1953), 132. The role of the *dueña* as the guardian of maidens is a venerable one. In Quevedo the *dueña* appears as a diabolical figure who is typically not above causing the fall of her charge, often for a price, as in "Advertencias de una dueña a un galán pobre" ("Advice of a duenna to a poor lover," 2.713). The *dueña* warns the penniless lover that "el romance sin dineros / es lengua que no se entiende" ("a romance without money / is a language that can't be understood," 23–24), a notion that Quevedo wants the gullible Apollo himself to understand.

29 Tillyard, *The Elizabethan World Picture,* 65.

30 Cf., for instance, *La hora de todos,* ed. López-Grigera, 138–39, where we have one of Quevedo's best satirical attacks on alchemy. For Quevedo's satire on alchemy, see Alessandro Martinengo, *Quevedo e il simbolo alchimistico* (Padua:

Liviana Editrice, 1967), 3–60 and Amédée Mas, ed., *Las zahurdas de Plutón* (Poitiers: S.F.I.L., 1956), 96–100.

31 See the note on the word *cruda* in James O. Crosby, *Poesía varia* (Madrid: Cátedra, 1981), 365.

32 Douglas Bush, *Mythology and the Renaissance Tradition in English Poetry* (1932; reprint, New York: Norton, 1963), 300.

33 See R. M. Price's analysis of the phrase *perro muerto* in Quevedo's sonnet "Que no me quieren bien todas, confieso" in "A Note on Three Satirical Sonnets of Quevedo," *Bulletin of Hispanic Studies* 40 (1963): 81–82. Here, as in the Daphne sonnet, the topic is linked to the refusal to pay a prostitute.

34 The combination of Apollo's lust with his miserliness is Quevedo's favorite way of ridiculing the god. This notion appears again in the ballad "Efectos del amor y los celos" ("The effects of love and jealousy"): "El Sol andaba tras Dafne, / con la luz en las alforjas, / en forma de cuadrillero, / con más saetas que joyas" ("The Sun wooed Daphne / with the light in his saddlebags, / like a bowman, / with more arrows than jewels," 3.768, 125–28).

35 Eugenio Asensio gives an excellent analysis of Quevedo's figures and types in his *Itinerario del entremés*, 2d ed., rev. (Madrid: Gredos, 1971), 177–97.

36 *La Caricature de la femme, du mariage et de l'amour dans l'oeuvre de Quevedo* (Paris: Ediciones Hispano-Americanas, 1957), 140.

37 See Alessandro Martinengo, *Quevedo e il simbolo alchimistico*, 32–48.

38 Cf. "Dafne . . . ninfa que los escabeches / y las aceitunas ronda" ("Daphne . . . the nymph who noses about marinades and olives," 2.682, 178–80); "Si el Sol, que, al revés, tras Dafne / siguió luz la mariposa, / te atisba, los escabeches / no fueran hoy de corona" ("If the Sun, who chases Daphne / in the reverse of the butterfly and the light, / should catch sight of you, marinades / would not have laurel leaves in them today," 3.860, 37–40).

Appendix

1 Blecua describes the Evora manuscript in *Obra poética* (Madrid: Castalia: 1969–81), 1:27–29. See also Eugenio Asensio, *Itinerario del entremés*, 2d ed., rev. (Madrid: Gredos, 1971), 255–56. This version of the Daphne sonnet also appears in an eighteenth-century manuscript (ms. 12717; in Blecua, 1:16).

2 In Blecua's edition, *Obra poética*, 2:19, the early version is labeled *B* and the revised version *A*. For purposes of clarity, I have followed a chronological progression and called the early version *A* and the revision *B*.

3 Blecua, *Poesía original* (Barcelona: Planeta, 1963), LXI–LXXXIV and *Obra poética*, 1:XVII–XXX; Crosby, *En torno a la poesía de Quevedo* (Madrid: Castalia, 1967), 17–42.

4 *Rabelais and His World*, trans. Hélène Iswolsky (Cambridge: MIT Press, 1968). I elaborate on Bakhtin's concept of "grotesque realism" and its relation to Quevedo later on in this section.

5 In Golden Age burlesques of Daphne, one popular technique to ridicule her metamorphosis is to transform certain parts of her body in order to make the event hilariously malicious. Polo de Medina, for instance, chooses her eyes and teeth: "viéndola con los ojos laureados / y de laurel los dientes traspillados" ("seeing her with her laureled eyes / and her teeth flattened into laurel leaves"). See *Obras completas* (Murcia: Tip. Sucesores de Nogués, 1948), 223.

6 On Rabelais, see Mikhail Bakhtin, *Rabelais and His World*; on Swift, see Nor-

man O. Brown, "The Excremental Vision," in *Life Against Death* (Middletown, Conn.: Wesleyan University Press, 1959), 179–201.

7 *Rabelais and His World*, 21.

8 *Rabelais and His World*, 13.

9 In a stimulating essay, "Quevedo: la obsesión excremental," in *Disidencias* (Barcelona: Seix Barral, 1977), 130–31, Juan Goytisolo regards Quevedo's use of scatology as liberating. The poet's obscenities are a confirmation of man's humanity against the sublimation imposed on the body by Catholicism.

10 *Totem and Tabu*, trans. James Strachey (New York: Norton, 1952), 140.

11 See *Obras en prosa*, ed. Luis Astrana Marín (Madrid: Aguilar, 1945), 185. The corrections for the text of the *Sueños* were done in such haste and with such lack of care that certain passages were mutilated to the point of incoherence. The *Buscón* also had to undergo revisions for its first edition (Zaragoza, 1626), when irreverent material had to be eliminated or toned down. Even though the revisions of the *Buscón*—in some cases as careless and as infelicitous as those of the *Sueños*—do not seem to have been made by Quevedo himself (see Fernando Lázaro Carreter's edition [Salamanca: Ediciones Universidad de Salamanca, 1980] LXII–LXVII), there is no doubt that those of the Daphne sonnet are Quevedo's own. These corrections show such impeccable poetic sense that they could have come only from someone as exceptionally gifted as our poet, and his editor González de Salas was no Quevedo.

12 Quevedo speaks of preparing his poetry for publication in his letters to Francisco de Oviedo in January and February, 1645 (Blecua, *Obra poética*, 1:XII). For the texts of these letters, see *Epistolario completo*, ed. Luis Astrana Marín (Madrid: Instituto Editorial Reus, 1946), 481–82, 485–86. Quevedo dies in September 1645, and the task of publishing his poems goes to González de Salas.

13 Alexander A. Parker correctly points to these attacks as a possible explanation for Quevedo's alleged repudiation of his *Buscón*. See *Literature and the Delinquent: The Picaresque Novel in Spain and Europe, 1599–1753* (Edinburgh: Edinburgh University Press, 1967), 161 n. 5. See also Lázaro Carreter's edition of the *Buscón*, LXVII.

14 See Blecua, *Obra poética*, 1:XIV–XV n. 16. González de Salas was not the only one to take material out of Quevedo's poems that was not considered fit for print. For instance, the ballad "Ya sueltan, Juanilla, presos" ("Prisoners are being freed, Juanilla")—which seems to have been enormously popular, for it circulated in numerous manuscripts and *impresos*—appears in printed texts (*Romances varios*, 1640, 1643, 1655) without its most obviously obscene images and words, such as the stanza that starts "Las putas y los caballos" ("Whores and horses"). For texts and variants, see Blecua, *Obra poética*, 3.776.

15 Here I have in mind well-known sonnets such as "La voz del ojo, que llamamos pedo" ("The voice of the eye, which we call a fart," in ms. 108 of the Biblioteca Menéndez Pelayo in Santander and in other mss.; see Blecua, *Obra poética*, 2.610); "Que tiene ojo de culo es evidente" ("That his eye is like an asshole is evident," Bib. Menéndez Pelayo, ms. 108; Blecua, *Obra poética*, 2.608); and "Puto es el hombre que de putas fía" ("A male whore is a man who trusts in whores," Biblioteca Menéndez Pelayo, ms. 108; Blecua, *Obra poética*, 2.600).

Bibliography

Alarcos García, Emilio. "El dinero en las obras de Quevedo." Discurso de apertura del curso 1942–43, Universidad de Valladolid.

——. "Quevedo y la parodia idiomática." *Archivum* 5 (1955): 3–38.

Allen, Archibald W. "Elegy and the Classical Attitude toward Love: Propertius I.1." *Yale Classical Studies* 11 (1950): 255–77.

Allen, Don Cameron. *Mysteriously Meant: The Rediscovery of Pagan Symbolism and Allegorical Interpretation in the Renaissance.* Baltimore: Johns Hopkins University Press, 1970.

Alonso, Dámaso. *Poesía española.* Madrid: Gredos, 1971.

Alphandéry, Paul. "L'Evhémérisme et les débuts de l'histoire des religions au moyen âge." *Revue de l'histoire des religions* 109 (1934): 5–27.

Altieri, Charles. "Ovid and the New Mythologists." *Novel: A Forum on Fiction* 7 (1973): 31–40.

Amandry, Pierre. *La Mantique apollinienne à Delphes: Essai sur le fonctionnement de l'oracle.* Paris: E. de Boccard, 1950.

Amsler, Samuel. "La Typologie de l'Ancien Testament chez Saint Paul." *Revue de Théologie et de Philosophie* 37 (1949): 114–28.

Antal, F. "Observations on Girolamo da Carpi." *Art Bulletin* 34 (1952): 81–103.

Anzulovic, Branimir. "Mannerism in Literature: A Review of Research." *Yearbook of Comparative and General Literature* 23 (1974): 54–66.

Asensio, Eugenio. *Itinerario del entremés.* 2d ed., rev. Madrid: Gredos, 1971.

Auerbach, Erich. "Figura." In *Scenes from the Drama of European Literature.* New York: Meridian, 1959.

——. "Typological Symbolism in Medieval Literature." *Yale French Studies* 9 (1952): 3–10.

Augustine of Hippo, Saint. *De doctrina christiana.* Edited by William M. Green. Vol. 80 of the *Corpus Scriptorum Ecclesiasticorum Latinorum.* Vienna: Hoelder-Pichler-Tempsky, 1963.

Bakhtin, Mikhail. *Rabelais and His World.* Translated by Hélène Iswolsky. Cambridge: MIT Press, 1968.

Barber, C. L. *Shakespeare's Festive Comedy.* Princeton: Princeton University Press, 1959.

Barnstone, Willis. *The Poetics of Ecstasy.* New York: Holmes & Meier, 1983.

Bartsch, Karl. *Albrecht von Halberstadt und Ovid im Mittelalter.* 1861. Reprint. Amsterdam: Editions Rodopi, 1965.

Beare, William. *The Roman Stage.* 3d ed. London: Methuen, 1964.

Bergmann, Emilie. *Art Inscribed: Essays on Ekphrasis in Spanish Golden Age Poetry.* Harvard Studies in Romance Languages, vol. 35. Cambridge: Harvard University Press, 1979.

Bersuire, Pierre. *Reductorium morale, liber XV: Ovidius moralizatus, cap. 1., De formis figurisque deorum.* Edited by Joseph Engels. Utrecht: Rijksuniversiteit. Instituut voor Laat Latijn, 1966.

―――. *L'Ovidius moralizatus di Pierre Bersuire.* Edited by Fausto Guisalberti. Studj Romanzi, vol. 23. Roma: Presso la Società, 1933.

Bieber, Margarete. *The History of the Greek and Roman Theater.* 2d ed., rev. and enl. Princeton: Princeton University Press, 1971.

―――. *Die Denkmäler zum Theaterwesen im Altertum.* Berlin and Leipzig: Vereinigung Wissenschaftlicher Verleger, 1920.

Blecua, Alberto. *En el texto de Garcilaso.* Madrid: Insula, 1970.

Boase, Roger. *The Origin and Meaning of Courtly Love.* Manchester: Manchester University Press, 1977.

Boccaccio, Giovanni. *Genealogia deorum gentilium.* 2 vols. Edited by Vincenzo Romano. Bari: Laterza, 1951.

Bode, Georg Heinrich, ed. *Scriptores rerum mythicarum Latini tres.* 2 vols. Cellis: E. H. C. Schulze, 1834.

Bömer, Franz. *P. Ovidius Naso. Metamorphosen: Kommentar.* Vol. 1. Heidelberg: C. Winter, 1969.

Boethius. *The Consolation of Philosophy.* Translated by Richard Green. New York: Bobbs-Merrill, 1962.

Boëthius, Axel. *The Golden House of Nero. Some Aspects of Roman Architecture.* Ann Arbor: University of Michigan Press, 1960.

Born, Lester K. "The Manuscripts of the *Integumenta* on the *Metamorphoses* of Ovid by John of Garland." *Transactions of the American Philological Association* 60 (1929): 179–99.

―――. "Ovid and Allegory." *Speculum* 9 (1934): 362–79.

Briganti, Giuliano. *Italian Mannerism.* Translated by Margaret Kunzle. Leipzig: Thomas & Hudson, 1962.

Brown, Norman O. "The Excremental Vision." In *Life Against Death.* Middletown, Conn.: Wesleyan University Press, 1959.

Buffière, Félix, ed. and trans. *Héraclite. Allégories d'Homère.* Paris: Les Belles-Lettres, 1962.

Bush, Douglas. *Mythology and the Renaissance Tradition in English Poetry.* 1932. Reprint. New York: Norton, 1963.

Calcaterra, Carlo. *Nella selva del Petrarca.* Bologna: Licino Cappelli, 1942.

Callimachus. *Hymns and Epigrams.* Edited and translated by A. W. Mair. Loeb Classical Library. 1955.

Campbell, Joseph. *The Hero with a Thousand Faces.* 1949. Reprint. Cleveland and New York: World Publishing, 1970.

Campbell, P. G. C. *L'Epître d'Othéa. Etude sur les sources de Christine de Pisan.* Paris: Librairie Ancienne Honoré Champion, 1924.

Cayol, A. "Un soneto de Garcilaso." *Garcilaso* no. 33 (1946): 12–13.

Chadwick, Henry. *Early Christian Thought and the Classical Tradition.* New York: Oxford University Press, 1966.

Champfleury. [Jules Fleury]. *Histoire de la caricature antique.* Paris: F. Dentu, 1879.

Christine de Pisan. *L'Epître d'Othéa.* Translated by Stephen Scrope and edited by Curt F. Bühler. London: Oxford University Press, 1970.

Clayborough, Arthur. *The Grotesque in English Literature.* 1965. Reprint. Oxford: Clarendon, 1967.

Clement of Alexandria. *The Exhortation to the Greeks.* Translated by G. W. Butterworth. 1919. Reprint. Loeb Classical Library. 1960.

———. *Stromata.* Migne, *Patrologia graeca* 9.9–602.

Clements, Robert J. *Michelangelo's Theory of Art.* London: Routledge and Kegan Paul, 1963.

———. *Picta Poesis. Literary and Humanistic Theory in Renaissance Emblem Books.* Rome: Edizioni di Storia e Letteratura, 1960.

Comparetti, Domenico. *Virgilio nel medio evo.* Edited by Giorgio Pasquali. Firenze: "La Nuova Italia" Editrice, 1955.

Cooke, J. D. "Euhemerism: A Mediaeval Interpretation of Classical Paganism." *Speculum* 2 (1927): 396–410.

Copley, Frank O. *Exclusus amator. A Study in Latin Love Poetry.* Madison: American Philological Association, 1956.

———. *"Servitium amoris* in the Roman Elegists." *Transactions of the American Philological Association* 78 (1947): 285–300.

Cossío, José María de. *Fábulas mitológicas en España.* Madrid: Espasa Calpe, 1952.

Cottino-Jones, Marga. "The Myth of Apollo and Daphne in Petrarch's *Canzoniere:* The Dynamics and Literary Function of Transformation." In *Francis Petrarch, Six Centuries Later: A Symposium,* edited by Aldo Scaglione. North Carolina Studies in the Romance Languages and Literatures, Symposia 3. Chapel Hill: Department of Romance Languages, 1975.

Coulter, Cornelia C. "The Genealogy of the Gods." In *Vassar Mediaeval Studies,* edited by Christabel Forsyth Fiske. New Haven: Yale University Press, 1923.

Courcelle, Pierre. *Late Latin Writers and Their Greek Sources.* Translated by Harry E. Wedeck. Cambridge: Harvard University Press, 1969.

Crosby, James O. *En torno a la poesía de Quevedo.* Madrid: Castalia, 1967.

Curtius, E. R. *European Literature and the Latin Middle Ages.* Translated by Willard R. Trask. 2d ed. New York: Harper & Row, 1963.

Dacos, Nicole. *La Découverte de la Domus Aurea et la formation des grotesques à la Renaissance.* Studies of the Warburg Institute, vol. 31. London: Warburg Institute, 1969.

Daniells, Roy. *Milton, Mannerism and Baroque.* Toronto: University of Toronto Press, 1963.

Daniélou, Jean. *From Shadows to Reality. Studies in the Biblical Typology of the Fathers.* Translated by D. W. Hibberd. London: Burns & Oates, 1960.

———. *Origène.* Paris: La Table Ronde, 1948.

Decharme, Paul. *La Critique des traditions religieuses chez les Grecs.* Paris: Alphonse Picard, 1904.

———. *Mythologie de la Grèce antique.* Paris: Garnier, 1879.

Demats, Paule. *Fabula. Trois études de mythographie antique et médiévale.* Genève: Droz, 1973.

Dölger, F. J. *Sol salutis. Gebet und Gesang im christlichen Altertum.* Münster: Aschendorff, 1925.

Dotti, Ugo. "Petrarca: il mito dafneo." *Convivium* 37 (1969): 9–23.

Duckworth, George D. *The Nature of Roman Comedy.* Princeton: Princeton University Press, 1952.

Dunchad. *Glossae in Martianum.* Edited by Cora E. Lutz. Lancaster, Pa.: American Philological Association, 1944.

Durling, Robert. "Petrarch's 'Giovene donna sotto un verde lauro.' " *MLN* 86 (1971): 1–20.

Duschke, Dennis. *Francesco Petrarca: Canzone XXIII from First to Final Version.* Ravenna: Longo, 1977.

Elliott, Kathleen O., and J. P. Elder. "A Critical Edition of the Vatican Mythographers." *Transactions of the American Philological Association* 78 (1947): 189–207.

Ellspermann, Gerard L. *The Attitude of the Early Christian Latin Writers towards Pagan Literature and Learning.* C.U.A. Patristic Studies, vol. 82. Washington, D.C.: Catholic University of America Press, 1949.

Engels, Joseph. "Berchoriana I: Notice bibliographique sur Pierre Bersuire." *Vivarium* 86 (1964): 62–112.

———. *Etudes sur l'Ovide moralisé.* Groningen: J. B. Wolters, 1945.

Enk, P. J. "Metamorphoses Ovidii duplici recensione." In *Ovidiana*, edited by N. I. Herescu. Paris: Les Belles Lettres, 1958.

Ettinghausen, Henry. *Francisco de Quevedo and the Neostoic Movement.* Oxford: Oxford University Press, 1972.

Farnell, Lewis R. *The Cults of the Greek States.* 5 vols. Oxford: Clarendon, 1896–1909.

Fernández de Navarrete, E. *Colección de documentos inéditos para la historia de España.* Vol. 16. Madrid, 1850.

Ferrante, Joan M. "*Cortes'Amor* in Medieval Texts." *Speculum* 55 (1980): 686–95.

Fletcher, Angus. *Allegory. The Theory of a Symbolic Mode.* 1964. Reprint. Ithaca: Cornell University Press, 1970.

Fontenrose, Joseph. *Orion: The Myth of the Hunter and the Huntress.* University of California Publications in Classical Studies, vol. 23. Berkeley: University of California Press, 1981.

———. *Python: A Study of Delphic Myth and Its Origins.* Berkeley and Los Angeles: University of California Press, 1959.

Foster, Kenelm. "Beatrice or Medusa: The Penitential Element in Petrarch's 'Canzoniere.' " In *Italian Studies Presented to E. R. Vincent.* Cambridge: W. Heffer, 1962.

Fränkel, Hermann. *Ovid: A Poet between Two Worlds.* Berkeley and Los Angeles: University of California Press, 1945.

Freccero, John. "The Fig Tree and the Laurel: Petrarch's Poetics." *Diacritics* 5 (1975): 34–40.

Fredericks, B. R. "Divine Wit vs. Divine Folly: Mercury and Apollo in *Metamorphoses* 1–2." *Classical Journal* 72 (1977): 244–49.

Freedberg, Sydney J. *Painting of the High Renaissance in Rome and Florence.* 2 vols. Cambridge: Harvard University Press, 1961.

Freeman, Rosemary. *English Emblem Books.* London: Chatto & Windus, 1948.

Freud, Sigmund. *Totem and Tabu.* Translated by James Strachey. New York: Norton, 1952.

Friedlaender, Walter. *Mannerism and Anti-Mannerism in Italian Painting.* 1957. Reprint. New York: Schocken, 1973.

Friedman, John B. *Orpheus in the Middle Ages.* Cambridge: Harvard University Press, 1970.

Friedrich, W. H. "Der Kosmos Ovids." *Festschrift Franz Dornseiff.* Leipzig: Bibliographisches Institut, 1953.

Fulgentius Planciades. *Mythologiarum libri tres Mythographi Latini.* Edited by Thomas Muncker. Amsterdam: Joannis à Someren, 1681.

Galinsky, G. Karl. "The Cipus Episode in Ovid's *Metamorphoses* (15.565–621)."
    Transactions of the American Philological Association 98 (1967): 181–91.
———. *The Herakles Theme: The Adaptations of the Hero in Literature from Homer to
    the Twentieth Century.* Oxford: Basil Blackwell, 1972.
———. *Ovid's Metamorphoses: An Introduction to the Basic Aspects.* Berkeley and Los
    Angeles: University of California Press, 1975.
Gallego, Morell Antonio, ed. *Garcilaso de la Vega y sus comentaristas.* Madrid: Gre-
    dos, 1972.
Garcilaso de la Vega. *Obras completas con comentario.* Edited by Elias L. Rivers.
    Madrid: Castalia, 1981.
Gheyn, J. van den, ed. *Epître d'Othéa . . . Reproduction des 100 miniatures du man-
    uscrit 9392 de Jean Miélot.* Brussels: Vromant, 1913.
Giovanni del Virgilio. "Giovanni del Virgilio, espositore delle *Metamorfosi*." Edit-
    ed by Fausto Guisalberti. *Il Giornale Dantesco* 34 (1933): 3–110.
Giraud, Yves. *La Fable de Daphné. Essai sur un type de métamorphose végétale dans la
    littérature et dans les arts jusqu'à la fin du XVIIe siècle.* Histoire des idées et
    critique littéraire, vol. 92. Genève: Droz, 1968.
Gombrich, E. H. *The Sense of Order. A Study in the Psychology of Decorative Art.* Ith-
    aca: Cornell University Press, 1979.
———. *The Story of Art.* 1950. Reprint. Oxford: Phaidon, 1972.
Goytisolo, Juan. "Quevedo: la obsesión excremental." In *Disidencias.* Barcelona:
    Seix Barral, 1977.
Grant, Robert M. *The Letter and the Spirit.* London: S.P.C.K., 1957.
Green, Otis H. *Spain and the Western Tradition.* 4 vols. Madison: University of
    Wisconsin Press, 1968.
Greene, Thomas M. *The Light in Troy. Imitation and Discovery in Renaissance Poetry.*
    New Haven: Yale University Press, 1982.
Gross, Nicolas P. "Rhetorical Wit and Amatory Persuasion in Ovid." *Classical
    Journal* 74 (1979): 305–18.
Guisalberti, Fausto, ed. "Arnolfo d'Orléans: un cultore di Ovidio nel secolo XII."
    Memorie del Reale Istituto Lombardo di Scienze e Lettere 24 (15 della serie III),
    fasc. 4 (1932): 157–234.
———. "Mediaeval Biographies of Ovid." *Journal of the Warburg and Courtauld In-
    stitutes* 9 (1946): 10–59.
Hagendahl, Harald. "Pagan Mythology and Poetry Applied to Christian Beliefs."
    In *Latin Fathers and the Classics.* Studia Graeca et Latina Gothoburgensia,
    vol. 6. Göteborg: Elanders Boktryckeri Aktiebolag, 1958.
Hagstrum, Jean H. *The Sister Arts. The Tradition of Literary Pictorialism and English
    Poetry from Dryden to Gray.* Chicago: University of Chicago Press, 1958.
———. *William Blake: Poet and Painter.* Chicago and London: University of Chica-
    go Press, 1964.
Haight, Elizabeth H. *The Symbolism of the House Door in Classical Poetry.* New
    York: Longmans & Green, 1950.
Hainsworth, P. R. J. "The Myth of Daphne in the *Rerum vulgarium fragmenta*."
    Italian Studies 34 (1979): 28–44.
Hanson, Richard P. C. *Allegory and Event.* London: S.C.M. Press, 1959.
Harpham, Geoffrey. *On the Grotesque. Strategies of Contradiction in Art and Litera-
    ture.* Princeton: Princeton University Press, 1982.
———. "The Grotesque: First Principles." *Journal of Aesthetics and Art Criticism* 34
    (1976): 461–68.

Hartt, Frederick. *History of Italian Renaissance Art.* New York: Harry N. Abrams, 1969.

Hatzfeld, Helmut. "Literary Mannerism and Baroque in Spain and France." *Comparative Literature Studies* 7 (1970): 419–36.

Hauréau, Barthélemy. "Mémoire sur un commentaire des *Métamorphoses* d'Ovide." *Mémoires de l'Academie des Inscriptions et Belles-Lettres* 30 (1883): 45–55.

Hauser, Arnold. *Mannerism: The Crisis of the Renaissance and the Origin of Modern Art.* New York: Knopf, 1965.

Henkel, Arthur, and Albrecht Schöne. *Emblemata.* Stuttgart: Metzler, 1967.

Henkel, M. D. "Illustrierte Ausgaben von Ovids *Metamorphosen* im XV., XVI. und XVII. Jahrhundert." *Vorträge der Bibliothek Warburg* 6 (1926–1927): 58–144.

Herrero-García, M. "Los rasgos físicos y el carácter según los textos españoles ul siglo XVII." *Revista de Filología Española* 12 (1925): 157–77.

Hibbard, Howard. *Bernini.* 1965. Reprint. New York: Penguin, 1976.

Hocke, Gustav René. *Manierismus in der Literatur.* Hamburg: Rowohlt, 1959.

———. *Die Welt als Labyrinth.* Hamburg: Rowohlt, 1957.

Holanda, Francisco de. *De la pintura antigua.* Translated by Manuel Denis (1563). Madrid: Jaime Ratés, 1921.

The Homeric Hymns and Homerica. Translated by Hugh G. Evelyn-White. Loeb Classical Library. 1954.

Horace. *The Satires and Epistles.* Translated by Smith Palmer Bovie. Chicago: University of Chicago Press, 1959.

Huizinga, Johan. *Homo Ludens: A Study of the Play Element in Culture.* Boston: Beacon, 1964.

———. *The Waning of the Middle Ages.* New York: Doubleday, 1954.

Iffland, James. *Quevedo and the Grotesque.* 2 vols. London: Tamesis, 1978–82.

Isidore of Seville. *Etymologiarum sive originum libri XX.* 2 vols. Edited by W. M. Lindsay. Oxford: Clarendon, 1911.

Jennings, Lee Byron. *The Ludicrous Demon. Aspects of the Grotesque in German Post-Romantic Prose.* Berkeley: University of California Press, 1963.

Johannes Scotus. *Annotationes in Marcianum.* Edited by Cora E. Lutz. Cambridge, Mass.: Mediaeval Academy of America, 1939.

John of Garland. *Integumenta Ovidii, poemetto inedito del secolo XIII.* Edited by Fausto Guisalberti. Messina-Milano: Giuseppe Principato, 1933.

John of the Cross. *St. John of the Cross: The Dark Night of the Soul.* Translated by Kurt F. Reinhardt. New York: Ungar, 1957.

Jones, J. W. "Allegorical Interpretation in Servius." *Classical Journal* 56 (1961): 217–26.

Kaibel, Georg. *Comicorum graecorum fragmenta.* Berlin: Weidmann, 1958.

Katzenellenbogen, Adolf. *Allegories of the Virtues and Vices in Medieval Art.* Translated by Alan J. P. Crick. Studies of the Warburg Institute, vol. 10. London: Warburg Institute, 1939.

Kayser, Wolfgang. *The Grotesque in Art and Literature.* Translated by U. Weisstein. Bloomington: Indiana University Press, 1963.

Keeble, T. W. "Some Mythological Figures in Golden Age Satire and Burlesque." *Bulletin of Spanish Studies* 25 (1948): 238–46.

Kennedy, Angus J. *Christine de Pizan: A Bibliographical Guide.* London: Grant & Cutler, 1984.

Lafaye, Georges. *Les Métamorphoses d'Ovide et leurs modéles grecs.* Bibliothèque de la faculté des lettres, vol. 19. Paris: F. Alcan, 1904.

Laistner, Max L. W. "Fulgentius in the Carolingian Age." In *The Intellectual Heritage of the Early Middle Ages.* Edited by Chester G. Starr. 1957. Reprint. New York: Octagon Books, 1966.

———. "Martianus Capella and His Ninth Century Commentators." *Bulletin of the John Rylands Library* 9 (1925): 130–38.

Lampe, G. W. H., and K. J. Woollcombe. *Essays on Typology.* Studies in Biblical Theology, no. 22. Naperville, Ill.: Alec R. Allenson, 1957.

Lang, Andrew. *Myth, Ritual and Religion.* 2 vols. London: Longmans & Green, 1913.

Langlois, Ernest. "Une Rédaction en prose de l'*Ovide moralisé.*" *Bibliothèque de l'Ecole des Chartes* 62 (1901): 251–55.

Laski, Marghanita. *Ecstasy. A Study of Some Secular and Religious Experiences.* Bloomington: Indiana University Press, 1961.

Lazar, Moshé. *Amour courtois et fin'amors dans la littérature du XIIe siècle.* Paris: C. Klincksieck, 1964.

Ledda, Giuseppina. *Contributo allo studio della letteratura emblematica in Spagna (1549–1613).* Pisa: Università di Pisa, 1970.

Lee, Rensselaer W. *"Ut pictura poesis:* The Humanistic Theory of Painting." *Art Bulletin* 22 (1940): 197–269.

Lesky, Albin. *A History of Greek Literature.* Translated by James Willis and Cornelis de Heer. London: Methuen, 1966.

Lewis, C. S. *The Allegory of Love.* 1936. Reprint. New York: Oxford University Press, 1958.

Lida, Raimundo. "De Quevedo, Lipsio y los escalígeros." In *Letras hispánicas.* México: Fondo de Cultura Económica, 1958.

———. "La 'España defendida' y la síntesis pagano-cristiana." In *Letras hispánicas.* México: Fondo de Cultura Económica, 1958.

———. "Sueños y discursos: el predicador y sus máscaras." In *Homenaje a Julio Caro Baroja.* Madrid: Centro de Investigaciones Sociológicas, 1978.

Liebeschütz, Hans. *Fulgentius Metaforalis, ein Beitrag zur Geschichte der antiken Mythologie im Mittelalter.* Studien der Bibliothek Warburg, vol. 4. Leipzig: Teubner, 1926.

Little, Douglas. "The Speech of Pythagoras in *Metamorphoses* 15 and the Structure of the *Metamorphoses.*" *Hermes* 98 (1970): 340–60.

L'Orange, H. P. *Domus Aurea, der Sonnenpalast.* Oslo: Serta Eitremiana, 1942.

Lowes, John L. "The Loveres Maladye of Hereos." *Modern Philology* 11 (1914): 491–546.

Luck, Georg. *The Latin Love Elegy.* London: Methuen, 1959.

Lutz, Cora E. "The Commentary of Remigius of Auxerre on Martianus Capella." *Mediaeval Studies* 19 (1957): 137–56.

Macrobius, Ambrosius Theodosius. *Saturnalia.* Vol. 1. Edited by James Willis. Leipzig: Teubner, 1963.

Magnus, Hugo. "Ovids *Metamorphosen* in doppelter Fassung?" *Hermes* 40 (1905): 191–239.

Marache, R. "La Révolte d'Ovide exilé contre Auguste." In *Ovidiana,* edited by N. I. Herescu. Paris: Les Belles Lettres, 1958.

Martianus Capella. *De nuptiis Philologiae et Mercurii.* Edited by James Willis. Leipzig: Teubner, 1983.

Martin, John Rupert. *Baroque.* New York: Harper & Row, 1977.

Martinengo, Alessandro. "La mitologia classica come repertorio stilistico dei concettisti ispanoamericani." *Studi di Letteratura Ispano-Americana* (Milan) 1 (1967): 77–109.

———. *Quevedo e il simbolo alchimistico.* Padua: Liviana Editrice, 1967.

Martínez López, Enrique. "Sobre 'aquella bestialidad' de Garcilaso (egl. III.230). *PMLA* 87 (1972): 12–25.

Mas, Amédée. *La Caricature de la femme, du mariage et de l'amour dans l'oeuvre de Quevedo.* Paris: Ediciones Hispano-Americanas, 1957.

Mazzotta, Giuseppe. "The *Canzoniere* and the Language of the Self." *Studies in Philology* 75 (1978): 271–96.

Mele, Eugenio. "In margine alle poesie di Garcilaso." *Bulletin Hispanique* 32 (1930): 218–45.

Mirollo, James. "The Mannered and the Mannerist in Late Renaissance Literature." In *The Meaning of Mannerism,* edited by Franklin W. Robinson and Stephen G. Nichols, Jr. Hanover, N. H.: University Press of New England, 1972.

———. *Mannerism and Renaissance Poetry. Concept, Mode, Inner Design.* New Haven: Yale University Press, 1984.

Munari, Franco. *Ovid im Mittelalter.* Zurich: Artemis, 1960.

Nash, Ernest. *Pictorial Dictionary of Ancient Rome.* 2 vols. New York and Washington, D.C.: Frederick A. Praeger, 1961.

Nicoll, Allardyce. *Masks, Mimes and Miracles.* London: George G. Harrap, 1931.

Nicoll, W. S. M. "Cupid, Apollo, and Daphne (Ovid, *Met.* 1.452 ff.)." *Classical Quarterly,* n. s., 30 (1980): 174–82.

Ogle, M. B. "Laurel in Ancient Religion and Folklore." *American Journal of Philology* 31 (1910): 287–311.

———. "The Classical Origin and Tradition of Literary Conceits." *American Journal of Philology* 34 (1913): 125–52.

Olivieri, Alessandro. *Frammenti della commedia greca e del mimo nella Sicilia e nella Magna Grecia.* 2d ed. Naples: Libreria Scientifica Editrice, 1946.

Osgood, Charles G. *Boccaccio on Poetry.* 1930. Reprint. New York: Liberal Arts Press, 1956.

Otis, Brooks. *Ovid as an Epic Poet.* Cambridge: Cambridge University Press, 1966.

Ovid. *Metamorphoses.* 2 vols. Edited by M. Haupt, O. Korn, J. Müller, and R. Ehwald, and revised by M. von Albrecht. Zurich and Dublin: Weidmann, 1966.

———. *Metamorphoses.* 2 vols. Edited and translated by F. J. Miller. Loeb Classical Library. 1966–68.

Ovide moralisé. Edited by C. de Boer. Amsterdam: Johannes Müller, 1915–1938.

Ovide moralisé en prose. Edited by C. de Boer. Amsterdam: Noord-Hollandsche, 1954.

Paetow, Louis John. *Morale Scolarium of John of Garland.* Berkeley: University of California Press, 1927.

Panofsky, Erwin. *Renaissance and Renascences in Western Art.* New York: Harper & Row, 1960.

———. *Studies in Iconology.* 1939. Reprint. New York: Harper & Row, 1967.

——— and Fritz Saxl. "Classical Mythology in Mediaeval Art." *Metropolitan Museum Studies* 4 (1933): 228–80.

Pansa, Giovanni. *Ovidio nel medioevo e nella tradizione popolare.* Sulmona: U. Caroselli, 1924.

Parker, Alexander A. *Literature and the Delinquent. The Picaresque Novel in Spain and Europe, 1599–1753.* Edinburgh: Edinburgh University Press, 1967.

Parry, Hugh. "Ovid's *Metamorphoses:* Violence in a Pastoral Landscape." *Transactions of the American Philological Association* 95 (1964): 268–82.

Patch, Howard R. *The Goddess Fortuna in Mediaeval Literature.* Cambridge: Harvard University Press, 1927.

Paterson, Alan K. G. "Ecphrasis in Garcilaso's 'Egloga Tercera.' " *Modern Language Review* 72 (1977): 73–92.

Pausanias. *Description of Greece.* Vol. 4. Translated by W. H. S. Jones. Loeb Classical Library. 1961.

Pépin, Jean. *Mythe et allégorie: Les Origines grecques et les contestations judéo-chrétiennes.* 2d ed. Paris: Etudes Augustiniennes, 1976.

Petrarch. *Africa.* Edited by Nicola Festa. Firenze: Sansoni, 1926.

———. *Africa.* Translated by Thomas G. Bergin and Alice S. Wilson. New Haven: Yale University Press, 1977.

———. *Le familiari.* Edited by Vittorio Rossi and Umberto Bosco. 4 vols. Firenze: Sansoni, 1933–42.

———. *Secretum.* Edited by Enrico Carrara. In *Prose.* Milano: Riccardo Ricciardi, 1955.

———. *Petrarch's Lyric Poems.* Edited and translated by Robert Durling. Cambridge: Harvard University Press, 1976.

Pickard-Cambridge, Arthur. *The Dramatic Festivals of Athens.* Oxford: Clarendon, 1953.

Pigman, G. W. "Versions of Imitation in the Renaissance." *Renaissance Quarterly* 33 (1980): 1–32.

Pinet, Marie-Josèphe. *Christine de Pisan, 1364–1430. Etude biographique et littéraire.* 1927. Reprint. Genève: Slatkine Reprints, 1974.

Platner, Samuel Ball. *A Topographical Dictionary of Ancient Rome.* London: Oxford University Press, H. Milford, 1929.

Pliny the Elder. *Natural History.* Vol. 2. Translated by H. Rackham. Loeb Classical Library. 1942.

Polo de Medina, Jacinto. *Obras completas.* Murcia: Tip. Sucesores de Nogués, 1948.

Porqueras-Mayo, Alberto. "La ninfa degollada de Garcilaso (Egloga III, versos 225–232)." In *Actas del Tercer Congreso Internacional de Hispanistas.* México: Colegio de México, 1970.

Post, Chandler R. *A History of Spanish Painting.* Harvard-Radcliffe Fine Arts Series, vol. 14. Cambridge: Harvard University Press, 1966.

Praz, Mario. *Studies in Seventeenth-Century Imagery.* Roma: Edizioni di Storia e Letteratura, 1964.

———. "Petrarca e gli emblematisti." In *Ricerche anglo-italiane.* Roma: Edizioni di Storia e Letteratura, 1944.

Preller, Ludwig. *Griechische Mythologie.* 2 vols. Berlin: Weidmann, 1860–61.

Price, R. M. "A Note on Three Satirical Sonnets of Quevedo." *Bulletin of Hispanic Studies* 40 (1963): 79–88.

Primmer, Adolf. "Mythos und Natur in Ovids 'Apollo und Daphne.' " *Wiener Studien* 10 (1976): 210–20.

Prudentius. *Psychomachia.* 2 vols. Edited and translated by H. J. Thomson. Loeb Classical Library. 1949–53.

Quevedo, Francisco de. *La vida del Buscón llamado Don Pablos.* 2d ed. Edited by

Fernando Lázaro Carreter. Salamanca: Ediciones Universidad de Salamanca, 1980.

———. *Epistolario completo*. Edited by Luis Astrana Marín. Madrid: Instituto Editorial Reus, 1946.

———. *La hora de todos y la Fortuna con seso*. Edited by Luisa López-Grigera. Madrid: Castalia, 1975.

———. *Obra poética*. 4 vols. Edited by José Manuel Blecua. Madrid: Castalia, 1969–81.

———. *Obras completas en prosa*. Edited by Luis Astrana Marín. Madrid: Aguilar, 1945.

———. *Obras completas*. Vol. 1, *Obras en prosa*. Edited by Felicidad Buendía. Madrid: Aguilar, 1961.

———. *El parnaso español*. Edited by José Antonio Gonzáles de Salas. Madrid, 1648.

———. *Poesía original*. Edited by José Manuel Blecua. Barcelona: Planeta, 1963.

———. *Poesía varia*. Edited by James O. Crosby. Madrid: Cátedra, 1981.

———. *Sueños y discursos*. Edited by Felipe C. R. Maldonado. Madrid: Castalia, 1982.

Rabanus Maurus. *De universo*. Migne, *Patrologia latina* 111.9–614.

Rahner, Hugo. *Greek Myths and Christian Mystery*. Translated by Brian Battershaw. New York: Harper & Row, 1963.

Rand, Edward Kennard. *Ovid and His Influence*. New York: Plimpton Press, 1928.

Raschke, Robert. *De Alberico mythologo*. Breslauer Philologische Abhandlungen, vol. 45. Breslau: M. & H. Marcus, 1913.

Realencyclopädie der classischen Altertumswissenschaft, s. v. "Daphne," 4:2136–40.

Reiss, Edmund. "*Fin'Amors*: Its History and Meaning in Medieval Literature." *Medieval and Renaissance Studies* no. 8 (1979): 74–99.

Remigius of Auxerre. *Commentum in Martianum Capellam*. 2 vols. Edited by Cora E. Lutz. Leiden: E. J. Brill, 1962–65.

Rhodes, Neil. *Elizabethan Grotesque*. London: Routledge & Kegan Paul, 1980.

Rigolot, François. "Nature and Function of Paronomasia in the *Canzoniere*." *Italian Quarterly* 18 (1974): 29–36.

Rivero, Albert J. "Petrarch's 'Nel dolce tempo de la prima etade.' " *MLN* 94 (1979): 92–112.

Rivers, Elias L., trans. *Renaissance and Baroque Poetry of Spain*. New York: Dell, 1966.

———. "The Pastoral Paradox of Natural Art." *MLN* 77 (1962): 130–44.

Robathan, Dorothy M. "Ovid in the Middle Ages." In *Ovid*. Edited by J. W. Binns. London and Boston: Routledge, 1973.

Robertson, D. W., Jr. *A Preface to Chaucer. Studies in Medieval Perspectives*. Princeton: Princeton University Press, 1962.

Romagnoli, Ettore. *Nel regno di Dioniso*. Bologna: Nicola Zanichelli, 1953.

Sant, Jeannette van't, ed. *Le Commentaire de Copenhague de l'Ovide moralisé*. Amsterdam: H. J. Paris, 1929.

Santayana, George. *The Sense of Beauty*. 1896. Reprint. New York: Dover, 1955.

Schapiro, Meyer. "The Joseph Scenes on the Maximianus Throne." In *Late Antique, Early Christian and Mediaeval Art*. New York: Braziller, 1979.

Schevill, Rudolph. *Ovid and the Renascence in Spain*. University of California Publications in Modern Philology, vol. 4, no. 1. Berkeley: University of California Press, 1913.

Segal, Charles. *Landscape in Ovid's Metamorphoses: A Study in the Transformation of a Literary Symbol.* Hermes Einzelschriften, no. 23. Wiesbaden: F. Steiner, 1969.
————. "Ovid's *Metamorphoses*: Greek Myth in Augustan Rome." *Studies in Philology* 68 (1971): 371–94.
————. "Myth and Philosophy in the *Metamorphoses*: Ovid's Augustanism and the Augustan Conclusion of Book XV." *American Journal of Philology* 90 (1969): 257–92.
Selig, Karl-Ludwig. "Garcilaso and the Visual Arts: Remarks on Some Aspects of Visualization." In *Interpretation und Vergleich: Festschrift für Walter Pabst.* Berlin: E. Schmidt, 1972.
Servius. *Servianorum in Vergilii carmina commentariorum.* 3 vols. Edited by Edward Kennard Rand et al. Lancaster, Pa.: American Philological Association, 1946–65.
Seznec, Jean. *The Survival of the Pagan Gods.* Translated by Barbara F. Sessions. 1953. Reprint. New York: Harper & Row, 1961.
Shearman, John. *Mannerism.* Baltimore: Penguin, 1967.
Smalley, Beryl. *English Friars and Antiquity in the Early Fourteenth Century.* Oxford: Basil Blackwell, 1960.
Smith, A. J. "Theory and Practice in Renaissance Poetry: Two Kinds of Imitation." *Bulletin of the John Rylands Library* 47 (1964): 212–43.
Smyth, Craig Hugh. *Mannerism and Maniera.* Locust Valley, N.Y.: J. J. Augustin, 1963.
Snell, Bruno. "Art and Play in Callimachus." In *The Discovery of the Mind.* Translated by T. G. Rosenmeyer. Oxford: Basil Blackwell, 1953.
Spencer, Theodore. *Shakespeare and the Nature of Man.* New York: Macmillan, 1942.
Spitzer, Leo. "Garcilaso, Third Eclogue, lines 265–271." *Hispanic Review* 20 (1952): 243–48.
————. "The 'récit de Théramène.' " In *Linguistics and Literary History: Essays in Stylistics.* 1948. Reprint. Princeton: Princeton University Press, 1974.
Stechow, Wolfgang. *Apollo und Daphne.* Studien der Bibliothek Warburg, vol. 23. Leipzig: Teubner, 1932.
Steig, Michael. "Defining the Grotesque: An Attempt at Synthesis." *Journal of Aesthetics and Art Criticism* 29 (1970): 253–60.
Struever, Nancy S. *The Language of History in the Renaissance: Rhetoric and Historical Consciousness in Florentine Humanism.* Princeton: Princeton University Press, 1970.
Sypher, Wylie. *Four Stages of Renaissance Style.* Garden City, N.Y.: Doubleday, 1955.
Tassoni, Alessandro. *La secchia rapita.* Edited by Giovanni Ziccardi. Torino: Unione Tipografico-Editrice Torinese, 1968.
Thomson, Philip. *The Grotesque.* London: Methuen, 1972.
Tillyard, E. M. W. *The Elizabethan World Picture.* New York: Vintage Books, n. d.
Traube, Ludwig. *Vorlesungen und Abhandlungen.* 3 vols. in 2. München: C. H. Beck, 1909–20.
Trendall, Arthur D. *Paestan Pottery: A Study of the Red-Figured Vases of Paestum.* London: Macmillan, 1936.
————. *Phlyax Vases.* Institute of Classical Studies, no. 19. 2d ed., rev. and enl. London: University of London, Institute of Classical Studies, 1967.

Tuchman, Barbara W. *A Distant Mirror: The Calamitous 14th Century.* New York: Knopf, 1978.

Tuve, Rosemond. *Allegorical Imagery: Some Mediaeval Books and Their Posterity.* Princeton: Princeton University Press, 1966.

———. "Baroque and Mannerist Milton?" In *Milton Studies in Honor of Harris Francis Fletcher.* Urbana: University of Illinois Press, 1961.

Vasari, Giorgio. *Le vite.* 9 vols. Edited by Gaetano Milanesi. Florence: Sansoni, 1906.

Viarre, Simone. *L'Image et la pensée dans les Métamorphoses d'Ovide.* Paris: Presses Universitaires de France, 1964.

Vickers, Nancy J. "Diana Described: Scattered Woman and Scattered Rhyme." *Critical Inquiry* 8 (1981): 265–79.

Vitruvius. *De architectura.* 2 vols. Edited and translated by Frank Granger. Loeb Classical Library. 1955–56.

Vollgraff, Carl Wilhelm. *Nikander und Ovid.* Groningen: J. B. Wolters, 1909.

Walsingham, Thomas. *De archana deorum.* Edited by Robert A. van Kluyve. Durham: Duke University Press, 1968.

Warnke, Frank J. *Versions of Baroque.* New Haven: Yale University Press, 1972.

Webster, T. B. L. "South Italian Vases and Attic Drama." *Classical Quarterly* 42 (1948): 15–27.

Whitman, Cedric H. *Aristophanes and the Comic Hero.* 1964. Reprint. Cambridge: Harvard University Press, 1971.

Wicksteed, Philip H., and Edmund G. Gardner. *Dante and Giovanni del Virgilio.* Westminster: A. Constable, 1902.

Wilamowitz-Moellendorff, Ulrich von. *Der Glaube der Hellenen.* 2 vols. Berlin: Weidmann, 1931–32.

Wilkins, Ernest H. "Descriptions of Pagan Divinities from Petrarch to Chaucer." *Speculum* 32 (1957): 511–22.

———. "The Genealogy of the Editions of the *Genealogia deorum.*" *Modern Philology* 17 (1919): 425–38.

———. *Studies in the Life and Works of Petrarch.* Cambridge, Mass.: Mediaeval Academy of America, 1955.

Wilkinson, L. P. *Ovid Recalled.* Cambridge: Cambridge University Press, 1955.

Wolfson, Harry A. *Philo: Foundations of Religious Philosophy in Judaism, Christianity, and Islam.* 2 vols. 1947. Reprint. Cambridge: Harvard University Press, 1948.

———. *The Philosophy of the Church Fathers.* Vol. 1, *Faith, Trinity, Incarnation.* 3d ed., rev. Cambridge: Harvard University Press, 1970.

Wright, Thomas. *A History of Caricature and Grotesque in Literature and Art.* 1865. Reprint. New York: Frederick Ungar, 1968.

Yardley, J. C. "The Elegiac Paraclausithyron." *Eranos* 76 (1978): 19–34.

Zaehner, Robert C. *Mysticism, Sacred and Profane.* Oxford: Clarendon, 1957.

Index

Achilles, 27, 116, 170 n.23
Actaeon, 34, 94, 104
Adam: as type of Christ, 61; and Eve, 61
Admetus, 169 n.6; and Alcestis, 52
Adonis: and Venus, 7, 116
Aeschylus, 141
Agon, 5, 6, 8, 80; in Arnulf of Orléans, 50–55; in Pierre Bersuire, 72–75, 78; in Garcilaso de la Vega, 8, 111; in John of Garland, 55; in Ovid, 5, 11, 19–20, 21–22, 43, 158; in the *Ovide moralisé*, 57, 65–68; in Petrarch, 7, 12, 82–83, 86, 88, 99, 101, 104, 109; in Francisco de Quevedo, 8, 131, 132, 134, 139–40, 150, 158
Alcestis, 52
Alciati, Andrea: *Emblematum liber*, 129
Alcmena, 171 n.26
Allegory, 5, 6, 45–49, 61; and typology, 61, 65
Alonso, Dámaso, 115, 145
Alpheus: and Arethusa, 103
Amyclas of Laconia, 15
Anaxagoras, 47
Anaxarete, 121
Aneau, Barthélemy: *Picta poesis*, 129, 186 n.18
Anthesteria, festival of, 28
Antipater the Stoic, 52
Antisthenes, 47
Aphrodite. *See* Venus
Apollo (Phoebus, Sol), 3, 31; in ancient Greece 14–17, 52–53; in Arnulf of Orléans, 51–55; in Pierre Bersuire, 71–75, 78; in Callimachus, 3; as Christ 65–68, 74, 75, 78, 80; in Chris-

tine de Pisan, 60, 63–64 (figs. 7–9), 78, 79 (fig. 12), 80; as the Devil, 75; in Garcilaso de la Vega, 8, 13, 111, 115–16, 126–29; grotesque in, 8, 10–11, 13, 20, 21, 25–26, 29–31, 152, 155, 160; origin of, 14; in Ovid, 6, 10–11, 20, 21, 22–27, 30–31, 34, 35, 40–43, 51, 86, 92–93, 99, 103, 105, 106, 108, 126, 131, 132, 138, 142, 150, 152, 153, 158; in the *Ovide moralisé*, 57–58, 62 (figs. 5–6), 65–68; in Pediment of the Siphnian Treasury (Delphi), 29, fig. 2; in Petrarch, 6–7, 82, 83, 104–6; in *phlyax* vases, 28–30, 32–33 (figs. 1, 3, 4); in Francisco de Quevedo, 13, 30, 132–39, 142, 143, 144, 145, 146–55, 158–61, 163; in John Ridevall *(Fulgentius metaforalis)*, 75
Apollonius: *Argonautica*, 9
Arachne, 39, 40, 43, 116
Arcimboldo, 110
Arcipreste de Hita: *Libro de Buen Amor*, 46
Arethusa, 34, 35; and Alpheus, 103
Aristophanes, 31, 142, 162; *Frogs*, 28
Arnulf of Orléans, 50–55, 107
Atellan farces, 30, 31
Athena (Pallas), 29, 47, 116
Athenagoras, 48
Auerbach, Erich, 61, 65
Augustine, Saint, 83, 86, 101, 180 n.1
Augustus, Caesar, 11, 19, 31, 42, 45, 53

Bakhtin, Mikhail, 13, 156–57, 161, 167 n.26

Mary E. Barnard is Assistant Professor of
Spanish and Comparative Literature at The
Pennsylvania State University.